A FAMILY
I

ALICE
born: Wed 20th June 1833
at 11am
married
JOHN LORD

ANN
born: Tue 14th February 1837
at 7am

ASHWORTH
born: Tue 28th July 1840
at 11am

RICHARD
married
ANNE REID

THOMAS
married
FLORENCE HILDA LORD

AMELIA (MILLY)
married
JOHN ASHWORTH

A baby son who died at an early age.

WINSTON

VERA

FLORENCE

LILIAN

MARGARET

ARNOLD

AMELIA

VERA

BARBARA

GEOFFREY WALKER
married
MARGARET LILIAN PEIRSON

PHILIP CUNNINGHAM
married
ELIZABETH SABINE

JAMES PRESTON
married
ALICE BRIDGE

ISOBEL MARGARET
married
ROLAND ERNEST SPARROW

THOMAS DOUGLAS
married
JEAN STOTT

SUSAN MARGARET
married
JOHN MICHAEL DAVIES

JOHN ROGER
married
MARGARET JEAN BRASH

KATE ELIZABETH

LOTTIE MARY

CHRISTOPHER JAMES

PETER THOMAS

SARAH MARGARET

FRANCES ALEXANDRA

James Haworth & Company

A Family in Print

John S. Haworth

FIRST PUBLISHED IN 1989 by JAMES HAWORTH LTD.
LONDON and LEICESTER.

Produced by James Haworth Ltd., Southgate, London.

Colour reproduction and print organisation by James Haworth (Leicester) Ltd., Fleet Street Works, Leicester.

Typesetting by Easi-Set Ltd., Enderby, Leicester.

ISBN No 0 9514227 0 7

CONTENTS

RIBBON DENTAL CREAM
COLGATE
COLGATE RIBBON DENTAL CREAM
6d 1/- 1/6

"NOW.... I'm Schoolgirl Complexion all over"
PALMOLIVE

INTRODUCTION

Through history there have been thousands of books recording the story for posterity of families rich and poor, famous and infamous.

One might well ask what makes this so very different that it could fall outside one of the above headings.

Many such family book sagas recount a rags to riches theme or, if concerning a business, how successfully it has consistently traded. Such books rarely seek to go below the surface to bring out the human drama that lies behind a business and the lives led by those who work within a family company.

The book seeks to "lift the curtain" behind which most families hide, to reveal the human endeavour by owner or employee in founding an individual business and to keep it functioning for some 75 years.

Portrayed are the family's attempts, over a hundred years, to overcome life's dangers, difficulties, frustrations and disappointments and how a business comes to dominate family life.

The tale unfolds in what might be called historical straight line chapters, concerning first the family, followed by chapters on individual parts of the company's history.

It is left to the reader to weave the story lines into a tapestry which portrays an unusual and perhaps unique description of a business family enwrapped by its products.

This story will appeal to those who are connected with or use the services of a family business. Such readers will feel they are looking at a mirror, possibly reflecting their own experiences.

Additionally, those whose interest lies with past and present advertising will appreciate the illustrations of display material, some of which could be described as masterpieces of the display designing art.

These illustrations, spread throughout the narrative, encompass a century's progress in window display manufacture. The striking cardboard showcard or display in a shop window or on a shop counter was the prime medium in the promotion of a manufacturer's product. Sadly the science of marketing, combined with commercial television advertising, plus the clinical approach in superstore appearance, has nowadays reduced nearly all such displays to a plain showcard or window banner.

Lastly, and making no apology for this approach, the story endeavours to record of those born between the two World Wars, an insight into life experienced, who would at that time be labelled as belonging to the commercial middle class. As a group in the past, they have not been fashionable to record in print; those less fortunately born, rightly deserving a full record of their hardship and plight prior to the 1950's, a hardship from which, to a great extent, the middle class of that time were protected. Likewise, the rich and the notorious have always in our society commanded maximum print coverage well outside their importance to the community.

This narrative sets out to be a contribution to the efforts put in by the population labelled as "middle class" in the days prior to the 1960's. In 1989 the picture is so very different with by far the majority of the population in the British Isles enjoying the luxuries of the 1930's now as commonplace in their standard of living and they too now in turn qualify for the title of "middle class".

James Haworth

THE FAMILY

Tuesday lunchtime, 7th April 1987. I have left the car by the entrance to the Bacup Recreation Ground as it is impossible to drive any further. Maden Road becomes no more than a rutted track after the well cared for, but now, in the pouring rain, deserted recreation ground. Donning water-proofs and walking boots seems the only way to approach Slip Inn Farm buildings, some three-quarters of a mile away. I pick my way along the track avoiding numerous puddles of uncertain depth; the Bacup golf course is on the right; even the hardy Lancashire golfers have deserted it in the biting cold. The rain is driven straight into my face by the wind. The low scudding clouds hug the higher hilltops and those overhead roll and pitch like an upturned sea. As the buildings of the Slip Inn loom closer on the horizon I am aware of walking almost within a time machine. Transported back a hundred years I can almost see grandfather, James Haworth, aged 17, walking back from the Wesleyan Chapel School where he is a pupil teacher, to his birthplace of farm and barns perched in bleak inhospitable countryside of dark rocks and boggy ground.

His father, (my great grandfather) also named James was, by all accounts a stern and God-fearing man who barely scraped a living by rearing a few cattle, bullocks and sheep over some 34 acres of this rock strewn area.

Great grandfather James Haworth (the 1st as I would like to call him) was born at Edgeside, Bacup, on the 26th January 1828, the son of George Haworth a woollen weaver. James (1st), one of eight children, was to follow his father's footsteps and take up the trade of a weaver, a trade he pursued for some 24 years, for he would have been put out to work from the age of 10, having had little or no education.

Work in these Lancashire valleys was at this period plentiful but extremely hard, for the Industrial Revolution had just begun. Lancashire and Yorkshire were the boom areas of England with mill and other business owners prospering beyond their wildest dreams. This prosperity was not to reach the workers; wages were deliberately kept low by agreement between the mill owners and long hours were expected; generally from 6a.m. to 6p.m. five days a week and perhaps finishing at 1p.m. on Saturday. To be without a job and a wage really meant no home and near starvation. Against this background, James (1st) married Ellen Walker on 27th November 1862, at the Parochial Chapel, Newchurch, in Rossendale.

Slip Inn Farm, Bacup, Forest of Rossendale, Lancashire.

The transition from mill workers to farmers began for the Haworth family when on 16th June 1832, Joseph Bullock, a farmer from the hamlet of Paythorne, gave his daughter Ellen in marriage to Richard Walker, also a farmer. The marriage was solemnised in the Parish Church of Gisburn. Richard Walker and Ellen came to live at Slip Inn Farm; how is undisclosed, Gisburn being some twenty miles to the north of Bacup.

The 1861 Bacup census shows living at Slip Inn, Richard Walker aged 61, farmer of 37 acres, wife Ellen, daughters Ellen, aged 27, Mary, aged 11 and Dedine (or Begine) aged 2. Registered also at this time as living at Slip Inn is another farmer, George Buckley aged 45, wife Ann, 6 daughters and 4 sons, three of whom work in the nearby coalmine: this was most likely the Hile Mine, within half a mile of the Slip Inn.

Ellen Haworth.

James Haworth (the First) Born 26th December 1828.

There were several other drift mines in the vicinity, each worked by a family or a few miners. These mines had been worked from the late 1700s to provide coal for the newly arrived steam power, which would drive machinery in the Rossendale Valley's new mills. Amongst these small mines with their miners there would be the requirement for a nearby ale house on the moor, to meet the needs of thirsty workers. The Buckleys were happy to provide beer and spirits within the building they lived, hence the aptly named "Slip Inn".

Slip Inn (left) still bleak in 1988.

Ten years later, the 1871 Bacup census cites the following as living at Slip Inn. James Haworth (1st) aged 41, farmer of 24 acres, born at Newchurch, and wife Ellen, born at Gisburn. Children Elizabeth E. aged 7, Sarah A. aged 6, Alice M. aged 3, James aged 1 year and a 12 year old girl Begine. The Buckleys had gone. The nearby mines were either being worked out or were unprofitable due to small coal seams. The Buckley's mining sons would have sought employment in larger mines elsewhere. With their going, together with the other miners, Slip Inn would cease to be an ale house, its closure hastened no doubt by James (1st), a devout Wesleyan who would not tolerate drinking.

Between 1861 and 1871, it would appear that Richard Walker, 62 years old in 1861, with no sons to follow him, would more than likely expect James Haworth (1st), on marrying his eldest daughter, Ellen, to join in helping to run the farm. Hence, James (1st) left the sweat shop of the mill as a woollen printer, only to change for the sweat and cold of Slip Inn farm. By 1870, both Richard Walker and wife Ellen would appear to have died, leaving James (1st) and Ellen the inheritance of Slip Inn. Mary Ann Walker appeared to have left, possibly to get married. Young Begine was still there, but we are to hear no more of her. James (1st) probably saw himself now as someone who by marriage and luck, was to come off the bottom rung of the ladder of life in Bacup. By all accounts, he was a devout Wesleyan and there is a record of a James Haworth as a Superintendent 1860 – 1867 of the Mount Pleasant Wesleyan Sunday School in Bacup.

As a description of life in the town, various extracts are reprinted on the next few pages from the issues of Bacup & Rossendale News and Bacup Times.

Mount Pleasant Wesleyan Chapel.

1863

6 Jun American Civil War.

The following ministers have expressed sympathy with the South.

John Howe - Waterbarn. Jonas Smith - Ebenezer.

Industry. Cotton Famine.

The Lancashire distress is decreasing. Due mainly to emigration to Australia.

27 Jun Industry.

If the number of mills running be a criterion the state of the cotton trade in the district has very materially improved during the past six weeks.
The work is bad for the workers, but they are glad to be in work.

18 Jul Employment.

In full work	-	-	*1,923*
4 or 5 days a week	-	-	*716*
3 days a week	-	-	*345*
Totally unemployed	-	-	*3,102*

(Note: Stacksteads not included).

Aug Religion - Primitive Methodists.

A Camp Meeting held in field belonging to Mr Edmund Lord in Burnley Road. 3,000 present.

Oct Empty Houses.

Some three years ago houses were very difficult to get. This is not the case now. Empty houses on all lands testify to the long and continued depression in trade.
Many have left for Yorkshire. Quite a few have emigrated. In some cases 2 or 3 families live together in one house to escape the rents and heavy rates which are now being made.

Bacup 1880.

Bacup Town 1877.

Quotes from the Bacup & Rossendale News.

1864

20 Feb British & Irish Magnetic Telegraph Co Ltd.

An office is now open at the Lancs & Yorks Rly. Station, Newchurch, for the transmission of messages to all parts of the UK.

2 Apl Punishment.

A youth of Lee Mill stole 4 pigeons. (Value 10/-d).
Committed for 14 days and to be afterwards flogged.

10 Dec **HOME!** Bacup & Rochdale News.

The majority of the dwellings of the poor are entirely destitute of means for the common decencies of life.

Open cesspools at every corner. No convenience for the dirt and refuse which is heaped up in the nearest place.

Ask any medical man, minister of religion etc or any of those brought into more intimate contact with the poor, and one and all will tell us that most of the causes of immorality are caused through want of the common decencies of life, and that the unhealthy dwellings drive the men into the streets and public houses.

At Bank-house, west of Newchurch Road, there is a plantation, and people are obliged to come from the town to obey the calls of nature. In King Street, some of the people use chamber utensils, and empty them into the streets. The smell is very offensive in summer. In Newchurch are some very superior cottages, but there are only two single privies for 16 houses.

In the door-stones, John Pillings wife makes tea-cakes for sale. She says 'The damp and water from the privy at the back comes through the wall. I stuffed a rag in to stop it, but still it runs on the floor'.

In Yorkshire Street there is one privy for 20 houses.

1865

1 Mar The Town.

The majority of the dwellings of the labouring classes are ill-arranged, devoid of proper ventilation and without efficient drainage.

As for our roads they are monstrous. St James Street, Irwell Terrace South Street. No one would believe we have borrowed £19,000 for the improvement of the town. A newly ploughed field would be infinitely cleaner.

£500 has been paid for paving Newchurch Road, yet the paths are as filthy as ever.

25 Feb Street Nuisance.

Young fellows obstructing the footpaths and insulting females. The nuisance has grown to an intolerable extent and it is impossible for respectable girls to walk the streets unprotected.

20 May Newchurch Road. Four - Storeys.

Such is the state of the sanitary arrangements here, that the probability for anyone walking past is that he will find his extremities deluged by a stream of slops.

Not less than a dozen pipes are constantly discharging upon the open street the slops, sink-water etc of the inmates of these four-storeys, emitting noxious odours.

The state of things is disgusting.

There is also food for speculation in the retaining wall abutting Newchurch Road, and should we address to some native a query as to how it is that the Local Board have not taken cognizance of this matter, he may probably receive the answer:

"Why, you see, thats Mesther Whitaker's job, but Mesther Whitakers is a rich man, an' the Local Board's flaid on' 'am".

We recommend the Board to deal summarily with him, as it does with poorer men.

1866

1 Jul Hygiene. (Letters).

.... there are hundreds in our locality who are possessed of so little self-respect as to almost neglect the practice of bathing.

I would entreat those who are restrained by fear and nervousness to put away unmanly timidity, assuring them that intimacy will engender confidence.

Those who may be deterred by indolence, merit no sympathy!

20 Oct Foreigners.

Now the harvest is got in, many from the east of England agricultural districts are beginning to arrive in search of employment in cotton mills.

13 Oct Bacup in the Rain.

G C Harrison Esq of FOREST HOUSE, Bacup, for the past three years has kept a record of the rainfall of Bacup. For the two years 1864/65 Bacup had 40 ins of rain both years. Rain fell on 165 out of the 365 days in 1865.

1867

5 Jan Industry.

Three factory operatives, employed by Messrs J Maden & Sons, Cotton Spinners, Bacup, were brought up on warrant charged with neglecting their work.

Mr R Dixon, the manager, proved the case, but the men promising to return to their work, the charge was withdrawn.

23 Feb Railway.

'I must congratulate the directors etc on the trains having attained the speed of a fast trotting donkey'.

1869

10 Jul Bacup Streets.

Residents of Bacup who have friends visiting them are advised to caution them to avoid the public streets as they would a pestilence.

Just now when the weather is favourable, we have mountains of dust all along the roads, and should we have heavy rain we shall soon have literally a sea of puddle.

A stranger walking from the station would doubt if we had approached anywhere near the first stage of civilisation.

Even when the roads are scraped it is often left in piles for at least a fortnight, and often much longer.

1874

26 Dec Industry.

Factories now start work 6.30am to 6pm.

At some of the mills notices have been posted that those now paid by the week, will now be paid hourly.

They will thus lose 3 hours a week.

From the census 1871 – 1881, the farm grew by 10 acres to 34 acres with an increasing number of cattle, a milk round, and a few more sheep. The farm appeared to be a successful enterprise which lasted for a period of 18 years. During the period 1864 – 1880 his wife Ellen gave birth to 8 children, as the 1881 census shows. James (1st) is now 51, Ellen 46, engaged on home duties, Elizabeth E. (Lizzie) aged 17, Sarah A. aged 16. Both these girls are cotton knitters, Alice M. aged 13 is on home duties. James 2nd, aged 11, Maggie aged 9 and George Richard aged 6 are all scholars, plus two other young children, Thomas W. aged 4, (of Richard and Thomas more later) and little Amelia aged 1. So poor wife Ellen was still child bearing aged 45.

The remarkable thing about these children is that they all survived well into middle and old age, when so many children in Bacup town during this period were dying from ill health and bad conditions. One must conclude that although the conditions at Slip Inn were obviously hard, there was no malnutrition and a freedom from killer diseases.

Bacup Cotton Mills.

Bacup dominated by Church and Chapel.

Mount Pleasant School 1879.
James Haworth (the Second) front row 5th from the left.

A letter published by the Sheffield Daily Telegraph.

1878 **Nov**

Reprint by the Bacup Times 9 Nov. 1878:

"The Forest of Rossendale".

There is a painful absence of 'forest' or anything approaching thereto. The eye roves over bleak, barren moors, or along bare ugly hills, searching in vain for vestiges of the alleged 'forest'.

Take a birds eye view from the highest eminence and what do you see most of all is — STONE. It crops up everywhere. Rossendale is still in the stone age, nor is there any expectation that it will ever emerge therefrom.

Mountainous dirt heaps — yawning quarries — lines of flag-laden trucks.

It is a dreary work-a-day place, in which a depressed, unintelligent population makes shift to exist in a variety of disagreeable ways. The people of the 'forest' are gaunt, tall, or lumpy and squat, with an expression on their faces as if their minds were constantly dwelling on the idea of suicide, or as if they had made a wager with someone that they would never look pleasant in their lives, and were determined to win.

Yet when the 'forrester' opens his mouth (or rather when he is of the humour to speak, for his mouth is ever open) he utters, not wise and witty words, but instead rolls out oaths and curses, which his wonderful dialect happily half conceals.

This is one of the reasons why the 'forest' offers a fine field for missionary labour. As a mission field, Rossendale has attractions which in Africa do not exist. The missionary here may go about, almost with the certainty that he will not be eaten. In the very worst times, when half the population was being slowly starved on parish allowance, a missionary would only be 'summat to eat'. This fact secures him immunity. Were he 'summat to sup' the matter would be different.

The 'factory hands' are an entirely different class. They are as insignificant physically as the 'brownbacks' (quarrymen) are prodigious. Cadaverous faces, sunken eyes, leaden looks and general ricketiness — such, and their clogs are the distinguishing peculiarities of the mill-workers. They are strangely ignorant.

They have not enough character to make them interesting as a study, but are just a dull stolid, depressed class, about whom no one would care to concern himself.

Of the outside world they know little, and care less — being wholly wrapped up in themselves. Their life reflected by their newspapers is one of beer-drinking and tea-drinking, both in extremes.

The Valley is inhabited chiefly by two classes — 'factory hands' and 'brownbacks'.

The 'brownback' is a picturesque, if not romantic being. He swears with perhaps more real grace, vigour and effectiveness than any other person whatever. Everything about him is massive, but for his understanding. His dress is primitive, consisting of a 'slop' (or overall) a red handkerchief and a hairy cap. If he wants to be particular he adds trousers, but these when first introduced were considered luxuries, and avoided by the steady conservative ones. The 'brownback' is engaged in the 'delphs' or quarries, and partakes of the roughness of the material among which he works. When not blasting on his employers behalf, he is 'blasting' on his own private account. He might be put forward to out-swear, out-drink and out-eat any competition. He is indifferent as to his lodging and will sleep anywhere. A saint existed in the old time in Cyprus who allowed the dirt to accumulate on his body till he was encased in it as a suit of armour. The 'brownback' imitates the saint largely not from love of sanctity, but love of ease.

The hours away from the delph he considers time for drinking beer, or if he has no money, to stand at street corners, envying those who have.

He fights policemen, and maltreats his wife, if he owns a slave of that description.

There are some churches and chapels, and clergymen and ministers, hence it is evident that the place is regarded as civilised and christian.

The Rossendale Valley might well be called the 'Valley of Tears' in respect to the spitting rain which continues 23 out of the 24 hours, the odd hour being devoted to comical attempts on the part of the sun to 'get up a shine'. The clouds from all quarters make a point of dissolving immediately over the unfortunate district. As a consequence the earth is sodden and soaked. The drenched natives are for ever looking as if they had by accident tumbled into a canal and just scrambled out.

Nature has hardly acted fairly by the Rossendalers; since she gave them such a climate, she ought in conscience to have made them waterproof.

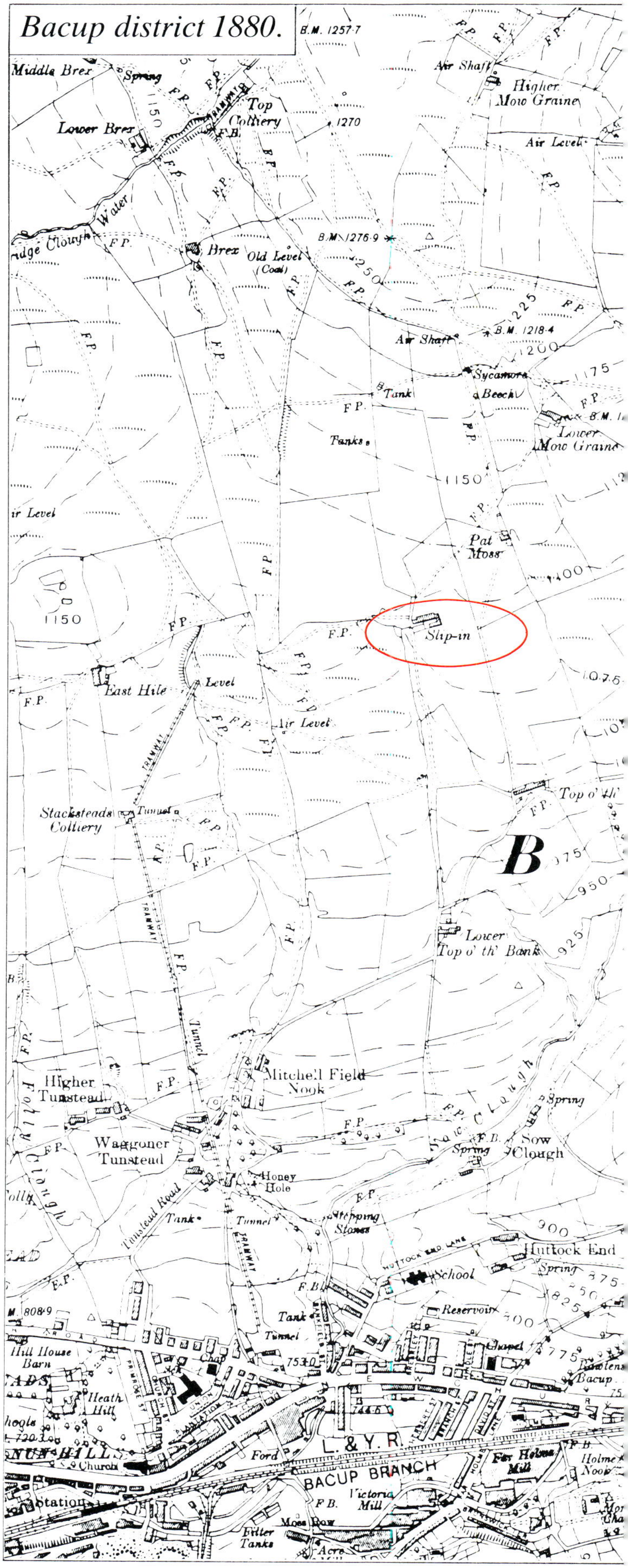

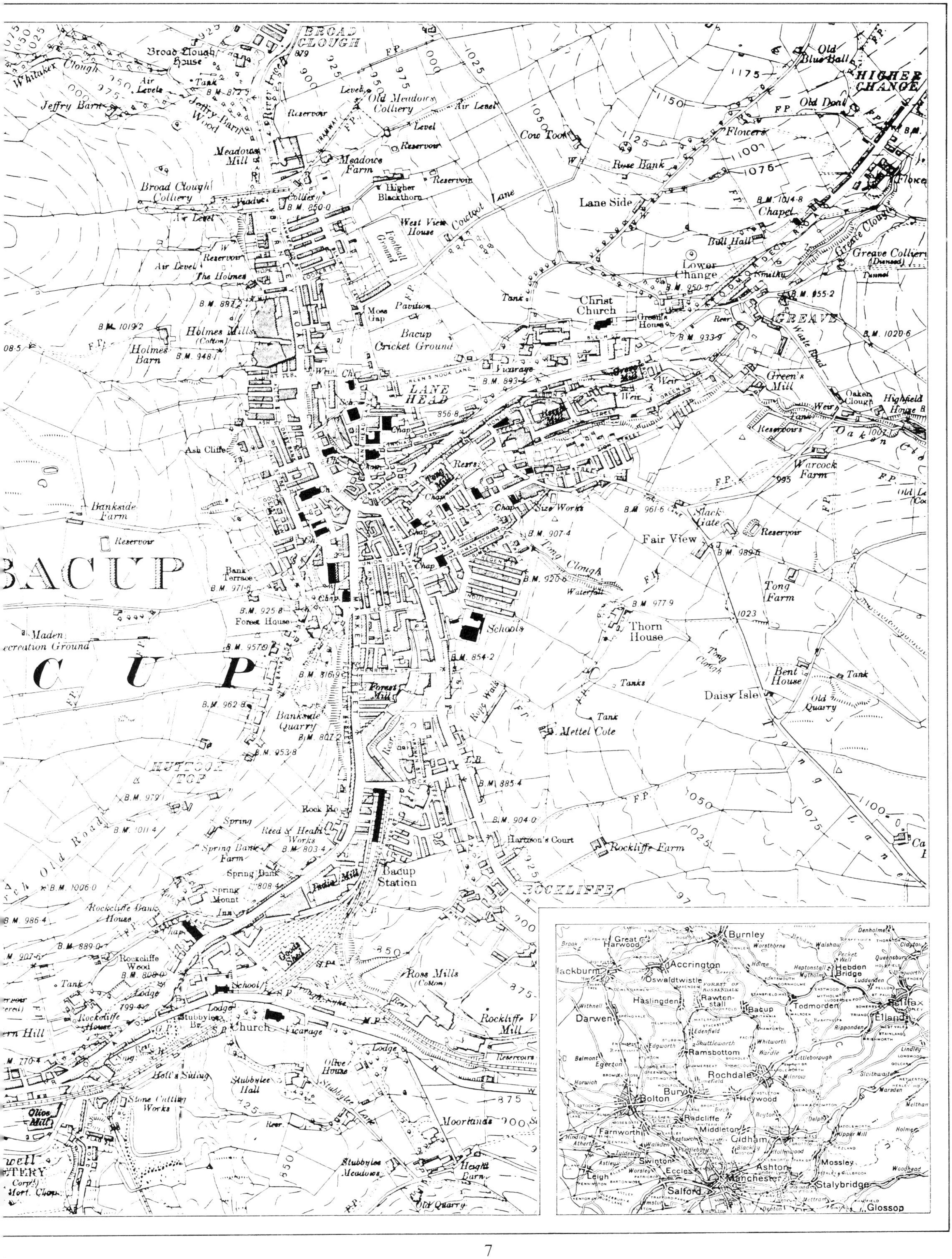
BACUP
BROAD CLOUGH
Broad Clough House
Whitaker Clough
Jeffry Barn
Jeffry Barn Wood
Old Meadows Colliery
Reservoir
Meadows Mill
Meadows Farm
Higher Blackthorn
Broad Clough Colliery
Viaduct
Colliery
Air Level
The Holmes
Holmes Mills (Cotton)
Holmes Barn
West View House
Football Ground
Cowtoot Lane
Cow Toot
Rose Bank
Lane Side
Old Blue Ball
HIGHER CHANGE
Old Dean
Flowers
Chapel
Bull Hall
Lower Change
Smithy
Greave Colliery
GREAVE
Christ Church
Green's House
Moss Gap
Pavilion
Bacup Cricket Ground
LANE HEAD
Vicarage
Green's Mill
Oaken Clough
Highfield House
Reservoirs
Warcock Farm
Ash Cliffe
Bankside Farm
Size Works
Slack Gate
Fair View
Tong Clough
Waterfall
Tong Farm
Bank Terrace
Forest House
Maden Recreation Ground
Schools
Thorn House
Bent House
Tank
Tanks
Daisy Isle
Old Quarry
Forest Mill
Bankside Quarry
Rope Walk
Mettel Cote
HUTCH TOP
Rock Ho
Spring
Reed & Heald Works
Spring Bank Farm
Spring Bank
Spring Mount
Inn
Hartleys Court
Rockliffe Farm
Bacup Station
ROCKLIFFE
Rockcliffe Bank House
Rockcliffe Wood
Goods Shed
Ross Mills (Cotton)
School
Lodge
Rockcliffe House
Stubbylee Br.
Church
Vicarage
Rockliffe V Mill
Holt's Siding
Stubbylee Hall
Olive House
Stubbylee Lane
Stone Cutting Works
Olive Mill
Moorlands
Stubbylee Meadows
Height Barn
Old Quarry
Old Road
Burnley
Great Harwood
Accrington
Oswaldtwistle
Haslingden
Rawtenstall
Bacup
Todmorden
Hebden Bridge
Halifax
Elland
Darwen
Edenfield
Shuttleworth
Whitworth
Wardle
Ramsbottom
Littleborough
Rochdale
Milnrow
Bolton
Bury
Heywood
Radcliffe
Middleton
Farnworth
Oldham
Swinton
Eccles
Ashton
Manchester
Salford
Stalybridge
Mossley
Glossop
Leigh

James' father, James (1st) died from a farm accident in January 1888: this was an event which was to change very much the direction of the Haworth family and in particular son James, now aged 18.

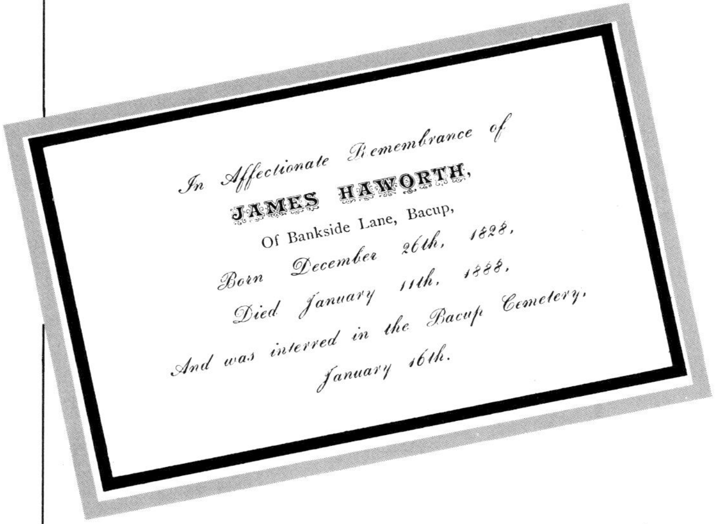
In Affectionate Remembrance of
JAMES HAWORTH,
Of Bankside Lane, Bacup,
Born December 26th, 1828,
Died January 11th, 1888,
And was interred in the Bacup Cemetery,
January 16th.

James had seen over the last 18 years the outside world come more and more to Bacup via the railway, and better roads. He was aware of Victorian progress in providing gaslighting, and in some cases even electricity. The telephone was putting in an appearance. Shops were beginning to stock, sell and advertise all kinds of new products and inventions in this boom era. England during this period was the industrial powerhouse of the world. Strangely enough at this boom time, Bacup and other cotton mill towns had suffered very much from unemployment. Demand for cotton had dropped, as mills started production in foreign countries and parts of the Empire.

1879

5 Apl Industry.

The Cotton trade is getting worse.

A general reduction of wages by 10% was enforced 6 months ago. After a meeting in the Mechanics it was resolved that another reduction of 10% should take place.

In Bacup a relief fund has been started and during the last few weeks between 400 and 500 distressed people have been relieved weekly.

There exists in Bacup, and Rossendale generally a mutual confidence between employees and employers. Trade Unions have never been at all encouraged in the district, and there is no likelihood that the proposed reduction will be resisted.

Two mass meetings of operatives are announced.

Mr William Pickup's mill, Newline, the hands turned out, but on being told that if they did not go in again in 10 minutes, they would be locked out, they returned to work.

1881

19 Mar Telephone.

Telephone communication has been fixed from Beech House to the Bacup Corn Mill for Mr J S Sutcliffe Esq. JP., thereby opening immediate communication from one place to the other without the aid of messengers.

We understand he also proposes to carry the connection forward to his Corn Mill at Rochdale.

We shall not be surprised to find the use of the telephone becomes general throughout the district.

1883

22 Oct Tramways.

Surveying commenced for Tramway from Rochdale to Bacup.

3 Dec Railway.

The first train from Bacup to Rochdale.
Thurs last – 7.15am.
Fares: Bacup to Rochdale – 2/6d – 1/10d – 1/5d. (Return).
Bacup to Manchester 6/-d – 4/4d – 3/2d. (Return).
The speed of trains between Facit & Bacup is limited to 10mph.

24 Dec Industry.

Now that the toll bars are abolished, Rossendale manufacturers are sending cotton pieces by road to Manchester, instead of by rail, and it is stated that the old-fashioned means of carriage is not only cheaper than L. & Y. Rly but actually quicker.

1884

21 Jun Sunday Gambling.

As rife on the tops as ever.

We are glad to note that the Bacup Police have been able to make an example of one batch of these most pernicious of Sabbath breakers, three of whom were on Wed fined 5/- and costs, for gambling on Brandwood Moor on Sunday last.

9 Aug Electric Light.

The first occasion on which the electric light has been made use of in the town.

Messrs Wm Sutcliffe & Sons, Corn Mill, Yorkshire St.

Gas entirely superseded in this mill. Sixty 20 candle power incandescent lamps.

Bacup Flood 1895.

The old Post Office occupying the corner site at the junction of Burnley Road with Market Street.

James, as the male head (aged 18 in 1888) of the family, now had to take stock. The farm was no longer viable due to cheaper meat, eggs and milk reaching Bacup via the railway and better roads. The future as a teacher with more study yet to do would provide no income for some time, so the family sold the farm to pay off debts. The family, 9 in number, moved to a newly built street of Co-op houses in Bacup, namely 35 Regent Street. This house was situated near the top of a row of terraced houses perched seemingly at an angle of 40 degrees from the horizontal. It consisted then of 4 rooms, (2 up and 2 down). Rent from the Co-op was 4s 4d per week or £150 to buy. James, the chief bread-winner, aged 18, and not more than 5ft tall, obtained a job behind the counter of stationers, Shepherd, Swyre and Markham in Market Street, (still very much in business in 1987 as Shepherd and Markham) and he so remained until March 1896.

James Haworth (the Second) aged 21 years.

James Haworth employed here 1888 – 1896.

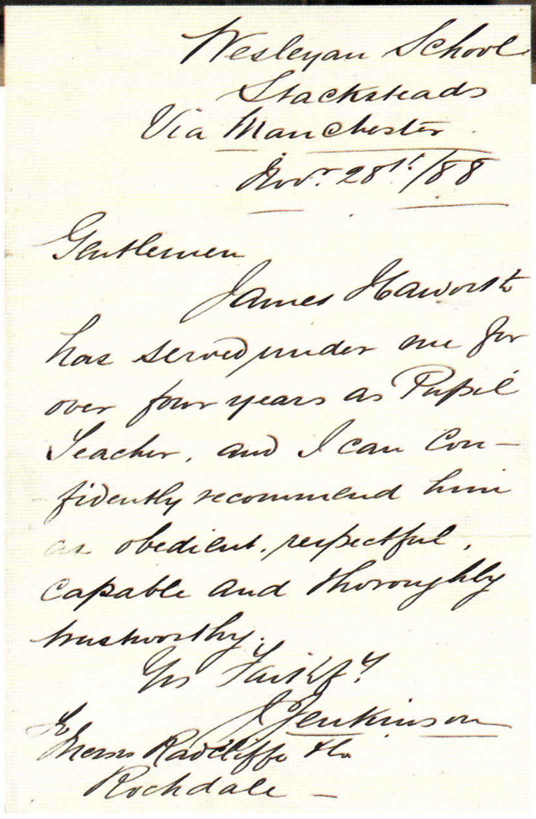
Wesleyan School
Stacksteads
Via Manchester
Nov. 28th/88

Gentlemen

James Haworth has served under me for over four years as Pupil Teacher, and I can confidently recommend him as obedient, respectful, capable and thoroughly trustworthy.

Yrs Faithy
J Jenkinson

To Messrs Radcliffe Ho
Rochdale

Recommendation for employment from James Haworth's Headmaster, which was unsuccessful.

No. 35 Regent Street (the third house on left).

1887

9 Jul Coal.

Rossendale mine-owners object to the Govt's ruling that the minimum age for starting work in the pit should be 12 years.

1889

3 Aug Electric.

In all probability we are on the eve of a great revolution in the matter of public and private lighting.

Two separate companies are applying to Parliament for powers to supply electricity to Bacup.

The Council ought to promote a Bill of their own.

If we get the electric light, perhaps the Gas Co will be glad to lower their prices.

10 Aug Tramways.

Opened last Sat. The event has long been looked forward to, and is hailed as a great boon to the district.

On Sat the trams were crowded.

In the early part of the week there was some unpleasantness at Waterfoot owing to the Company having fixed upon Glen Terrace as the terminus of the stage from Stacksteads, instead of Waterfoot Railway Station.

Burnley Road, Bacup.

We are glad to say that the directors have altered the stage to the railway station.

21 Sep Phonograph.

Mr Edison has succeeded in perfecting a mailing phonograph. People could now speak their letters into instruments, take off the impressed cylinder, open it flat, and send it away in an ordinary envelope.

The receiver could fit the cylinder to the machine and reproduce the message without there being need to write a single word.

1890

13 Dec Electric Light.

The Queen has discontinued the use of the electric light, as it is injurous to the eyes.

1893

2 Sep Licensed Houses.

Bacup has 79.
One to every 297 of the population.

7 Oct Football.

Professionalism. The wages of an Association player ranges higher than that of many men who have spent hundreds of pounds in education and many years of study.

It is said that in one town a half-back has been obtained at a cost of £250 down, £150 a year and an outside post of £70 a year.

Such demands as these are outrageous.

1894

2 Feb Industry – Destitution.

Soup for the destitute served at the Police Station to about 100. Expenses have been defrayed by a fund raised by the Police Force.

Soup will be served out daily as long as the severe weather lasts.

Since Tues about 81 gallons of soup, half a load of potatoes, 52 loaves, 54 cwt of coals and a quantity of clogs, boots, clothing (bed) to exceptionally needy cases, have been dispensed by the Bacup Police Force.

From 100 to 150 families have been assisted daily.

Stringent inquiry is made into each case so that none but the really needy may participate.

Contributions have been received from the Mayor and several Bacup tradesmen.

1895

9 Mar Industry – Half-timers.

Proposed to raise school leaving age from 11 to 12.

The Town Council is against raising the age.

The Mayor said they were so happy at their work that he would be sorry to deprive them of it until they were 12.

(Comment by Times – 'If it is so splendid I wonder why well-to-do people keep their children away?').

Bankside, Bacup, looking across Market Street and Plantation Street 1882.

His sales assistant position, held for nearly eight years, brought him very much into contact with travellers selling account books, notebooks and the newly produced coloured greeting cards which were just becoming popular for birthdays and Christmas. James obviously gleaned much from the printing travellers selling these items on behalf of the printing firms in Lancashire and Yorkshire, whose salesmen worked their way up the valleys, from mill town to mill town. No doubt the travellers were pleased to have someone who showed interest in their job whilst they waited their turn to show their samples to Mr Shepherd or Mr Markham and hopefully obtain their orders. One particular traveller from the printers Richard Johnson & Sons of Manchester noted young James' interest in becoming a print traveller and arranged an interview for James, one March Saturday afternoon with his Managing Director, James duly attended and perhaps to his surprise was told he could have a traveller's job if he could supply three good references. To this end, James went to the then Mayor of Bacup, John Henry Maden, M.P., his headmaster J. Jenkinson and the Wesleyan Minister. James obtained these references by the Tuesday and posted them off to his intending employer.

On the Wednesday, the Minister was taking refreshment in the back room of the stationers with Mr Shepherd and acquainted him with the news that his counterhand had asked him, the Minister, for a reference as he was apparently seeking a new job. On the Minister leaving, Mr Shepherd called James into his back room and on learning it was indeed true that he had applied for a traveller's job, immediately dismissed him.

1896

15 Feb Bacup Streets.

They are a standing disgrace to the town. All the thoroughfares in the centre of the town, including Market St, Bridge St, St. James St, and Union St, have been filled with a surging mass of young men and young women, boys and girls who seem to take delight in marching round jostling each other about, and also all others with whom they come in contact, so that it has been next to impossible for decent people to pass along.

We are glad to observe that the police and magistrates have decided to make a determined effort to put an end to this disgraceful state of affairs.

Several cases have come before the bench last Wed.

It was stated that the young women were nearly as bad as the young men.

7 Mar Police.

The Town Council are to purchase a bicycle for the use of the police in serving summonses, catching furious riders and for sergeants to visit constables on their beats.

13 Jun Cycling – Women.

Cycling by women is becoming quite fashionable among the ladies in Bacup.

Already a few have ventured to appear in public.

1 Aug Cycling – Women.

Women ought not to cycle.

It is a useless, and unwomanly craze, and will go out just as quickly as it came into fashion.

Girls and women who are well brought up, and really nice, but who have taken to the cycle only because it is the fashion for the moment ought not to be allowed to lay themselves open to being obliged to mix with the bold and mannish class of women who are the real patrons of this sport.

29 Aug Motor Cars.

14 miles per hour the limit. (It had been 4).

5 Dec Motor Car.

The first in Rossendale.

Propelled by Benzoline.

James was now unemployed but only for the Thursday, and Friday following his dismissal. For in the first post on Saturday came a letter to say that the salesman's job was his. The relief was great for he was hoping soon to marry Ann Unwin, whom he had been courting for the last 4 years, beginning with his poignant letter to her of 28th July 1892. Ann, also aged 26 lived with her mother, father and 3 sisters at 6 Christchurch Street, Bacup. Ann had since 12 years old been a typical mill girl of the period, working long hours as a knitter. Along with a thousand or two others, her clogs contributed to a cacophony of sound as the girls went to begin work in the early hours of each morning.

Ann Unwin, mill girl.

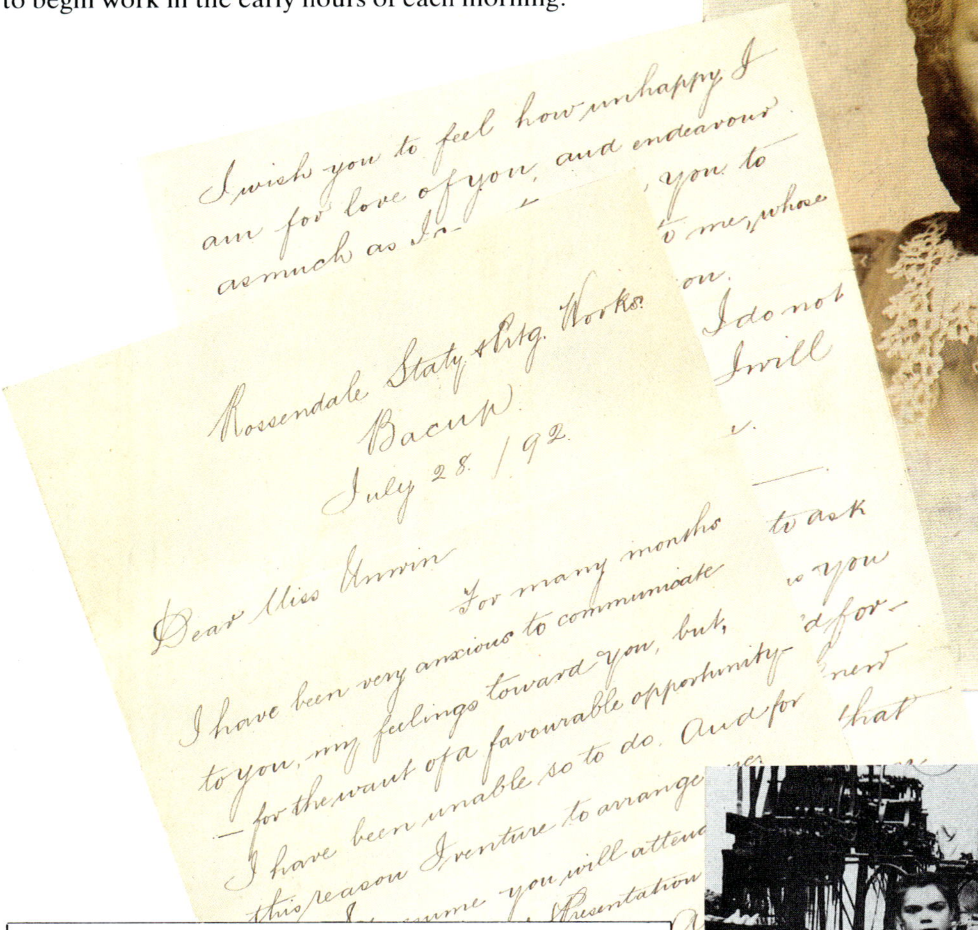

I wish you to feel how unhappy I
am for love of you, and endeavour
as much as I ... you to

Rossendale Staty & Ptg. Works
Bacup
July 28/92

Dear Miss Unwin
For many months
I have been very anxious to communicate
to you, my feelings toward you, but,
— for the want of a favourable opportunity
I have been unable so to do. And for
this reason I venture to arrange
I presume you will attend ... Presentation

Dear Miss Unwin

For many months I have been very anxious to communicate to you, my feelings toward you, but, – for the want of a favourable opportunity – I have been unable so to do. And for this reason I venture to arrange one.

I presume you will attend the Meeting at Mount. (Presentation of xxxxxx) next Saturday Evening. After the meeting will you meet me in Earnshaw Road? I am sorry to send this note, because I know it may give you pain & unrest, but I am selfish enough to send it, because I wish you to feel how unhappy I am for love of you and endeavour as much as I can to entice you to give up your whole heart to me, whose whole existence hangs upon you.

I am greedy of you Annie. I do not think of anyone but you. I will give up anything for you.

Do not forget me Annie –.

But have I any right to ask you to remember me? Perhaps you do think of me? You would forgive me asking this if you knew the extreme passion I have that you should love me as I do you.

Consoling myself with the hopes of soon seeing you I remain

faithfully yours

James Haworth

Type of machinery Ann Unwin worked.

July 28th 1892
Letter written by James Haworth to Ann Unwin using his employer's address to create a good impression.

John Unwin – Ann's father.

The George and Dragon Inn, Bacup 1880.

Ann (centre), Mother (right) and younger Sisters.

Ann aged 21 years.

No. 6 Christchurch Street (third house up from bottom).
Home of the Unwin family from 1880.

45 Pursuant to the Acts for the Re...

96. Marriage SOLEMNIZED AT Wesleyan Chapel Mount Pleasant, in the District of Bacup

No.	When Married.	Name and Surname.	Age.	Condition.	Rank or Profession.	Residence at the time of Marriage.		
90	Eleventh June 1896.	James Haworth	26 years	Bachelor	Commercial Traveller	35 Regent Street Bacup	James Haworth Deceased	Farmer
		Ann Unwin	26 years	Spinster	Heald Knitter	6 Christ Church Street Bacup.	John Unwin	Traveller

Married in the Wesleyan Chapel according to the Rites and Ceremonies of the Wesleyan Methodists by Certificate, by me, Walter H Mayer Wes Minister

This Marriage was Solemnized between us: James Haworth, Ann Unwin. In the Presence of us, Thomas Walker Haworth, Esther Unwin. Robert Scholfield, REGISTRAR.

I hereby Certify the above to be a True Copy of the Entry No. 90, in the Marriage Register, No. 22, for the said District of Haslingden. Witness my Hand this 11th day of June 1896. Robert Scholfield, Registrar.

This Certificate being signed and certified as a true copy by an officer in whose custody the original is intrusted, is admissible in evidence in any Court of Justice.

The marriage of James and Ann took place on 11th June 1896, at the Wesleyan Chapel, Mount Pleasant, Bacup, where they had first met. Ann's father, John Unwin, appeared also to have been a traveller, so perhaps he had some influence on James choosing that profession.

There is no record of any honeymoon and it was more than likely back to work on the Monday, but at least they had their own home at 6 Rose Hill Street, Bacup. This again was a house on a 40 degree slope, the front door straight onto the street with direct entry to the living room. The privy would be at the back, along with the coal shed and a rough back alley led to a rear entrance. Ninety-two years later the home is still of the same size. The street seems to have a warm and friendly atmosphere. This cannot be said for the soulless so-called modern estates and high-rise flats that are today to be seen in parts of Rossendale Valley.

James and Ann were, I recall, never to lose their Bacup accent which, even in 1987, seems not to have been diluted by the present inhabitants of Bacup. This was clearly instanced to me by the fair lady assistant in Shepherd and Markham who was most helpful to my queries on literature of old Bacup. Likewise, with the ladies of the Library and Friends of the Bacup Natural History Society, all of whom took great trouble to help me on my visit to Bacup. As a Southerner, I always had to listen with great care to make sure I understood what was said and I recall as a young boy experiencing very much the same difficulty with my grandfather and grandmother.

Wedding Day 11th June 1896.

No. 6 Rose Hill Street, Bacup (third house up). Photo 1987.

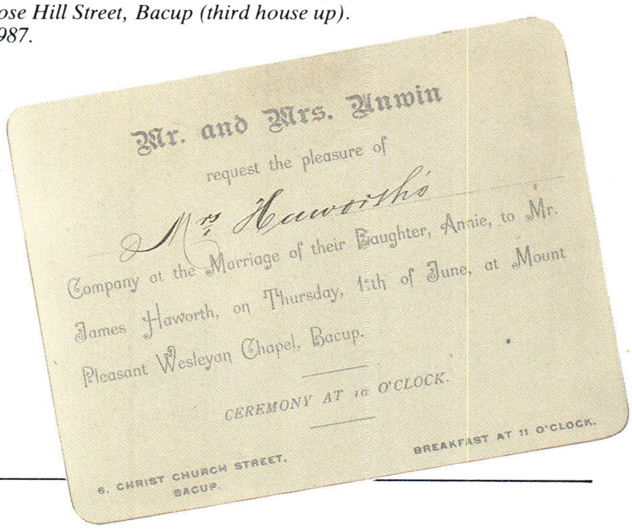
Mr. and Mrs. Unwin
request the pleasure of
Mr Haworth's
Company at the Marriage of their Daughter, Annie, to Mr. James Haworth, on Thursday, 11th of June, at Mount Pleasant Wesleyan Chapel, Bacup.

CEREMONY AT 10 O'CLOCK.

6, CHRIST CHURCH STREET, BACUP.

BREAKFAST AT 11 O'CLOCK.

James, newly married, now had to prove himself as a salesman of print, account books and general stationery. His salary would have been very small, probably £2 per week and he would have to pay all his travelling expenses out of that. Any further real income would depend on commission from sales.

The first train of the morning from Bacup would perhaps take James to Rochdale or Bolton. Leaving the station, there would be no alternative, carrying heavy bags of samples, but to walk miles per day in each town. Calling on existing customers and endeavouring to find new business, would often entail fruitless calls and walking in the wrong direction due to bad information. As James had to pay for his own travelling expenses, walking was the only way to conserve his salary; to take a tram was a luxury indeed.

It is perhaps difficult to imagine how James felt leaving behind the compactness and confines of Bacup for the hustle and noise of the larger towns down the valleys, plus the meccas of Manchester and Liverpool. Their streets filled to capacity with pedestrians, carriages and horsedrawn carts carrying loads of every size and description. The clanging of trams and occasionally the sound of a horseless carriage back-firing, frightening man and beast alike.

James must have been successful in the short time he had been given to prove himself – at the most it would have been one month's trial.

Market Street was originally known as Market Stede Lane, but in the early 19th century it was renamed Market Street. In its original state Market Street was extremely narrow, unsuited to the increased use made of it as Manchester grew in size and importance. In 1821, the Police Commissioners obtained an act of parliament which enabled them to widen the road and reconstruct the buildings along its line. Although work started in 1822, it was not completed until 1834, as the Police Commissioners had to wait for money to become available. The total cost of the work was a quarter of a million pounds. The result was a wide thoroughfare enabling the free movement of traffic between one end of Manchester and the other. The photograph shows Market Street around 1890 and the buildings to be seen on the Royal Exchange side at that time.

Piccadilly, one of the best known parts of Manchester, received its name in the early years of the 19th century, but there is nothing to indicate why it was so called. The road had originally been called Lever's Row, whilst that part of Piccadilly occupied by the Esplanade and Infirmary had been called the Daub Holes, from the 16th century, if not earlier.

Cannon Street was one of the principal business streets of Victorian Manchester linking High Street with Corporation Street. Between 1830 and 1880, Cannon Street declined from being an attractive street to one which gave the impression of an overcrowded dirty slum, which the visitor was glad to pass through as quickly as possible.

As the months and years went by, being a successful traveller for Richard Johnson & Sons, he would have noticed that full halftone colour was becoming very much apparent for advertisements and sales literature in shops as well as poster sites. He began to envy such productions which were being produced in anything up to 16 colours by the new Chromo Litho process. Such printing was not within the capacity of Richard Johnson & Sons, who were stationery printers. They were confined to black and white, with colour used occasionally.

James now had a family with the birth of daughter Lucy and a son, to be John James, was on the way. His wife Annie (as she was now known) could no longer go out to work. He was the sole bread-winner, but with increasing frustration at not being able to bid for the full colour print orders with their greater value in money terms and thereby more commission and salary.

It was the custom for commercial travellers when seeking a meal or staying overnight in a hotel (a temperance one in James' case), to sit together. The senior traveller, by custom, presided over an open discussion about success, experiences and conditions.

During the year 1900 James met travellers from the now famous Leeds print firm of Alf Cooke, who were justifiably proud of their company. With their wide range of colour printing and by the award of the Royal Warrant as Chromo Lithographers to Her Majesty Queen Victoria in 1885, they were the only printing firm then to have such an award.

James, with 4 years of hard stationery print selling behind him, was now very sure of himself. He felt able to apply for a traveller's position with the illustrious firm of Alf Cooke. Nothing ventured, nothing gained, he wrote direct to Mr Alf Cooke at Christmas 1900. Mr Cooke, being always a gentleman, acknowledged the letter by return but with it came no promise of an interview.

However, at the end of January came a letter which awaited James on a cold Thursday evening, after his return from selling in Manchester, stating if he cared to present himself at 11a.m. that coming Saturday at Crown Print Works, Leeds, he would be granted an interview.

As luck would have it, Saturday morning arrived with a heavy snowfall during the night. The carrier with whom he had arranged to get a lift into Todmorden for the Leeds train, was not willing to risk the journey. The interchange connections by the very slow Lancashire and Yorkshire Railway from Bacup to Leeds, would not have got James to Leeds on time, even in fine weather. There was, therefore, nothing for it but to walk out into the dark early morning, with still falling snow, and trudge the 7 miles of moorland road to Todmorden Station. Clutching his bag with change of clothes and boots, he reached the station. James was fortunate enough to find that although the trains were slow, their drivers were dedicated enough to make sure they ran to time in such conditions. James made Leeds with time to spare to locate Crown Print Works at Hunslet, through the still falling snow flurries.

Todmorden Station, where trains still connect with Leeds. Photo 1987.

Bacup – Todmorden Road.

Arriving at the most imposing entrance, James saw the florid decorations at the main entrance to the Alf Cooke powerhouse of print. It was surmounted in those days by a huge Royal Coat of Arms flanked by flags, whilst the name of the company was spelled out in letters some 15ft in height affixed to the roof edge.

Once inside, he would have been aware of the hum of machinery, the smartness and opulence of the interior, brilliantly lit by electricity powered by the Company's own steam engine.

At the appointed hour he would have been ushered into Mr Alf Cooke's large oak panelled office, with a roaring fire to one side. Seated behind a large desk, a man of medium build, prematurely white haired for his age of 58, and possibly not looking too well with an impending illness, immaculately dressed, he came forward to greet James.

Alf Cooke was born in Leeds of a father who kept a shop in Meadow Lane, which combined the functions of stationer, printer, bookseller and newspaper vendor. Brought up under a rigid discipline imposed by his God-fearing father, he went to the Collegiate Institute for a sound education.

Alf Cooke had gone into business on his own account, aged 24, by renting a shop to sell stationery and newspapers. He undertook simple letterpress printing, but 12 months later he installed one of the new lithographic presses and thereby introduced coloured printed almanacs for shop-keepers to give to their customers.

Specimen from the Alf Cooke Album of Colour Printing.

Extracts from the Bacup Circuit Wesleyan Record Vol. I No. 10 October 1900.

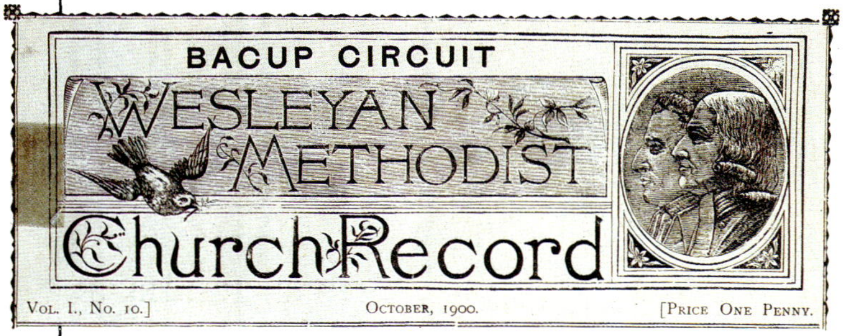
BACUP CIRCUIT
WESLEYAN METHODIST
Church Record
VOL. I., No. 10.] OCTOBER, 1900. [PRICE ONE PENNY.

BAPTISMS.

HAWORTH. – On September 3rd, at Mount Pleasant, John James, son of James and Ann Haworth, 8, Rosehill Street. Born May 3rd 1899.

September 23rd was observed as Band of Hope Sunday. Instead of the usual lessons we had three addresses of lofty tone and great usefulness. Mr. Longthorn Cockcroft spoke some strong, plain and kindly words. Mr. Jas. Hy. Ashworth dwelt upon the great dignity of man in virtues of his kinship with God, and showed that proper self respect could not be maintained if men became slaves to strong drink. The elder scholars especially were urged to an intelligent acceptance of temperance principles. The remainder of the time was profitably utilised by the Superintendent.

The very successful sale of these coloured almanacs in the early 1870s enhanced his business. With the profits, he bought premises on the east side of Hunslet Road near to Crown Point Bridge; hence the name Crown Point Works.

Alf Cooke survived two disastrous fires in 1880 and 1894 which more or less destroyed his printing works on both occasions. On the latter occasion he chartered a special train to take him from Scarborough, where he had been visiting his fishing boat interests, to Leeds. Surveying the smoking ruins, he immediately planned his re-building to start printing again, which he was to do within 10 days. Consequently, he built an even better and more spacious factory within 10 months, which still stands today in 1989, with modern additions.

Crown Works, Hunslet, Leeds.

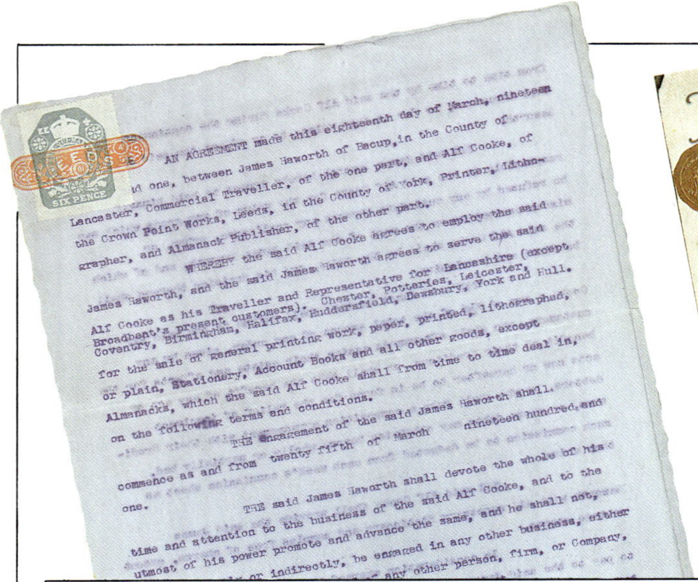
AN AGREEMENT made this eighteenth day of March, nineteen
d one, between James Haworth of Bacup, in the County of
Lancaster, Commercial Traveller, of the one part, and Alf Cooke, of
the Crown Point Works, Leeds, in the County of York, Printer, Litho-
grapher, and Almanack Publisher, of the other part.
WHEREBY the said Alf Cooke agrees to employ the said
James Haworth, and the said James Haworth agrees to serve the said
Alf Cooke as his Traveller and Representative for Lancashire (except
Broadbent's present customers). Chester, Potteries, Leicester,
Coventry, Birmingham, Halifax, Huddersfield, Dewsbury, York and Hull.
for the sale of general printing work, paper, printed, lithographed,
or plain, Stationery, Account Books and all other goods, except
Almanacks, which the said Alf Cooke shall from time to time deal in,
on the following terms and conditions.
THE engagement of the said James Haworth shall
commence as and from twenty fifth of March nineteen hundred and
one.
THE said James Haworth shall devote the whole of his
time and attention to the business of the said Alf Cooke, and to the
utmost of his power promote and advance the same, and he shall not,

Agreement between James Haworth and Alf Cooke 18th March 1901

AN AGREEMENT made this eighteenth day of March, nineteen hundred and one, between James Haworth of Bacup, in the County of Lancaster, Commercial Traveller, of the one part, and Alf Cooke, of the Crown Point Works, Leeds, in the County of York, Printer, Lithographer, and Almanack Publisher, of the other part.

WHEREBY the said Alf Cooke agrees to employ the said James Haworth, and the said James Haworth agrees to serve the said Alf Cooke as his Traveller and Representative for Lancashire (except Broadbent's present customers). Chester, Potteries, Leicester, Coventry, Birmingham, Halifax, Huddersfield, Dewsbury, York and Hull, for the sale of general printing work, paper, printed, lithographed, or plain, Stationery, Account Books and all other goods, except Almanacks, which the said Alf Cooke shall from time to time deal in, on the following terms and conditions.

THE engagement of the said James Haworth shall commence as and from twenty fifth of March nineteen hundred and one.

THE said James Haworth shall devote the whole of his time and attention to the business of the said Alf Cooke, and to the utmost of his power promote and advance the same, and he shall not, either directly or indirectly, be engaged in any other business either on his own account or on behalf of any other person, firm, or Company, whatsoever, during the continuance of this Agreement.

THE said James Haworth shall not collect or receive from the customers of the said Alf Cooke any coin, bills, drafts, cheques or documents representing money, in payment of any account with the said Alf Cooke, but the said James Haworth shall decline same if tendered to him, any breach of this clause by the said James Haworth be considered as a sufficient reason for the instant dismissal of the said James Haworth and the immediate recision of this Agreement by the said Alf Cooke.

THE said James Haworth shall defray and pay all Railway, Hotel, and other expenses incurred by him whilst engaged in the business of the said Alf Cooke.

THE said James Haworth shall abide by the General Rules to be observed by all persons employed at the Crown Point Printing Works of the said Alf Cooke now in force, and to all alterations and variations therein and additions thereto, which may be made from time to time by the said Alf Cooke during the continuance of this Agreement, so far as they relate to or effect the said James Haworth.

THE said James Haworth hereby agrees to hold himself responsible to the said Alf Cooke for the value of any goods which may be refused by any customers through any negligence, error, or misrepresentation on the part of the said James Haworth, and of which the said Alf Cooke shall be the judge, and his decision thereon shall be final and conclusive.

THE said James Haworth shall refund to the said Alf Cooke a sum of 7½% of the total amount of any order, given by any customers, who shall afterwards assign their estate and effects for the benefit of their Creditors, or shall take the benefit of any act or acts now or hereafter to be in force for the relief of insolvent debtors, or who shall make a composition arrangement with their Creditors, or whose debts may otherwise become wholly or partially bad, such commission to be deducted from each week's commission sheet as they arise.

THE said Alf Cooke shall provide the said James Haworth with all necessary stationery and samples free of charge, except postage stamps.

In consideration whereof the said Alf Cooke agrees to pay to the said James Haworth, during the continuance of this Agreement a salary of £3.10.0. per week, and a commission of 3¾% on all orders obtained by the said James Haworth, and executed by the said Alf Cooke.

IN case the said James Haworth shall neglect or refuse to perform his services as aforesaid, the wages hereinbefore agreed to be paid to him by the said Alf Cooke shall cease and be no longer payable, during such time as the said James Haworth shall not perform such services as aforesaid, or be unable to do so from illness or any other cause whatever, but the following holidays are excluded from this provision and the wages shall be payable, namely:- A vacation not exceeding fourteen days in length, Good Friday, Easter Monday, Whit Monday, Bank Holiday in August, Christmas Day and the day following in each year.

IF either party to this Agreement desires to determine and put an end to the same, he shall do so by giving to the other party, twenty eight days previous NOTICE in writing thereof expiring on any Saturday, to be delivered personally or sent by Registered letter through the General Post to the last known address of the party to whom such Notice shall be addressed, provided that the said Alf Cooke may at any time summarily discharge the said James Haworth without giving him any Notice whatever, for any breach by him of any clause or provision in this Agreement, or for flagrant misconduct, or for wilful neglect of duty, and of which events and contingencies the said Alf Cooke shall be the sole judge, and his opinion thereon final and conclusive.

Signed by the said Alf Cooke
in the presence of
W. Sowrey,
Woodbine Cottage,
Horsforth

ALF COOKE

Signed by the said James Haworth
in the presence of
T. W. Haworth,
35, Regent Street,
Bacup.
Bank Cashier

JAMES HAWORTH

This slight, short young man James Haworth, aged 30 with a moustache, must have impressed Alf Cooke from the first moment. Both shared the same God-fearing background, the church and one's faith being so important when obtaining a job. James' stationery experience and selling was an added bonus. The interview would have been a very searching one of young James' character, by Alf Cooke, former Mayor of Leeds, Justice of the Peace and Alderman, one of the most powerful and respected men in Leeds, if not the whole of Yorkshire.

Alf Cooke was a man of instant decision. James had a salesman's position subject to an agreement being drawn up, satisfactory references and notice to Richard Johnson & Sons.

The area to be allocated was Lancashire, Yorkshire, Cheshire and Derbyshire. James was to give his all to this High Temple of Print – Crown Works (see Agreement).

James would have retraced his snowbound journey: the seven-mile walk would have passed in a flash in his happiness and satisfaction of working for the best printer in the North of England, if not the whole of the country. His wife Ann would have been pleased for him, though I doubt whether they would have realised at the time, the vision of wider horizons that lay ahead in saying farewell to the severe life of Bacup which they, and their parents had known all their lives. Daughter Lucy would have welcomed her father home. John James, still very much a babe in arms (born May 3rd 1899) would not have known their destinies (including the writer's) were to be changed by this printer in Leeds, giving James a salesman's position.

Wife Ann, children Lucy and John would not have seen much of their head of the household. Six days of the week would have been a round of constant travelling, from 6a.m. in the morning to 8p.m. at night. Many nights were spent away in temperance lodging houses in York, Hull, Birmingham and Coventry. Sunday, they would go to Chapel at least twice and then there would be written reports to Alf Cooke of progress made and orders secured.

Within two months, as seen by Alf Cooke's letter to James, whilst rapping his knuckles over discounts, he was praising his tact, ability and industry (see text of letter).

Despite James' tenacity in bringing in orders combined with ever-increasing salary through commission, he was however, mindful in his success of the difficulties of travelling by train from Bacup. A move could now be afforded. Such a move should be nearer the scene of action and that meant Manchester. Consequently in 1903, a house, No. 5 Vine Street, Prestwich, then a well-to-do suburb of Manchester, was chosen, with the greenery of Heaton Park nearby.

This meant leaving behind at 35 Regent Street, Bacup, – mother Ellen, brother Thomas (now a cashier with the Lancashire and Yorkshire Bank's branch in Bacup) brother Richard and five sisters both married and unmarried.

Alf Cooke's letter to James Haworth with complaint and praise.
Alf Cooke shortly to die from ill health in 1902.

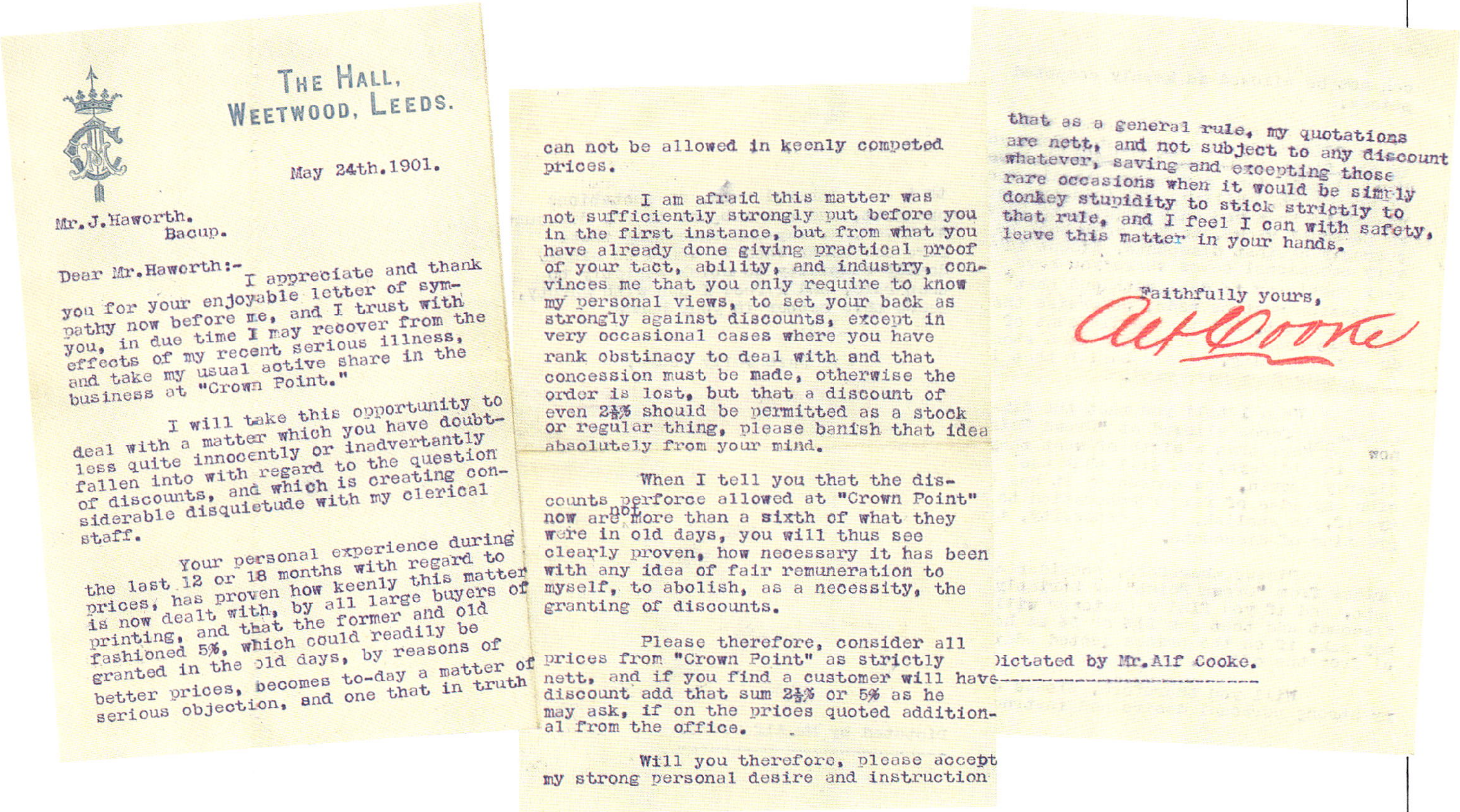

THE HALL,
WEETWOOD, LEEDS.

May 24th.1901.

Mr.J.Haworth.
Bacup.

Dear Mr.Haworth:-
I appreciate and thank you for your enjoyable letter of sympathy now before me, and I trust with you, in due time I may recover from the effects of my recent serious illness, and take my usual active share in the business at "Crown Point."

I will take this opportunity to deal with a matter which you have doubtless quite innocently or inadvertantly fallen into with regard to the question of discounts, and which is creating considerable disquietude with my clerical staff.

Your personal experience during the last 12 or 18 months with regard to prices, has proven how keenly this matter is now dealt with, by all large buyers of printing, and that the former and old fashioned 5%, which could readily be granted in the old days, by reasons of better prices, becomes to-day a matter of serious objection, and one that in truth can not be allowed in keenly competed prices.

I am afraid this matter was not sufficiently strongly put before you in the first instance, but from what you have already done giving practical proof of your tact, ability, and industry, convinces me that you only require to know my personal views, to set your back as strongly against discounts, except in very occasional cases where you have rank obstinacy to deal with and that concession must be made, otherwise the order is lost, but that a discount of even 2½% should be permitted as a stock or regular thing, please banish that idea absolutely from your mind.

When I tell you that the discounts perforce allowed at "Crown Point" now are not more than a sixth of what they were in old days, you will thus see clearly proven, how necessary it has been with any idea of fair remuneration to myself, to abolish, as a necessity, the granting of discounts.

Please therefore, consider all prices from "Crown Point" as strictly nett, and if you find a customer will have discount add that sum 2½% or 5% as he may ask, if on the prices quoted additional from the office.

Will you therefore, please accept my strong personal desire and instruction that as a general rule, my quotations are nett, and not subject to any discount whatever, saving and excepting those rare occasions when it would be simply donkey stupidity to stick strictly to that rule, and I feel I can with safety, leave this matter in your hands.

Faithfully yours,
Alf Cooke

Dictated by Mr.Alf Cooke.

On the 14th February, 1904, son Harry was born. There had never been a Harry in the Haworth family before and I just wonder if he was named after Harry Cooke, who had taken over the control of Alf Cooke Printing on the death, in 1902, of his father.

James would have missed that special confidence he had enjoyed with Alf Cooke in working with a man who had come up the hard way as he had done. Now he would be reporting to a man similar in age to himself, but spared the hardship of James' background.

James by now, through introductions, was pursuing business in London, as others from Alf Cooke had been doing for some time. Amongst James' customers was Oxo whose business warranted a weekly call. This was usually in the afternoon, after having come from a morning call to Cadbury's at Bournville, Birmingham.

London, long the banking, insurance and goods importing centre of Britain, was by 1900 only just beginning to attract businesses based on new technology. Many firms whose head office and factories were in the Midlands and the North, felt that they needed a London office. This for prestigious reasons, as London was then the hub of the greatest Empire the modern world had ever known, as well as keeping close contact with the newly formed advertising agencies. Such agencies were required to organise and handle the placing of the ever-increasing amount of all types of advertising, created for companies required to maintain and increase their expansion, when England was at her peak as an industrial nation.

Alf Cooke Ltd were no exception in wanting a London office and in 1905 an office with clerk and typist was opened in Old Serjeant's Inn Chambers, Chancery Lane, London WC.

James, of course made use of this base from the very first, as did Harry Cooke and others from Leeds who were seeking business in the South. James, meanwhile, was spreading his business-getting expertise; companies such as Huntley & Palmer, Fry's of Bristol and Cadbury's were under his belt and he was able to see their buyers very easily. Buyers also had London offices and on certain days "held court" for would-be supplying printers.

Lucy Haworth, John James Haworth, 1903.

Whilst the move to Prestwich brought improved surroundings for children Lucy and John James, it also meant that their father could see yet more customers in the time available. Trams from the bottom of the road took him to Manchester's main line stations, from which fast trains would steam to the towns he had to cover.

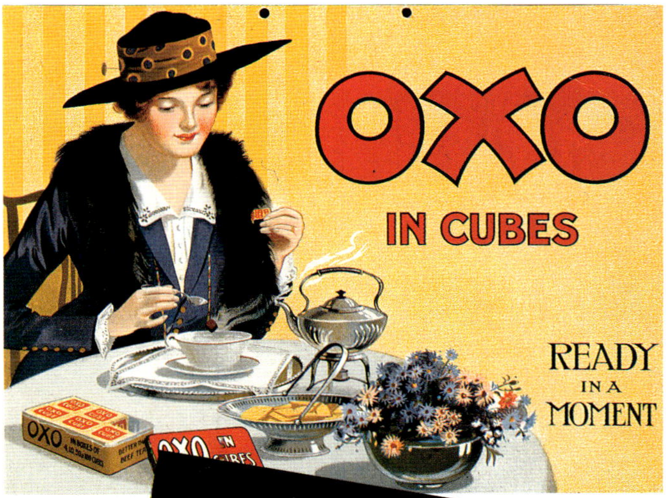

Right: Letter to James from brother Thomas illustrating the bond between these two brothers. This bond was to result thirteen years later in their own business.

Below right: Lucy, Harry and John, 1906 Prestwich.

The early 1900s saw buyers very much wanting to see advertising ideas and designs to promote their products. Prior to this time it was mainly the owners of businesses who suggested their own designs and produced them for reproduction. Now they no longer had the time or the skill, so they gave the problem to their employed buyers, who in turn, had not the skill either to prepare the designs. They therefore had to seek the designs required from printers.

Probably to their surprise, they found printers willing to submit ideas on speculation and without payment, on the understanding that if the submitted design was successful, it would obtain the business without a competitive quotation against the design. The price however had to be reasonable and obviously not too high. The print business could then be obtained with a reasonable profit margin – much more than in competitive quoting.

However, there was a problem – your sketch had to be the best and if it was not, you had an immediate direct loss on your hands – that of the artist's costs.

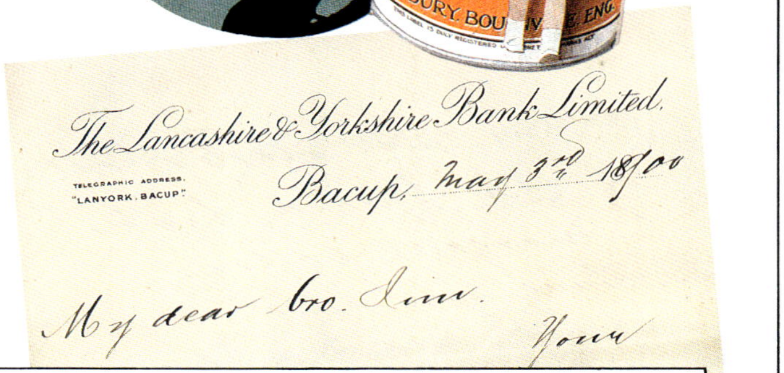

May 3rd 1900

My dear bro. Jim.

Your letter to hand. In it I could see you were in a good mood. Early rising is good for one. I have proved it and hope to try it again. It is all a habit (and a bad one).

Staying up late, but I feel I can't sleep without having a good read before going to bed. However I feel I must put a stop to it. It did me good to read your letter, in breathed goodness and happiness and a considerable brotherly feeling which, without you telling me, I know you bear towards me, and indeed all of us. I realise this more and more every day. I am glad it is a characteristic of our family and I esteem its value more when I so often find it is lacking with many families.

The views have not yet come. Did you find Smith's (wst) place? They supply them I think. I have not read the President's sermon yet but will do so this evening. When your letter came I had just started one Jim Barries books - Margaret Ogilvy have you read any of his books? If not, I commend them to you. Read the Little Minister.

At home we are in the midst of spring cleaning all upset - but with a little outside assistance we, or to speak truthfully, they hope soon to have finished.

I trust you are having a good week booking orders galore.

With best wishes

Believe Me

Your loving bro.

Tom

Advertisement for Gong Soup for which John J. was the model.

Usual dress for John J.

Harry Haworth aged 4 about to go to London.

James, by 1905, was already in touch with advertising design artists and, with their artwork had obtained considerable business from London-based companies. It was, and perhaps still is the case, that those whose roots are in the North of England are very reluctant to move to London and the South, despite the apparent opportunities presented.

The cost of such a move in those days was not a significant factor. Reluctance to move was apparent with those at Alf Cooke Ltd, who were endeavouring to obtain business with daily sallies by train from their lair in Leeds, James Haworth included. But James had at least changed his roots just recently from Bacup to Prestwich. He, therefore, having already forsaken some of his roots, could possibly make an easier change than those at Leeds who might have considered coming to London, to organise the sales of print based on the London office.

Heaton Chapel School 1905. John J. Haworth – middle row, next to teacher.

John James Haworth in Sunday best, 1906.

The family break-up on James Haworth moving to London 1907.
Ellen Haworth's children. Back row - Margaret, Richard, Alice, Amelia.
Front row - James, Sarah, Ellen, Elizabeth, Thomas Haworth.

Ellen Haworth's grandchildren — 1907
Back row - left to right - Jenny Holt, Alan Witham, Stanley Holt, Irene Smith.
Middle row - left to right - Edith Haworth, John J. Haworth, Harry Haworth,
Grandmother Ellen Haworth, Lucy Haworth, Denis Witham.
Front row - left to right - Leslie Smith, Phyllis Hayworth, Tom Holt, Jack Holt.

"Avondale" (now No. 84) The Mall, Southgate. Lucy, John J. and Harry soon after arriving in London 1907.

So, with the blessing and with no opposition from his seniors at Crown Point, Leeds, James moved to London in 1907. He decided to live in a newly built house, "Avondale", (now 84) The Mall, Southgate, North London. Southgate was then a country village surrounded by country estates and farms. The village lay between the main Great Northern Railway line out to New Barnet and the North of England, and the branch line opened in 1871 from Wood Green to Enfield.

James was to take charge of all sales based on the London office at Chancery Lane. He organised a studio of two or three artists to prepare designs and could engage any suitable London travellers to secure further new business.

How James came to choose Southgate as a home has never been fully explained. I had heard my father say that on one of James' visits to London by train from Leeds, the line was blocked by a derailment at New Southgate. It was suggested however that ticket holders could walk to Palmers Green Station to get the branch line train to Kings Cross. To have done so would have involved walking through rural Southgate. Anyway, James discovered Southgate and this is perhaps as good an explanation as any.

One can imagine the family of wife Annie, with 3 wide-eyed children; Lucy aged 11, John 8, and Harry 3, arriving at Euston one afternoon from Manchester. A quick trip on the electric Metropolitan line to Kings Cross and then by local steam train to Palmers Green. Finally, a hired cab up Aldermans and Cannon Hill to the newly built Mall, by Southgate Green. The furniture would have arrived by railway wagon container the previous day, James supervising its unloading. A new world to be discovered for the entire family, equal almost, as far as wife Annie and the children were concerned, as if they had gone to Australia, America or Canada, as so many had gone from Bacup in recent years.

Their accents and their dress would have made them very much foreigners in the soft-speaking South and the children the butt of ridicule from the resident children.

Sleepy Southgate 1900.

Southgate "En Fete" 1903 on occasion of Sir Thomas Lipton leaving his nearby country estate to compete for the America's Cup in his yacht, Shamrock.

Palmers Green Station 1906. Great Northern Railway branch line from Wood Green to the then terminus at Windmill Hill, Enfield.

Main Line train, New Southgate.

Form III Southgate C. of E. Boys School 1907. John J. is to be found 2nd row from the front 5th from the right in polo-neck jersey.

Far right: Rear of "Avondale" 1907.
Left to right - Maid, Lucy, Harry in barrow, John J. Ann Haworth.

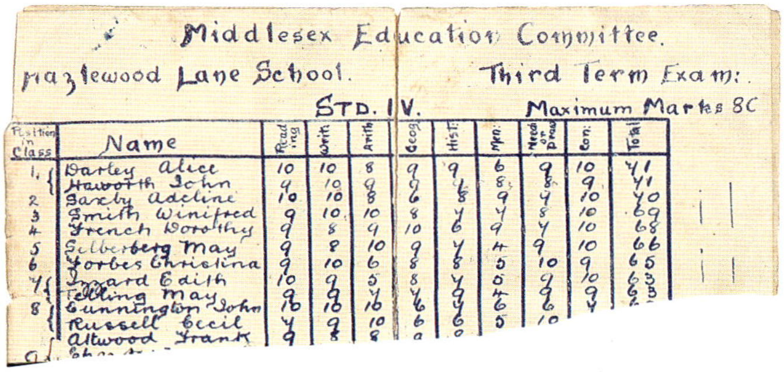

Middlesex Education Committee.
Hazlewood Lane School. Third Term Exam:
STD. IV. Maximum Marks 80

Position in Class	Name	Reading	Writ:	Arith	Geog	Hist:	Men:	Needle or Draw	Con:	Total
1. {	Darley Alice	10	10	8	9	9	6	9	10	71
	Haworth John	9	10	9	9	7	8	8	9	71
2	Saxby Adeline	10	10	8	6	8	9	7	10	70
3	Smith Winifred	9	10	10	8	7	7	8	10	69
4	French Dorothy	9	8	9	10	6	9	7	10	68
5	Selberberg May	9	8	10	9	7	4	9	10	66
6	Forbes Christina	9	10	6	8	8	5	10	9	65
7 {	Izzard Edith	10	9	5	8	7	5	9	10	63
	Telling May	9	9	7	7	9	4	9	9	63
8 {	Gunnington John	10	10	10	6	7	6	6	7	[illegible]
	Russell Cecil	7	9	10	6	6	5	10	[illegible]	[illegible]
	Altwood Frank	9	8	8	[illegible]	[illegible]	[illegible]	[illegible]	[illegible]	[illegible]

James, as father, would not have very much time to give to house or family matters. He had to make sure of his continued success and thereby commission income from Alf Cooke Ltd. The family would see no less or no more of James than they had for the last ten years.

John J. Haworth was despatched to Hazelwood Lane School, Palmers Green, where in his first term (the Christmas term) in the fourth form, he achieved first position, equal with Alice Darley, out of 40 children. In 1909 he transferred to the Boys' School, Southgate; this was not to last long, despite a good letter from the Headmaster. In 1910 there was a further move to Southgate County School in Fox Lane, Palmers Green where the fees were £2. 2s. 0d per term and where he seemed to be able to keep himself in the top third of boys as the terms went by. He remained there until 1914.

Form IV Hazelwood Lane School, Palmers Green. John J. front row in sailor suit.

High Street, Southgate – traffic 1907.

Farming was to appear once again in James' life. In 1909 he purchased and rented land that now constitutes The Greenway Estate, between The Bourne, Fox Lane and the High Street, Southgate. The Mall practically overlooked this area. Cows were bought and a milk round established. There were chickens and eggs for sale and calves were reared for market. The two eldest children, John J. and Lucy were, of course, expected to work as unpaid hands, both before and after school. As a reward for milking the cows, John J. at Christmas 1909 was presented with a Robinson Crusoe book. Young Harry was to get a rather scary American comic strip book – "Buster Brown, his dog Tige and their Troubles" – his reward for feeding the chickens.

First farm in Southgate 1910 opposite The Mall, Southgate, now the tree-lined Meadway housing estate.

Harry and calf, opposite "Avondale" The Mall, 1912.

James Haworth, printer and farmer with son John J. on farm opposite their home in The Mall, Southgate 1911.

Southgate village, 1909.

Chase Side, Southgate, near Avenue Road, 1908.

John J. played football for the school and probably the only other excitement in his life at that time occurred on a foggy December 6th, 1912, when a plane crashed into the roof of 75 Derwent Road, Palmers Green, just around the corner from The Mall. This was witnessed by John J. and two other boys who dashed back to the County School, got an extending ladder and rescued the pilot, who, none the worse for his accident, was stuck on the roof. Incidentally, the pilot's name was de Manio, whose son, Jack de Manio became the well-known BBC radio personality of the 1960s.

Southgate County School football team. 1913-1914.
Front row - left to right - John Haworth, Arthur Furrow, Reginald Addison (who became an Air Vice Marshall) Doug Cook.

The Bourne, Southgate 1907. James Haworth's first farm lay within land to the left-hand side of the road.

Life at "Avondale" was, by all accounts, enjoyable. A pony and trap was available to take James to and from Palmers Green Station. There was a live-in housemaid to prepare meals and do the washing, as well as a daily lady for the cleaning. James, through commission, was well off and by the beginning of 1913 was one of the highest earners in the Alf Cooke Company, thanks to the 3¾% commission rate in his original terms of appointment.

Lucy Haworth – 1912.

Winter 1912 in low cloud pilot Manio, lost his way to Hendon Aerodrome, crashing into Mr Andow's home, 75 Derwent Road, Palmers Green.

Silver trowels presented to John and Harry Haworth on laying the foundation stone of the Wesleyan Church, Winchmore Hill, 16th March 1912.

"The Cherry Tree" 1908, The Green, Southgate. Entrance to The Mall on extreme right.

Harry Cooke could not have failed to notice James' rising income and his empire building down at the London office. The many artists turning out order-winning designs on behalf of James' customers produced an ever spiralling increase in business with James at the same time increasing his income.

There was also another problem for Alf Cooke Ltd, due to all this business from London, – that of communication with the factory. The great variety of work obtained through successful artists' designs, meant that an increasing number of orders fell outside the scope of Alf Cooke's machinery. For example: Posters, Showcards and Cut-out Displays.

These had to be passed to outside finishers, which reduced profit margins. With consequential delays and loss of quality, James was beginning to get complaints. There was in the making a collision course between James and Harry Cooke, particularly when the latter changed the financial rules by making James, London General Manager with a fixed salary and reducing his calling area! On the other hand, James was wanting to go ever onward, increasing business on his own account.

James Haworth

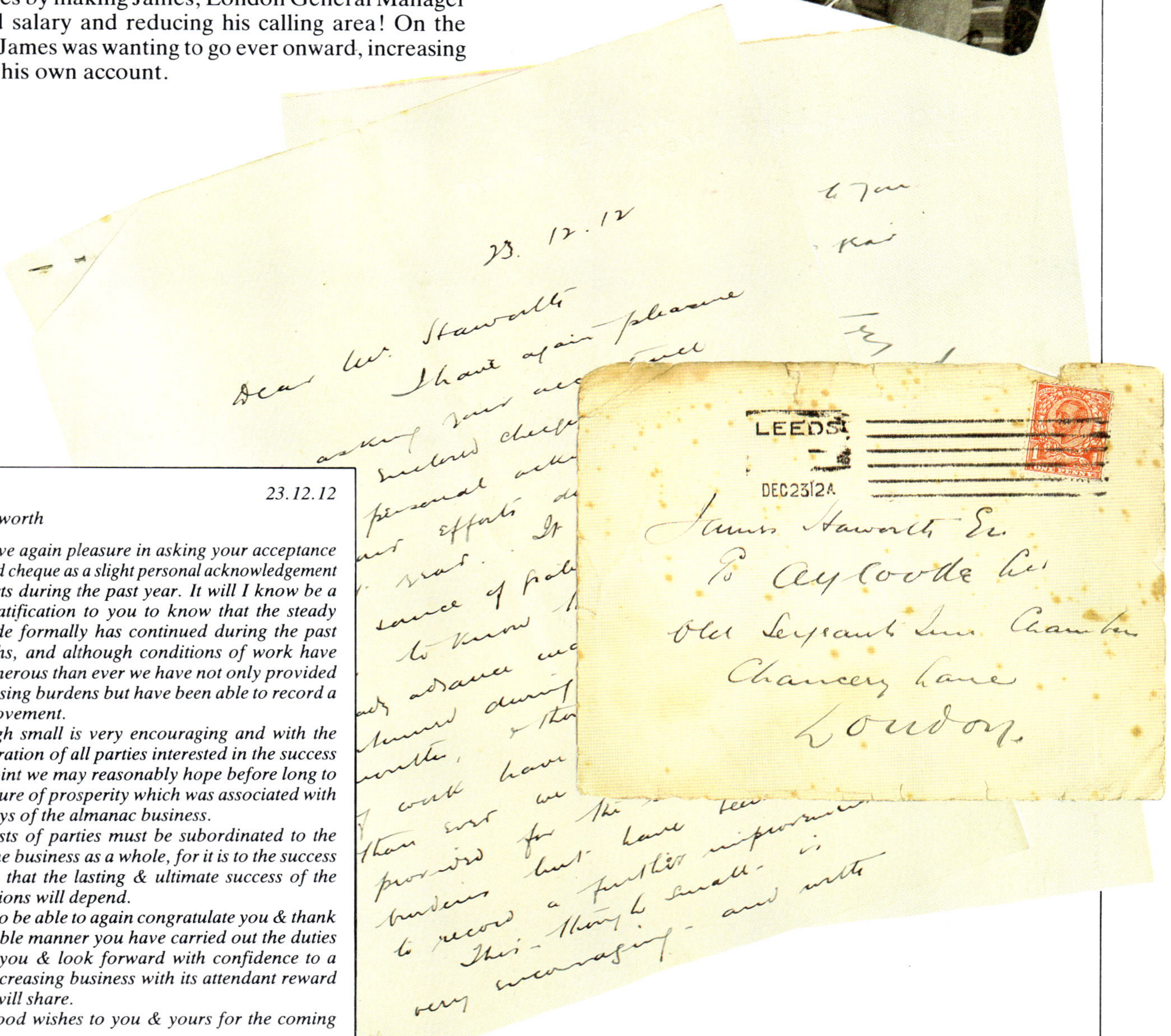

23.12.12

Dear Mr Haworth

I have again pleasure in asking your acceptance of the enclosed cheque as a slight personal acknowledgement of your efforts during the past year. It will I know be a source of gratification to you to know that the steady advance made formally has continued during the past twelve months, and although conditions of work have been more onerous than ever we have not only provided for the unceasing burdens but have been able to record a further improvement.

This though small is very encouraging and with the loyal co-operation of all parties interested in the success of Crown Point we may reasonably hope before long to enjoy a measure of prosperity which was associated with the balmy days of the almanac business.

The interests of parties must be subordinated to the interests of the business as a whole, for it is to the success of the whole that the lasting & ultimate success of the different sections will depend.

I am glad to be able to again congratulate you & thank you for the able manner you have carried out the duties entrusted to you & look forward with confidence to a constantly increasing business with its attendant reward in which all will share.

With all good wishes to you & yours for the coming year.

Believe me
Yours very truly
Harry Cooke

Letter of appreciation from Harry Cooke with a hint of changes to come in James Haworth's Terms of Employment.

Perhaps Harry Cooke should have negotiated more with James and offered a Directorship to such a successful salesman, and even brought him back to Leeds as Sales Director. But this was 1913 and masters still had to keep successful workers in their place.

James could see the writing on the wall and that come what may, his wings were going to be clipped. He was, however going to be as tough as Harry Cooke.

Harry Cooke

It was October 1913 when he decided to contact his brother Thomas. James had persuaded Thomas in 1906 to leave the safety of the Lancashire and Yorkshire Bank at Urmston in order to take over basically James' northern territory in the Alf Cooke company when he went to London.

Prior to this, in 1903, Thomas Haworth with his mother Ellen, had moved to 30 Queen's Road, Urmston, on his change of bank branch. Ellen was to die on October 10th 1911 and was interred in Bacup cemetery. Thomas married Miss Florence Lord on 14th February 1912 and they made their home at "Ribblesdale", Queens Road, Urmston, where a son, Geoffrey was born in 1913, who subsequently joined James Haworth Ltd in 1931.

From the correspondence of Harry Cooke, it would seem that James was channelling Thomas's northern orders through the London office, rather than direct with Leeds. Another reason for wing-clipping!

So James, in the space of less than eight weeks and with brother Thomas party to his plans, set about forming their own business as originators and suppliers of advertising and general colour print. What an awesome thought, with no financial backing, other than their own money, to try and start from a point that had taken Alf Cooke & Company 50 years to reach.

Thomas Haworth

The die was quickly cast, and the unease at the London office due to customer difficulties persuaded the majority of the artists and travellers, as well as some office personnel to go with them to 55 Chancery Lane. Thus commenced the business of James Haworth & Brother in December 1913. That story is told later.

Returning to "Avondale", Southgate, life there in late 1913 must have been very fraught; the house mortgaged with the bank to raise money to finance the new company, endless letters to organise the engagement of staff and production of print by the P.P. Press in Liverpool.

P.P. Press was a print company owned by the large Joseph Bibby Company, soap manufacturers, whom James and Thomas had come to know through business and religious contacts. It was hoped P.P. Press would handle their printing, allowing discounts and extended credit to the would-be new company of James Haworth.

Children being children, whilst very conscious of tension within a household are often not aware of the origins of such tension, especially if the reasons are business or work worries outside the home. It's only when such children themselves enter the family business they begin to understand such worries. John J. and Harry were not to be involved for six years at least.

Ellen Haworth, "Ribblesdale", Urmston.

Extracts from some of the letters written by James Haworth whilst working for Alf Cooke, Printers, Leeds. These were sent to his brother Thomas, also working for Alf Cooke as one of their Northern print travellers.

These letters dated between 12th September and December 26th 1913 trace the reason, speed, frustration and anguish it took to create a printing business within a period of three months.

There are also a few extracts of letters from others affected by James' crucial decisions.

As well as the letters quoted, there were perhaps a hundred more written by James during this period. Many were to the staff at Alf Cooke's asking if they would join him in his new business enterprise. To customers, advising them of his intended change and hoping they would support him with design and print enquiries, this salesman about to become a proprietor of a printing business.

Lastly, to friends and relations, to see if they had spare finance to risk in this embryo company.

Many, of course, would reply, necessitating yet another letter.

One can perhaps, on reading these few extracts, understand the single-mindedness of purpose, mixed with ruthlessness, to achieve his success, which as a memorial to his effort has lasted, to date, seventy-five years.

JH/NM. *Sept. 12th 1913*

Mr. T.W. Haworth,

VISIT TO LONDON. I am sorry that both these have gone down. I gather that the order was settled before our estimate arrived and I shall be glad if you will make enquiry, and if it was late, let us follow this up.

I may say that a large lot of Lino Work they have taken at Leeds has seriously dislocated business at this end, and we are in bad repute at Colmans, Liebigs & Cadburys. The attention to the orders at Leeds during the last 2 months is nothing short of a scandal, and I shall loose thousands of pounds worth of work in consequence.

Yours faithfully,

FROM ALF COOKE, LTD., LONDON. *Sep. 27 1913*

My Dear Bro. Thomas,

They have been disputing my right to go there since the Belgian agent has been calling though he has done nothing. I have however recently sent them an Est. direct from this office (unknown to Leeds) and several sketches and asked for an appointment. If my right is challenged seriously to call on them simply on account of their agent there, it will lead to a rupture but even if this does not happen I am strongly tempted by another offer I have had this week from the P. P. Press. I have been in correspondence and have had an interview with Jas Prescott on Thursday last. I have arranged to go to Liverpool on Friday next to look over their factory and if they are satisfactory and are prepared to add litho plant I shall enter serious negotiations with them. They have parted with their London man. I shall therefore come on from Birmingham on Thursday night to Urmston where I should like an hours very serious talk with you and I think you might accompany me there.

I have been messed about both at Oxo and Cadburys with deliveries. We have the novelty of a works manager trying to compete with us in getting work and I get no help - if only they would carry out the orders and could manage.

I am much more keen on this than I was on Hazel Watsons. It will be much better for us. My staff here will go with me. I have already mentioned it to Byatt and Jack. By the way Jack will most likely come on to .... on Friday next and go on possibly with you to Liverpool. What proposals can you make. Sit down and think hard and write me fully.

Polly arrived alright and is enjoying herself well, had a good nights sleep last night.

With fondest love to you and yours,
Your ever affect. Bro.
James

My dear Bro. Tom, *Oct. 21st 13.*

I was very glad to have your letter this morning. You are mistaken in thinking there was anything between Leeds and myself when I was last up. Had there been I should certainly have told you - why not? Since I saw you H.C. (Harry Cooke) has been on the representation business again & wishes to commence the New Year on the New Lines, i.e. you are to be direct with Scotland taken off & to have not more ground than you are able to look after, this is the one thing which is causing the unrest.

I know as you do it has long been on his chest to make the alterations & I am sure he will make it at all costs. He has invited me to write him and make proposals, but I think it would be more to the point if he would write me?

There is no doubt we shall have to face it & I shall be glad to hear, or much better still if you could come & talk things over. Could you come for a day or two Thursday. I wish you could. Am longing just for a good chat with you. The sooner the better or we shall be in a hole if we are not careful. It concerns you as much or more as it does me and it has filled me with a considerable anxiety.

With fondest love
Your affect. Bro.
James

p.s. Your letter was very welcome.

---

comment - after Oct. 21

Several previous letters to Thomas had voiced a thought about "going it alone" by reason of continuing frustration with Alf Cooke's production problems.

Oct. 25th 13.

My dear Bro. Tom,

Sorry I can't see you this weekend. Should much have liked. Can't you come next? or any day next week. You are quite forgetting the "Old Fit" which meets you half way. I have some things on at Oxo - 2 lots of books of 5 million worth about £8,000. Poor Leeds can't do it & I am at Mr. Mallwoods request getting prices from the trade including P. P. -

I have mentioned the matter to Mr. Mallwood which has approval - If we can fix up with say 2 or 3 lpress & 2 or 3 litho. houses we shall be I think alright. The more I think of it the better it goes - there is only one thing - Capital - for the first 6 months - How much will it take? If we could get over the first 6 months I think we should be much better off than we are at present. I should prize your council in these important considerations. I shall meet Prescott on Monday noon - he is in town. Can you write me tomorrow?

With fondest love
Always your affect. Bro.
James

Nov. 12 1913

My dear bro Tom,

I am very much pained by your letter this morning & I wish I could see and talk to you instead of writing. Every day I have been intending writing you but the progress of the business we have on hand has made but very little headway since I saw you that I have waited day after day in the hope of having something good to write you. Last night I began the enclosed note about 10p.m. & decided not to post it until this morning. You totally misunderstand me - I have always been & still am ready to stand or fall by you.

Whilst I have been planning and working quietly here I have felt all the time that you have been doing the same. I confess I ought to have written you if only to say I have not much to tell you. I want you to withdraw your remarks. I value your council and help more than any other, & I cannot bear to think of us parting - remember the advice given us by our dear Mother.

I have had a lot to worry and distract me during the week - things going wrong - bad work going to Cadburys & young Alf going there. I shall be glad when we get on our own, to which end I am working with all my powers & am relying upon you doing the same, trusting each other whether we hear from each other or not for a few days. I saw Mr. Lord yesterday morning & had a conversation re the change of which he takes a favourable view. I was sending a message with him but found he would not return for a fortnight.

This is the first letter this day. I was so upset by yours. It should not be I know. I trust you will overlook it & be as we always have been in days past.

With love and best wishes,
Ever your affectionate bro.
James

Comment

No doubt there had been a letter to James from brother Thomas expressing doubts about the whole enterprise of starting a new business, hence tone of replies.

Nov. 12/13

My dear Bro. Tom,

Now Tom, I want you to have more faith in me and never to write a letter such as the one received this a.m. It was a stab to my heart. I feel angry with Leeds for the way they have treated you, and although I have not said much I have felt it keenly - when they strike you, they strike me much more. I have not forgot my responsibility in bringing you from the Bank and you may rely upon my faithfulness. We shall enter gladly, freely and unfettered upon the campaign awaiting us for it will be the campaign of our lives and I have little doubt of the results. During the weekend and in the trains I have read The Life of Cromwell by Dr. Horton - a book in season.

If you were not in the campaign with me and which I am now bent upon, the loss would be great indeed - but it is unthinkable and I will not say more.

Prescott remarked that they were Methodists and Liberals - just an aside - and thought that if we kept close together we should all do well.

May I hear from you by return and then after your visit write me fully on Sat. to Avondale and I will call for the letter on Sunday a.m.

There are just one or two other queries -

1. *Will they carry our address on their heading and our name also?*
2. *Is it desired that we should carry their name and address on our heading such as -*

Selling Agents for the
P. P. Press
Liverpool

Personally I favour the above. Do you?
Perhaps two kinds of headings?

3. *If we had a bad time and were towards end of 6 or 9 months to get rather tight for money, owing to paying wages, rent etc. would they be prepared to give us extended credit and how long. Is it not desirable to raise this? I think it is.*

Now Tom I am confident you will address yourself right manfully to this important task and bring it to a speedy and successful termination.

Again I express my deep regret at the negligence in writing which I had been daily expecting to do and to have something to write about.

With fondest love
Ever your loving bro. James

TELGS. ALCUIN, FLEET, LONDON.
TELEPHONE 1131 HOLBORN.
HEAD OFFICE & FACTORY,
CROWN POINT PRINTING WORKS,
LEEDS

PERSONAL

OLD SERJEANTS' INN CHAMBERS,
CHANCERY LANE,
LONDON. W.C.

Nov. 14 1913

Dear Mr. Haworth,

I have been expecting to hear from you with your views as to my proposal for further representation. I am desirous to begin the New Year on the new lines and am also naturally desirous to give favourable consideration to your views as well, that the new arrangement may be satisfactory to both of us.

My proposal is, your position should be that of General Sales Manager, and that your influence should be felt over all our staff and your experience and facilities in the way of sketches and artists should be available for every district. In short, that your interest should not be confined to any particular area, or to any particular traveller. The London business would be conducted practically as at present. You and the London staff would be available for country travelling as now and probably even extended. Your remuneration would be based on your net earnings, on the average of say this and last year. These two years will I think represent the most favourable returns to you. Afterwards, all expenses would be met from here, either clerical, travelling or assistance.

Your brother would then be employed as a direct and independent traveller, as our other travellers. His ground would be arranged so that his services would be used to the best & fullest advantage, and his remuneration would of course be balanced, in estimating the respective remuneration earned by him over a similar period. In his case a portion of his remuneration would be on a commission basis. At present he has too much ground and I propose removing him from Hull and Scotland. I should leave him his York accounts.

I think the above indicates my views in a general way. Let me have your suggestions as soon as possible, as time is getting on, and I want to have this matter cleared up and out of the way.

Faithfully yours,
H.C.

Comment - 14.11.1913

Letter from Mr Harry Cooke to James Haworth curbing his and brother Thomas's empire building via the London office. This new control and position would greatly reduce their salaries from commission. In James Haworth's case from something like £4,000 income based on the old 1901 Agreement with Alf Cooke to £2,000 maximum as General Sales Manager.

A £4,000 salary in 1913 would have been in the highest bracket of incomes most likely a great deal more than Harry Cookes!

Nov. 16 1913

My dear Bro. Tom,

I was glad to have your letter yesterday morning reporting your interview of Friday. You are quite right in your conclusion that the whole business hangs upon Finances. In my interview of Thursday I left him under the impression that they were favourable to the proposed arrangement i.e. of waiting for payment until we ourselves were paid. This is very much the same as an ordinary traveller who collects a/cs. With you I can quite understand their position - by being servants only.

Office

I am in treaty for 2 or 3 places - but can't fix until finance is settled. I gave Jack the job of finding an office - but shall have I fear to take it on myself or Robinson or Alan. I have asked him again re money, but couldn't tell - "nothing much" - "practically nothing". He is the least enthusiastic and no doubt would be glad if the thing fell thro'. To us it means more than I can describe.

Orders

I have some fine enquiries for January and it would be a thousand pities to miss the golden chance - I must confess to feeling very nervous lest it should fall thro' with P. P.

Money

We reckoned it would cost us at least £1,700 the first year and so far as I can see there is only £500 - your £212 and mine.

Could we get a loan from Pollie of £250 or so. We ought to have £1,000 at least to begin with. Give your whole heart and mind to the business for it will be a desperate struggle. I must confess to a feeling of disappointment that the P. P. have allowed things to drift so long. We have a bare fortnight in which to settle all up.

I have not yet decided upon a name - Vandyke I like very well. Have applied for an office in Regent House. We could then have Regent Press? Have a big list of other names - this can soon be settled. We could have Carlton Press (London) Limited.

Be assured, if you are anxious - I am much more so. Do your best and I will do the same.

Let me hear from you again on Monday night and I will write you.

With fondest love - ever your loving Bro.
James

My dear Bro. Tom, *Nov. 22 1913*

I was glad to have your letter this morning. On Thursday last I got home about 10, needless to say rather tired out but greatly relieved and gladdened. The more I think of it the better I am pleased and satisfied. How is it with you now that you have had time to turn it over and over again?

We have booked the offices for 7 years, determinable at 3, 5 or 7 years on our part for £125 including cleaning. The agreement will be ready for signature on Wednesday next. It will be advisable for you to come forward on Friday afternoon next, to finally clear all up. We shall then be ready to deal with Notice etc. and the above agreement etc.

The landlord will paint and decorate the offices and will have it ready for tenancy in two weeks after. In the office there were several items left by previous tenant - safe, roll top desk, 3 chairs, table, also carpet and oil cloth - the lot we have got at £10.

Jack and Robinson and Alan as well as the artists are all very well pleased at the settlement - of course they don't know the financial arrangements - this is our business only - but I have assured them that it is highly satisfactory. I put it to them plainly - Jack as well - if they preferred they could stay where they were. They want to come with me - every one of them.

Stationery

We will get to this next week. A colour business card is preferable. I told them of P. Ps attitude to name - they now know that it is to be James Haworth & Bro. - I trust this may live on for many generations - an honoured name.

Calendar

I should like a calendar to send out - a figure subject preferably. Bibby used a beautiful picture for one of their Quarterlies - a pretty girl of 14 or 16 seated in furs. Something of this sort for Calendar, Business Card, etc. etc.

Annie and the children are all pleased at the course we are taking and I hope it will be well for them.

Shall be glad to hear from you and to learn that you are able to come Thursday. I think it would be better than Friday.

Leeds have already had ample measure from J. H. if they get no more this year.

Write soon.

With fondest love,
Your affect. Bro.
James

Dear Mr. Cooke, *Nov. 28 1913*

Referring to your letter of the 14th inst. I have taken time to give my most careful and serious consideration to the views expressed therein.

I may say that in addition to those views, unsettling as they have been, the unsatisfactory way in which orders have been executed during the past 6 months have given me considerable worry and caused much unrest.

In consequence, I propose to commence business on my own account, and in this I am being joined by my brother, Mr. Robinson and Mr. Witham together with Mr. Byatt and Mr. Bertram and therefore with reluctance and regret I respectfully beg to give you notice that I shall terminate my engagement with you at the end of the present year.

I beg to remain,
Respectfully yours,
James Haworth

My dear Bro. Tom, *Dec. 2 1913*

I was glad to have your letter this a.m. Altho rather brief it was welcome. I got an acknowledgement of our letter this morning as you will see keeping us both until the end of the year - but Alan & Robinson are to terminate on December 15th - Byatt & Bertram also got their letters acknowledged all in a very formal way - ours especially - H.C. (Harry Cooke) did write to Alan & Robinson - but I have not had a word. He has also written Stapleton - contents I don't know.

Pullan put in an appearance at 2 o'clock today and has been policeman. He has to remain the month out. He was extremely nice and showed genuine sorrow at what has taken place. He is of course out for all the information he can get. He has taken Jack to the hotel with him tonight and he has asked Whincap to meet him tomorrow night. No doubt he will get a good deal of information from these two. — H.C. (Harry Cooke) has placed Whincap in a stew he hardly knowing what to say and he will hand his notice in on the 15th. I'll advise him further tomorrow. Byatt & Bertram & Alan & Robinson are remaining faithful hence - and we are absolutely united which is great comfort.

Robinson & Alan & Byatt & Bertram will be in harness before we can possibly be but every day I am paving the way and I am amply satisfied with results. All in best of spirits - not a bit cast down as we (or I) appeared on Saturday last.

The artists chose the paper for the rooms this a.m. and things are going apace in the rooms. We shall want the Stationery very badly & am glad Prescott (of P. P. Press) is coming up tomorrow & hope to see him.

Pushing on at a good rate with all things & I have no doubt you are. Will write you again after seeing Prescott.

Couldn't get letter in sooner. You will see how I am fixed. Please write to Avondale.

With fondest love
James

My dear Bro. Tom, *Dec. 4 1913*

Sorry I've no chance to write you other than here, when I get home. Pullan is in charge, he is the policeman, watching, & spurning & quizzing for information - some pains of things here you will no doubt imagine. Jack looks more scared than anyone & the way he is asking all manner of things, together things which have been lying about for 6 months & things which will not be req'd for 3 or 4 months - have suddenly become urgent is amusing. He appears dreadfully frightened - & in consequence is dangerous - i.e. he will not stop at a trifle to save his skin.

Whilst I've been away Pullan has had Whincap out to lunch - Holborn Restaurant! today before I left I warned him to be on his guard & I think he will be true. It will be a further shock next week when he resigns along with Miss Langstrom, Jack has been at him, whether persuading him to stay I could not find out - but evidently presuming he was staying. Should see tomorrow?

Don't forget to write fully Am feeling rather tired out - long day - but high in spirit. Robinson & Alan are all that could be desired and are a great comfort in these anxious days. - They are 2 gallant lads - viewing who can serve the most.

Excuse more it is so late.

Ever your affect. Bro.
James

Reference to Pullan. Was to Mr. J.G. Pullan, who had commenced with Alf Cooke in 1885 as a young man and was to become a director, serving the company for 50 years.

My dear Bro. Tom, *Dec. 5/13*

I am also sending you a copy of a letter to North and if you get this in for time tomorrow I can go forward to see him by all means do. You really ought to have taken this matter in your own hands & secured him - he will mean so much to you. The position calls for desperate efforts. During the next few weeks they will do their best to kill us. Were I in your position, North would be mine.

Things have gone on much as usual today. H.C. (Harry Cooke) is coming next week and desperate effort will be made to get Byatt.

I feel sorry now that I did not prepare a legal agreement duly stamped and signed I'll do this with Baxter.

Yesterday, whilst I was away in Birmingham Whincap was out to lunch with Pullan & Jack, & today he has been with me. They were suggesting that if he could get Byatt to join him, together they could have the management of the artist room & were prepared to offer better terms. Whincap is prepared to hand in his notice next week on my giving him an assurance of performance.

With fondest love
Your ever affect. Bro.
James

Avondale
Dec. 8 1913

My dear Bro. Tom,

From tomorrow we will conduct our correspondence from 55 Chancery Lane. The painters and paper hangers are only out tonight. The offices look splendid now. The electric fillings are being put in and the office furniture made for artist room. Two of them will be in next Monday.

North I very dearly wish we could get him. He will with his work be the most formidable. Especially on your northern ground and by all means go and see him at home in York even if you have to stay over night there.

Letters are a poor substitute for talk. Will you feel your way with him re terms. He would be worth £5 plus 5%. This is what Holiday got and he is a far better man and he could get the same orders as at Cookes or better. We should be prepared to give him an agreement and he could work at home or in a studio in York or Liverpool where he liked to live. Go for him and get him.

Byatt Sealed and settled. We will talk over things - salaries etc when you come.

Whincap - is alright not so much concerned about him as the others.

Pullan There was a letter from Colemans addressed to me this am. He did not open it.

I will write immediately I hear from North and if you would like will go to York on Saty afternoon or better still if he will come here. Shall be glad to hear from you again.

With fondest love and best wishes
I am your affect. Bro.
James

H.C. (Harry Cooke) is here tonight - Pullan has been across to see him - and I believe Jack has gone later he will be at the office for the first time in the morning since the fateful day.

JAMES HAWORTH & BRO. *Dec. 9 1913*

My dear Bro. Tom,

Just another line or two further to my letter of this evening.

I am glad to find things on the improve at home, Harry is better altho confined to bed and I think Annie is also rather better - she is I am sorry to say far from being well. The doctor told her to take more rest. They are all in bed now. I very heartily wish Cookes would call me off and give me a fortnight holiday - but alas no such luck. They will keep me chained up until the last. Have no doubt they will go round to several of our customers - but when our forces are called up and the artillery is in action, they will then realise what it means to have us in opposition.

I am writing to North tonight making an appointment for Saturday and I should like you to join me. If so you will scarcely be able to come this week but please write me and let me know by Thursday - as I am going to Norwich on Thursday and on Friday would like to be in Leicester, in the afternoon and then should like to come forward to York and return in good time for Saturday night. Let me know what you suggest. We could make our plans a very long way ahead.

Things are going very well indeed for us and I am delighted with the prospects. Mr. Maltwood (of Oxo) in his fatherly way told me how well I might do if I only follow high principals and industry.

I hope I shall not disappoint him or disappoint those who are nearer and dearer to me. I had a letter from Pollie tell her I will write her soon. I trust Floss and baby are well.

With fondest love
Your ever affect. Bro.
James

These are just temporary headings.

Norwich
Dec. 11 1913

My dear Bro. Tom,

I intend finishing off here tomorrow morning and going on to Leicester and returning home in the evening. - Then coming on to you to arrive there early afternoon and shall be glad if you will join me - will wire you tomorrow or Saty morning the time I shall arrive. So far things look decidedly promising don't they? We can have an hour or two's chat and compare notes and then you can come forward on the following week - next week end. I think they will release us probably next week end. It would I think pay them to do so.

I am pleased to say that Harry is better than he was on Tuesday but not yet right. I am sorry to say Annie is far from being what she should be - got run down. I am hoping she will soon be better. Lucy and John James are quite well.

What did you think of North's reply? Possibly we may meet Baxter saty. I have just written him saying I may be in the North saty. - You don't of course breathe a word to North.

I shall be glad to join to things with you saty. Am feeling very tired tonight.

With fondest love,
Your affect. Bro.
James

---

55 Chancery Lane
Dec. 23 1913

To T.W. Haworth
Manchester

All going well, saw Prescott of P.P. Press, he is pleased the way things are shaping, furniture coming tomorrow, arranging calendar tomorrow, artists getting into stride, wish you were here - it feels splendid to be on your own.

Fondest love and best wishes for a right Merry Christmas.
Yours as ever
James

Dec. 26 1913

My dear Bro. Tom,

I had been expecting to hear from you the last few days, but take it you are having a rest, as I am myself previous to the great campaign.

It is now late on Friday - we have had a most enjoyable Xmas. All to ourselves and I feel most benefited by this rest these 2 days.

If you get to Liverpool fairly early on Monday, possibly you will be able to leave in the evening, if not stay until Tuesday and then come on direct.

I am eagerly, looking and longing with my brother, along with artists am expecting a bright and prosperous time. I trust this will be so with you in the north.

With fondest love Dear Tom
Your affect. Bro.
James

Chancery Lane - Dec. 16 1913

My dear Bro. Tom,

You will begin to wonder where I am - Got home about 1.30 Sunday am very tired out.

Yesterday evening had a very good interview with both the Prescotts - every thing so far is going satisfactorily. They will have the furniture from their London place transferred to ours. They will have the conversation duly typed out and signed. They are anxious to give us every possible support and I am looking forward to good and I trust happy times for us all.

Mr. H.C. will be here tomorrow - I learn he is taking it badly - been ill this week end. With you I feel sorry - how different it all might have been.

Shall be glad to hear from you. Glad to say that Harry is now nearly alright - and Annie is improving but not yet up to the mark.

Trust you are all well.
With fondest love
Your loving Bro.
James

Chancery Lane - Dec. 17 1913

My dear Bro. Tom,

Thank you for your letter this morning. In regard to sketches you hold it will not be necessary to retain these pending settlement of Comm a/c. I have seen H.C. today and his disposition is not at all in this direction. He sent Pullan and the typist into the next room and I had acomplished conversation. I must say, I feel extremely sorry for him and could have cried. He spoke of me in a higher tone than ever I have heard him before - all the others he said - indicating Byatt and Baxter - would not make much difference and could be replaced but dispaired of replacing me. I exposed and opened my mind fully to think of the causes. He said he would always be glad to see me if I would call. Of course what we have done, we have done and the arrangement made is a good one.

Harry is better and Annie is far from being herself -
When can you come up? How would saty do? or next Monday?
I am finishing I think on Friday.

With fondest love
Your affect. Bro.
James

Avondale, Dec. 22 1913

My dear Bro. Tom,

They are quoting for the Window Bills - The sketches only arrived this morning - Allen's (another printing company) are greatly interested in us and told me all about Lloyds beginning. He also asked me whether I had gone too far to open negotiations with them ie. to join them as a traveller they were prepared to make me a good offer and would consider it - I told them it was no use we had gone too far.

Pullan has today given me a cheque on salary and they will pay comm. weekly as hitherto as the goods are delivered. Poor Pullan he does seem down hearted. They are closing the artists room for 6 months to see if they can do without it. They have an idea that this is about the time we shall last. No idea at all who is backing us. They think Mallwood & H.C. (Harry Cooke) has been asking someone at Liebigs if it is so - this has got to Mr. Mallwood's ears - and he is annoyed - at H.C. of course. It looks a deserted place only Jack and the typist when Pullan has gone - every artist gone, even Swinburn - to whom they are returning his indentures and who is joining us in the new year. Misses Wright and Hocknell we are not taking. Rest this week and come prepared to settle all up that we may get into action by Janry 1st. Every thing is going well and satisfactory so far. The prospects are good.

Wishing you a right Merry Xmas and all at Ribbendale.

With fondest love
Your affect. Bro.
James

Avondale,
The Mall, Southgate,
Dec. 27 1913

My dear Bro. Tom,

Thank you for your letter of the 23rd which I only got this morning. Sorry to learn that baby is having a bad time just now and giving you one too.

Cooke's are sending their circulars out Monday and Tuesday next week - so we should issue ours Wednesday night at latest.

P.P. are I fear "at sea" in quoting for litho work and I think it will be better for us to deal with it all in London with British Color, David Allen etc. thro' Baxter until they get a plant of their own. I have sent them some Oxo enquiries and they are off - it may be they are dislocated with holidays - L'press they are alright on. Get to know when they are going to put down machinery.

I will write you more fully and address the letter to you at P.P. for Monday.

I hope that you have had more rest and are feeling in rare form for the task which awaits you this week. Finish up the points I will write you on, even if you have to return on Tuesday.

Shall be glad to see you and have your help next week.

We are improving here. Annie rather better - although Harry not so well again today. Hope you are better at Ribblesdale.

Fondest love,
Yours ever,
James

Jan. 1, 1914

Messrs. Scots & Brown Ltd.,
Stone Cutter Street,
Ludgate Circus, E.C.

Dear Sirs,

I have resigned my position as London Manager for Messrs. Alf. Cooke Ltd, and have entered into partnership with my brother, Mr. T.W. Haworth who has acted for the last 10 years as Northern representative for Messrs. Alf. Cooke Ltd. - and the style of the firm will therefore be JAMES HAWORTH & BRO.

Also I have been able to retain the services of the several clever artists and copy writers, who have worked so successfully under my direction in London for many years past.

You may therefore confidently expect from us sketches and designs of high artistic merit, and sound advertising value.

JAMES HAWORTH & BRO. will also be in a position to produce printing of exceptional merit, either letterpress, or litho - at prices which will always be worth your serious consideration.

So that you would have at your service a highly trained staff of artists, perfect printing equipment, and my own lifelong experience of advertising and printing.

That it will be worth your while to afford us the opportunity to quote on your next printing order - and submit designs - is the firm conviction of,

Yours very faithfully,
FOR JAMES HAWORTH & BRO.
James Haworth

To Mr. Thomas Haworth from H. Baxter one of the first travellers for James Haworth.

8 Ashirele Grove,
Cardigan Road,
Leeds
24.1.14

Dear Mr. Haworth,

I hear that Cooke's are feeling the blow badly, they have decided to dispose of their Rotary machine and close the Pamplet Dept. Mr. Kempton who had charge of the Rotary & Perfector machines has been advised to look out for another berth. They (Cooke's) have been very very slack for the last few weeks.

Many kind regards and best wishes for your early recovery,
Sincerely yours,
H. Baxter

Alf Cooke were to survive the breakup of their London studio and sales office. After the first world war they amalgamated with the large quality printers, Bemrose, who in turn became a member of Universal Printers a public quoted company.

The Alf Cooke factory at Leeds went through further changes and in 1987 is still a printing factory, under the title Bonar Cooke Cartons Ltd.

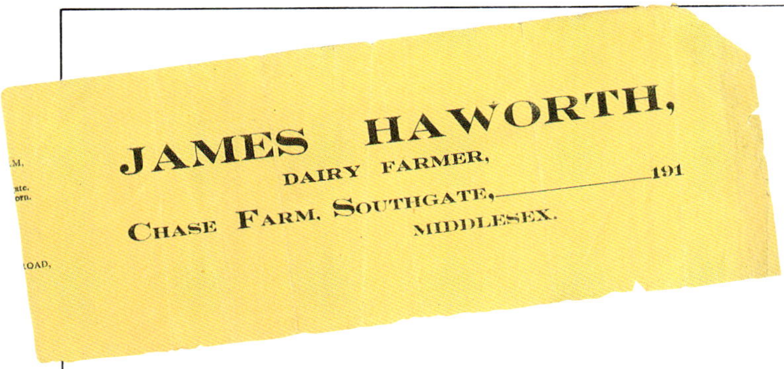

As well as the trauma, worry and the work load involved in making a success of the business, there was the worry of war with Germany. War clouds began to gather early in 1914, depressing business throughout the country. On 14th August war became a reality – a World War that in four horrific years was to affect every family in Britain and cost Britain the flower of her manhood in the slaughter of the trenches of the Western Front and Gallipoli, as well as in sea battles.

1914 to 1923. Farming New Farm, Oak Lodge, and Chase Farms, Southgate.

The U Boat menace, meant that farming was a booming industry, with cheap imports no longer possible through shipping losses. Despite the difficult business climate, James was courageous enough to expand his renting and leasing of farms in the Southgate area, adding New Farm, Enfield Road in October 1914. Oak Lodge Farm in March 1917, and Chase Farm in September 1917.

By Christmas 1917 the Haworth farms covered over 303 acres. There were 86 head of cattle, 10 horses, 29 sheep, 10 pigs and 3 working horses for the ploughs, reaping, drilling and mowing machines.

Forty acres had been given to the growing of cereals. There were two milk rounds. John J. aged 18 became Farm Manager, assisted by two cowmen, a horseman, a labourer, two hands under 18, plus girl and women helpers. Occasionally recovering wounded soldiers were seconded for farm work.

Oak Lodge Farm, Chase Road, Southgate.

Douglas Mould (centre) from Westpole Farm, a great friend of John J. Haworth.

First World War staff, John J. on right. Seated - Frank Dork Cowman, Harry Jeffrey and George Ward Milkmen.
Richard Haworth, James Haworth's second brother, had been brought down from Bacup, to manage New Farm in 1914.

War wounded soldier helping with the Massey Harris Binder. August 1917.

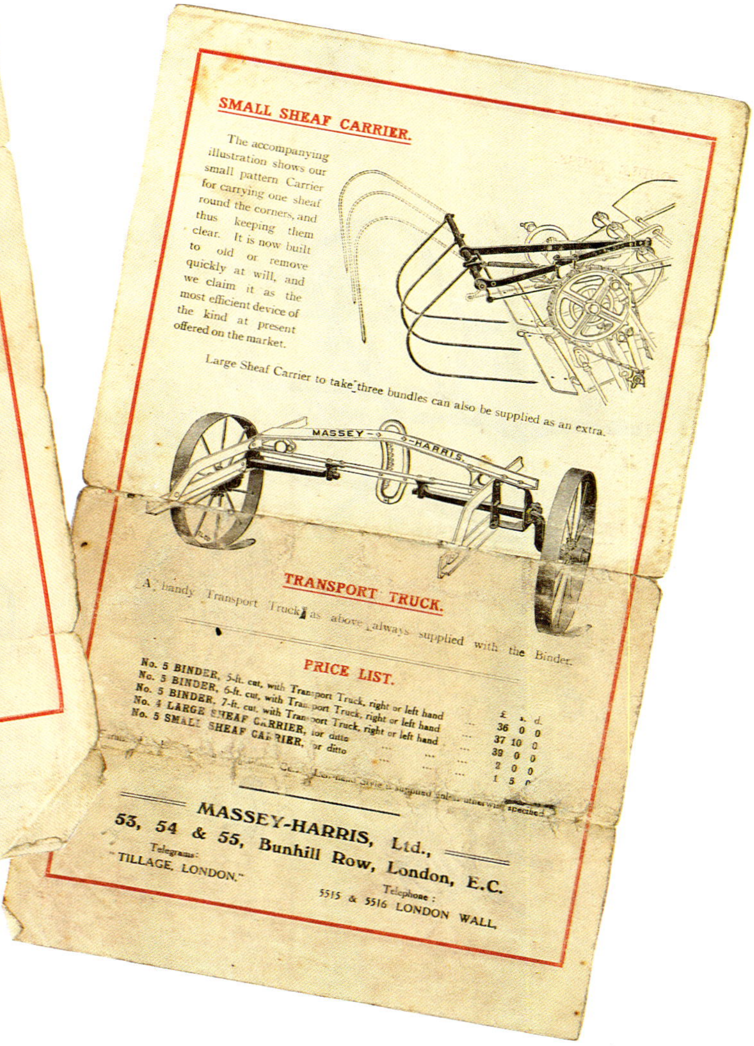

Oak Lodge Farm. The track is now Merrivale, Southgate and the Piccadilly Tube Line crosses the field.

John J. at present site of Oakwood (previously Enfield West) underground station.

Oak Lodge Farm residents.

New Farm Pasture, Enfield Road.

John J.

Visit to Hendon by John J. to meet pilot Reg Addison on right.

John Elliott
Airman friend of John J.

Certificates of Exemption for John J. as Farm Manager.

TELEPHONE VICTORIA 4400.

Appeal Tribunal for the County of Middlesex.

GUILDHALL, WESTMINSTER, S.W.

S. W. 1.

27th, June, 1917.

I beg to inform you that it will be unnecessary attend the Tribunal to-morrow for the hearing al.

Yours faithfully,

R. 62. Local Tribunal for SOUTHGATE.

Applicant (If not Man himself). Address Council Offices,

R. 66. Appellant or other party (Not Military Representative).

Appeal Tribunal for COUNTY OF MIDDLESEX,

Address GUILDHALL WESTMINSTER, S.W.

Date 22 JUN 1917

If not already examined by a Medical Board, please present yourself for examination by the Medical Board of your District before the hearing. Production of this notice will facilitate your examination.

NOTICE OF HEARING.

Notice is hereby given that the appeal against the decision of ... Local Tribunal in r...

SA 35301

Army Form W. 3236.

NOTICE PAPER to be sent to men who belong to the Army Reserve under the provisions of the Military Service Acts, 1916.

[In accordance with the provisions of Section 24 (2) of the Reserve Forces Act, 1882, "evidence of the delivery at the last registered place of abode of a man belonging to the Army Reserve of a Notice, or of a letter addressed to such man, and containing a notice, shall be evidence that such Notice was brought to the knowledge of such man."]

Christian Names J. J.

Surname Haworth

Address "Avondale" The Mall Southgate

No. in Milty. Register (A.B. 414) 1062

Class Number B

You are hereby warned that you will be required to join for service with the Colours on the 19 May 191 7.

You should therefore present yourself at ... on the above date, not later than 8am o'clock, bringing this paper with you.

RECRUITING OFFICE WOOD GREEN, N.

Signature.

Rank.

Appointment.

Section 15 of the Reserve Forces Act, 1882, which ... Army Reserve is called out on Permanent service, and such sickness or other reasonable excuse as may be ... appear at any time and place at which he is required ... according to the circumstances, of deserting ... absenting himself without leave within the meaning ...

Wt. W14660/M1864. 750m 2/17 Drayton Mill. (816)

REGIONAL No. 93203 No. of Voucher 3247M

BOARD OF AGRICULTURE AND FISHERIES VOUCHER. MILITARY SERVICE.

County Agricultural Executive Committee.

This is to Certify that :—

Name and Address (of man) J. J. Haworth, Southgate

Occupation of man Foreman

Name and Address (of employer) J. Haworth

is engaged in Agriculture one of the occupations and fulfils the conditions ... notes issued with the Military Service ... so engaged ...

A. F. W. 3291.

L^x_1 328

Mr. John James Haworth was medically examined at Holloway No 3 on 7 JUN 1918 and classified as: Grade ...

NATIONAL SERVICE MEDICAL BOARD No. 3 HOLLOWAY. 7 JUN 1918

Chairman (Medical Board).

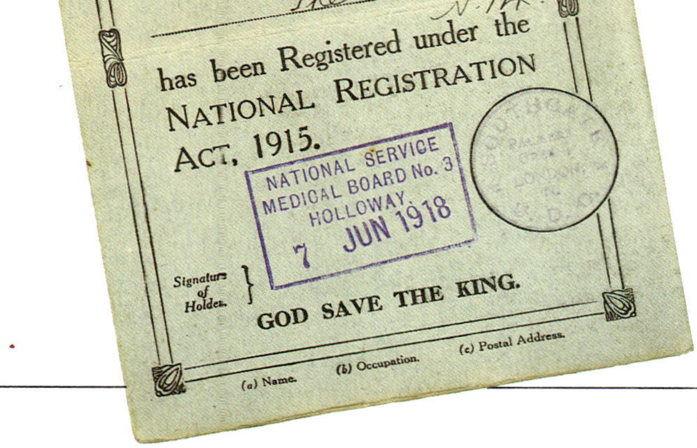

This is to Certify that

(a) John James Haworth

(b) Farm Workers Foreman

(c) of Avondale The Mall N.14

has been Registered under the NATIONAL REGISTRATION ACT, 1915.

NATIONAL SERVICE MEDICAL BOARD No. 3 HOLLOWAY 7 JUN 1918

Signature of Holder.

GOD SAVE THE KING.

(a) Name. (b) Occupation. (c) Postal Address.

The idea of a volunteer army had by 1916 been abandoned and conscription was the order of the day, though farming was an essential occupation and carried with it a certain exemption from call-up. Death at the front by 1917 meant that all young men in farming could no longer be exempted and John J. had to report for a medical. He was classed as A.4 which eliminated him from immediate call-up, but he would have to report to Hounslow Barracks by December 1918. The war, however, fortunately finished on 11th November 1918 and as a farmer John J. was told not to report.

Lloyd George with Middlesex and Hertfordshire Farmers.

Bottom left: Southgate County School friends in the Navy and Royal Flying Corps.

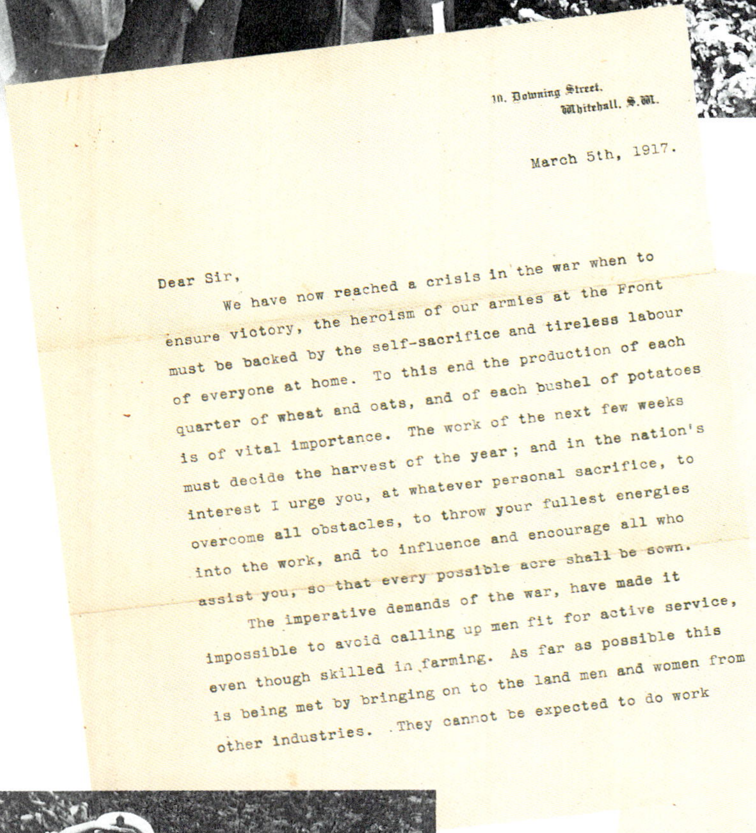

10, Downing Street,
Whitehall, S.W.

March 5th, 1917.

Dear Sir,

We have now reached a crisis in the war when to ensure victory, the heroism of our armies at the Front must be backed by the self-sacrifice and tireless labour of everyone at home. To this end the production of each quarter of wheat and oats, and of each bushel of potatoes is of vital importance. The work of the next few weeks must decide the harvest of the year; and in the nation's interest I urge you, at whatever personal sacrifice, to overcome all obstacles, to throw your fullest energies into the work, and to influence and encourage all who assist you, so that every possible acre shall be sown.

The imperative demands of the war, have made it impossible to avoid calling up men fit for active service, even though skilled in farming. As far as possible this is being met by bringing on to the land men and women from other industries. They cannot be expected to do work

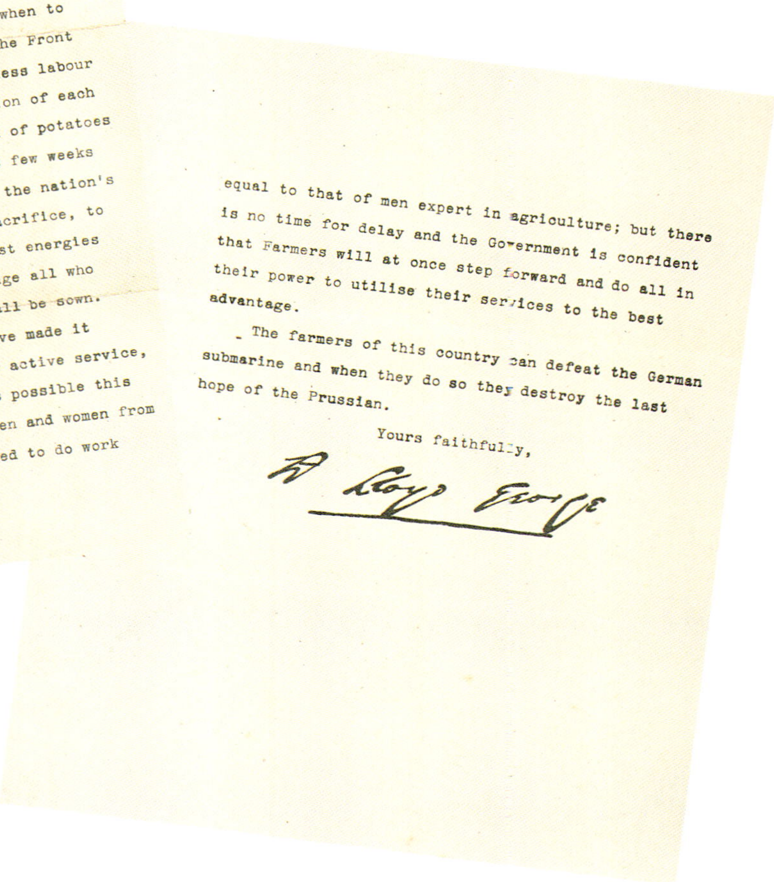

equal to that of men expert in agriculture; but there is no time for delay and the Government is confident that Farmers will at once step forward and do all in their power to utilise their services to the best advantage.

The farmers of this country can defeat the German submarine and when they do so they destroy the last hope of the Prussian.

Yours faithfully,

D Lloyd George

He continued the management of the farms, which were still a profitable enterprise. But, cheap imports were again becoming available and the farms became unprofitable. They were sold off finally in 1923 after having been supported with money from the print business.

The machinery and stock from the last farm sold on 25th September 1923 raised £5,686–19s–0d. I have no record of the money received for the land, or the buyer, except to say it was more than likely bought on behalf of the Piccadilly Line which ended then at Finsbury Park. Already plans were in hand to extend the line to Cockfosters. Chase Farm was an ideal site for Enfield West (later Oakwood) Station, with of course houses on the remainder of the area. With hindsight, a lost fortune! But life is full of that cry.

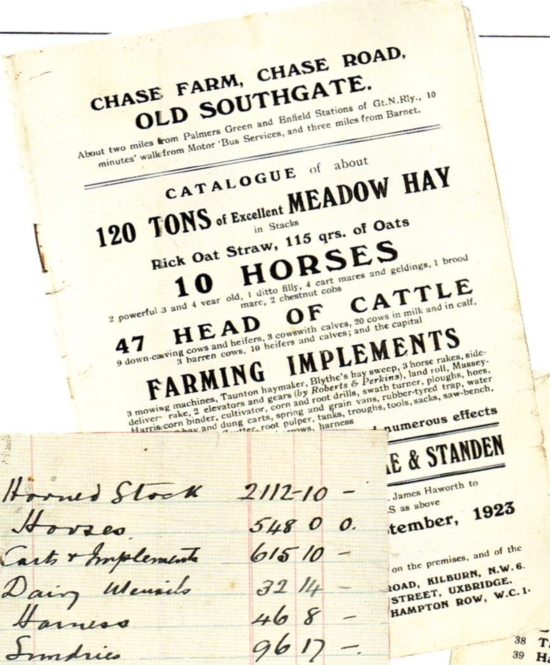

CHASE FARM, CHASE ROAD,
OLD SOUTHGATE.
About two miles from Palmers Green and Enfield Stations of Gt.N.Rly., 10 minutes' walk from Motor 'Bus Services, and three miles from Barnet.

CATALOGUE of about
120 TONS of Excellent MEADOW HAY in Stacks
Rick Oat Straw, 115 qrs. of Oats
10 HORSES
2 powerful 3 and 4 year old, 1 ditto filly, 4 cart mares and geldings, 1 brood mare, 2 chestnut cobs
47 HEAD OF CATTLE
9 down-calving cows and heifers, 3 cows with calves, 20 cows in milk and in calf, 3 barren cows, 10 heifers and calves; and the capital
FARMING IMPLEMENTS
3 mowing machines, Taunton haymaker, Blythe's hay sweep, 3 horse rakes, side-delivery rake, 2 elevators and gears (by *Roberts & Perkins*), land roll, Massey-Harris corn binder, cultivator, corn and root drills, swath turner, ploughs, hoes, ... hay and dung carts, spring and grain vans, rubber-tyred trap, water ...cutter, root pulper, tanks, troughs, tools, sacks, saw-bench, ...rrows, harness
...numerous effects
...E & STANDEN
... James Haworth to
...S as above
...tember, 1923
... on the premises, and of the
...ROAD, KILBURN, N.W.6.
...STREET, UXBRIDGE.
...HAMPTON ROW, W.C.1.

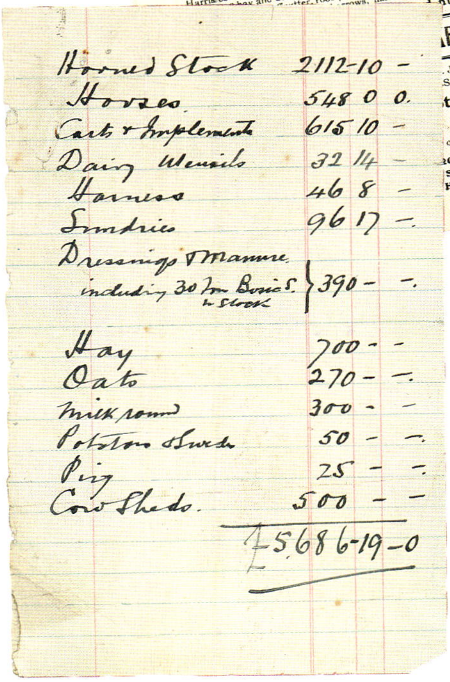

Horned Stock	2112-10 -
Horses	548 0 0.
Carts & Implements	615 10 -
Dairy Utensils	32 14 -
Harness	46 8 -
Sundries	96 17 -
Dressings & Manure including 30 Ton Basic S. in Stock	390 - -
Hay	700 - -
Oats	270 - -
Milk round	300 - -
Potatoes & Swedes	50 - -
Pig	25 - -
Cow Sheds.	500 - -
	£5686-19-0

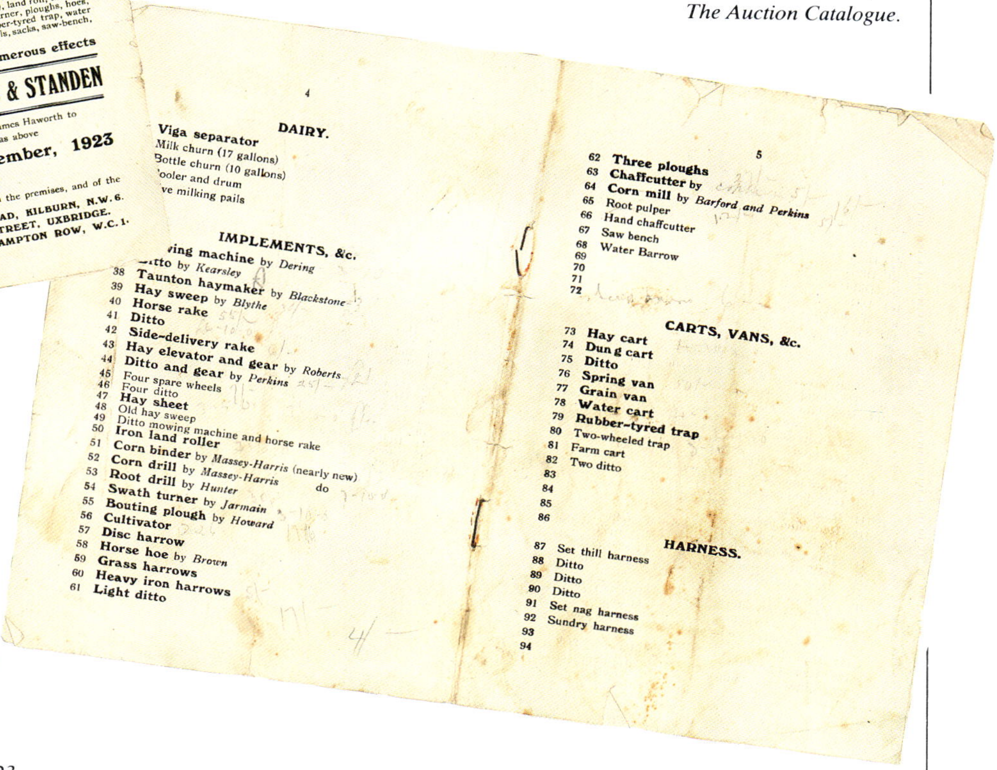

4

DAIRY.
Viga separator
Milk churn (17 gallons)
Bottle churn (10 gallons)
Cooler and drum
...ve milking pails

IMPLEMENTS, &c.
...wing machine by *Dering*
Ditto by *Kearsley*
38 Taunton haymaker by *Blackstone*
39 Hay sweep by *Blythe*
40 Horse rake
41 Ditto
42 Side-delivery rake
43 Hay elevator and gear by *Roberts*
44 Ditto and gear by *Perkins*
45 Four spare wheels
46 Four ditto
47 Hay sheet
48 Old hay sweep
49 Ditto mowing machine and horse rake
50 Iron land roller
51 Corn binder by *Massey-Harris* (nearly new)
52 Corn drill by *Massey-Harris* do
53 Root drill by *Hunter*
54 Swath turner by *Jarmain*
55 Bouting plough by *Howard*
56 Cultivator
57 Disc harrow
58 Horse hoe by *Brown*
59 Grass harrows
60 Heavy iron harrows
61 Light ditto

5

62 Three ploughs
63 Chaffcutter by
64 Corn mill by *Barford and Perkins*
65 Root pulper
66 Hand chaffcutter
67 Saw bench
68 Water Barrow
69
70
71
72

CARTS, VANS, &c.
73 Hay cart
74 Dung cart
75 Ditto
76 Spring van
77 Grain van
78 Water cart
79 Rubber-tyred trap
80 Two-wheeled trap
81 Farm cart
82 Two ditto
83
84
85
86

HARNESS.
87 Set thill harness
88 Ditto
89 Ditto
90 Ditto
91 Set nag harness
92 Sundry harness
93
94

The Auction Catalogue.

John J. says goodbye to his friends, September, 1923.

Farming finished – empty fields 1923.

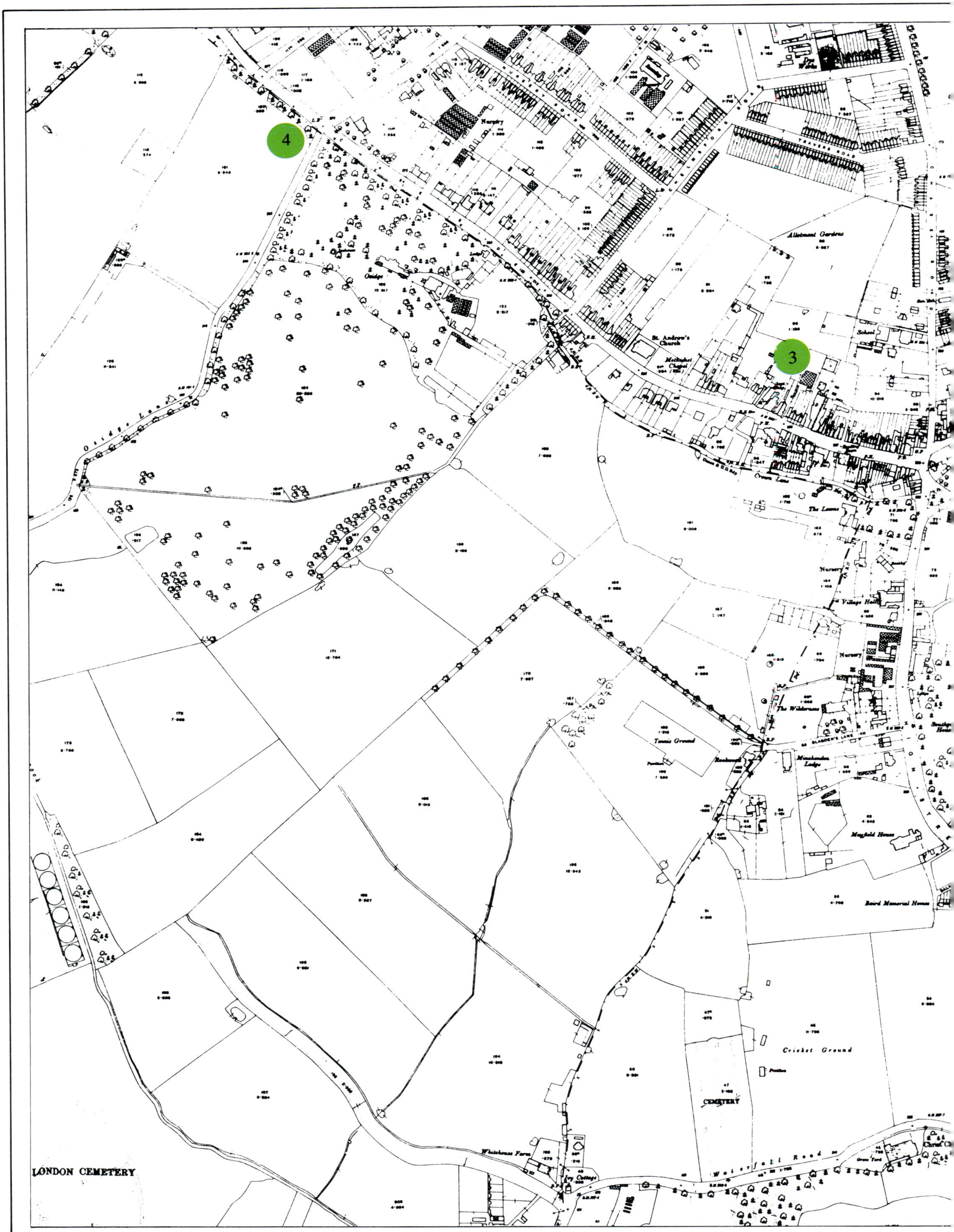
4
3
Nursery
Allotment Gardens
St. Andrew's Church
Methodist Chapel
School
Crown Lane
The Lawns
Nursery
Village Hall
Nursery
The Wilderness
Tennis Ground
Mayfield House
Baird Memorial Homes
Cricket Ground
CEMETERY
Whitehouse Farm
Ivy Cottage
Waterfall Road
LONDON CEMETERY

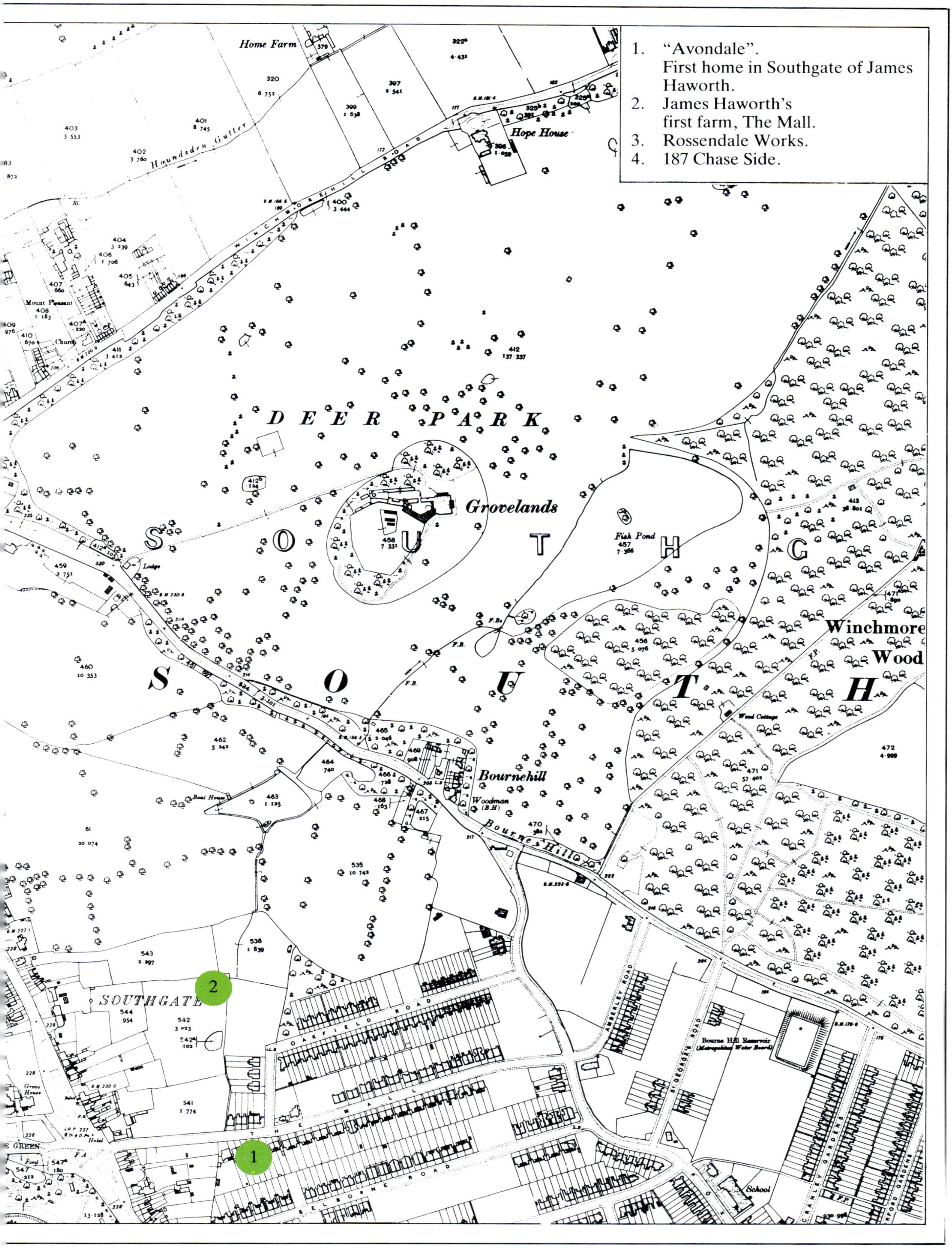

1. "Avondale".
First home in Southgate of James Haworth.
2. James Haworth's first farm, The Mall.
3. Rossendale Works.
4. 187 Chase Side.
Home Farm
Hope House
Houndsden Gutter
Winchmore Hill Road
Mount Pleasant
Church
DEER PARK
Grovelands
Fish Pond
SOUTHGATE
Winchmore Wood
Lodge
Wood Cottage
Bournehill
Woodman (B.H)
Bourne Hill
Boat House
SOUTHGATE
Oakfield Road
The Mall
Belborne Road
Amberley Road
St. George's Road
Bourne Hill Reservoir (Metropolitan Water Board)
School
Cranley Gardens
Grove House
Hotel
GREEN
Pond
1
2

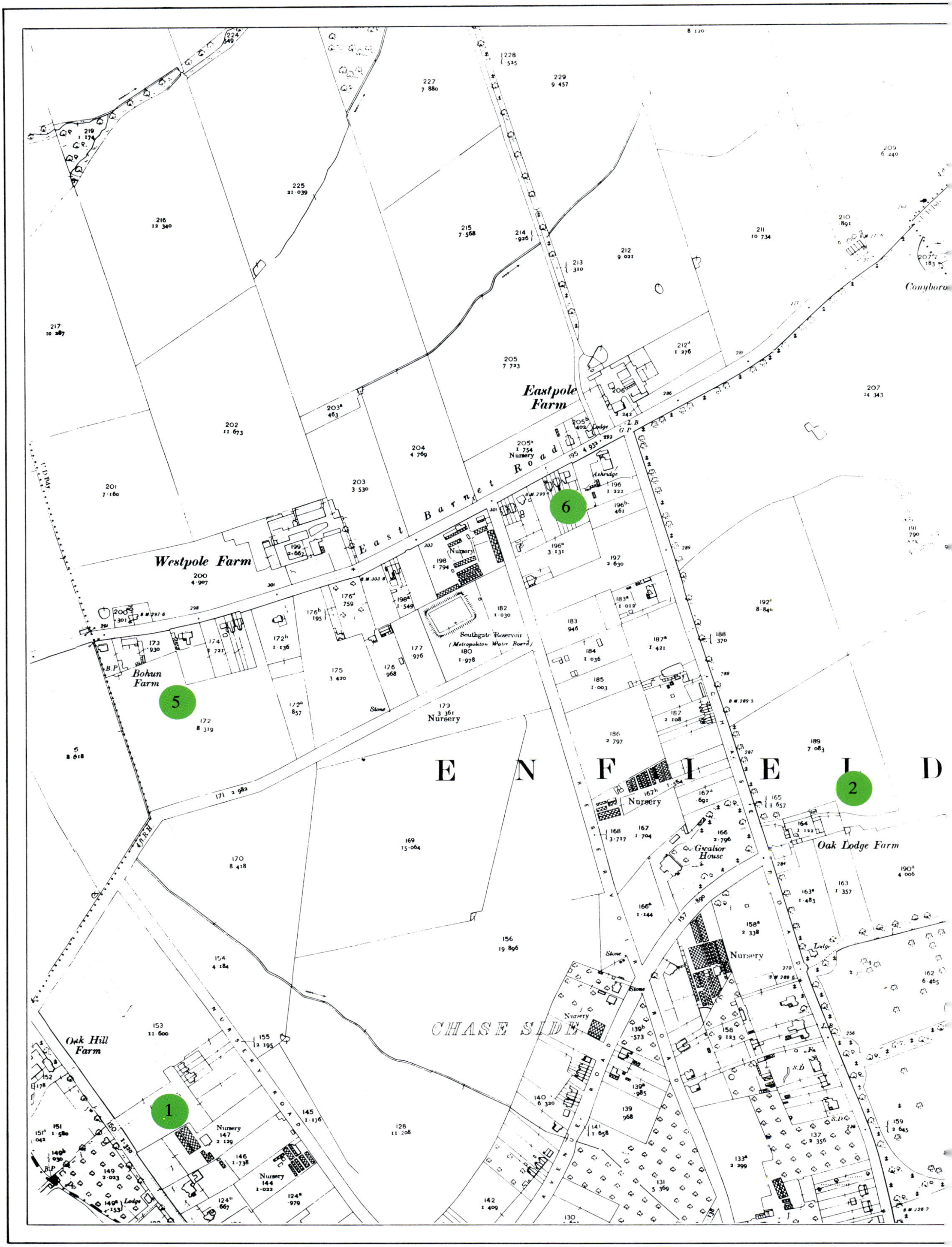

Westpole Farm
Eastpole Farm
East Barnet Road
Bohun Farm
Southgate Reservoir (Metropolitan Water Board)
Nursery
E N F I E L D
Oak Lodge Farm
Gralior House
CHASE SIDE
Oak Hill Farm
Nursery Road
Avenue Road
Lodge
1
2
5
6

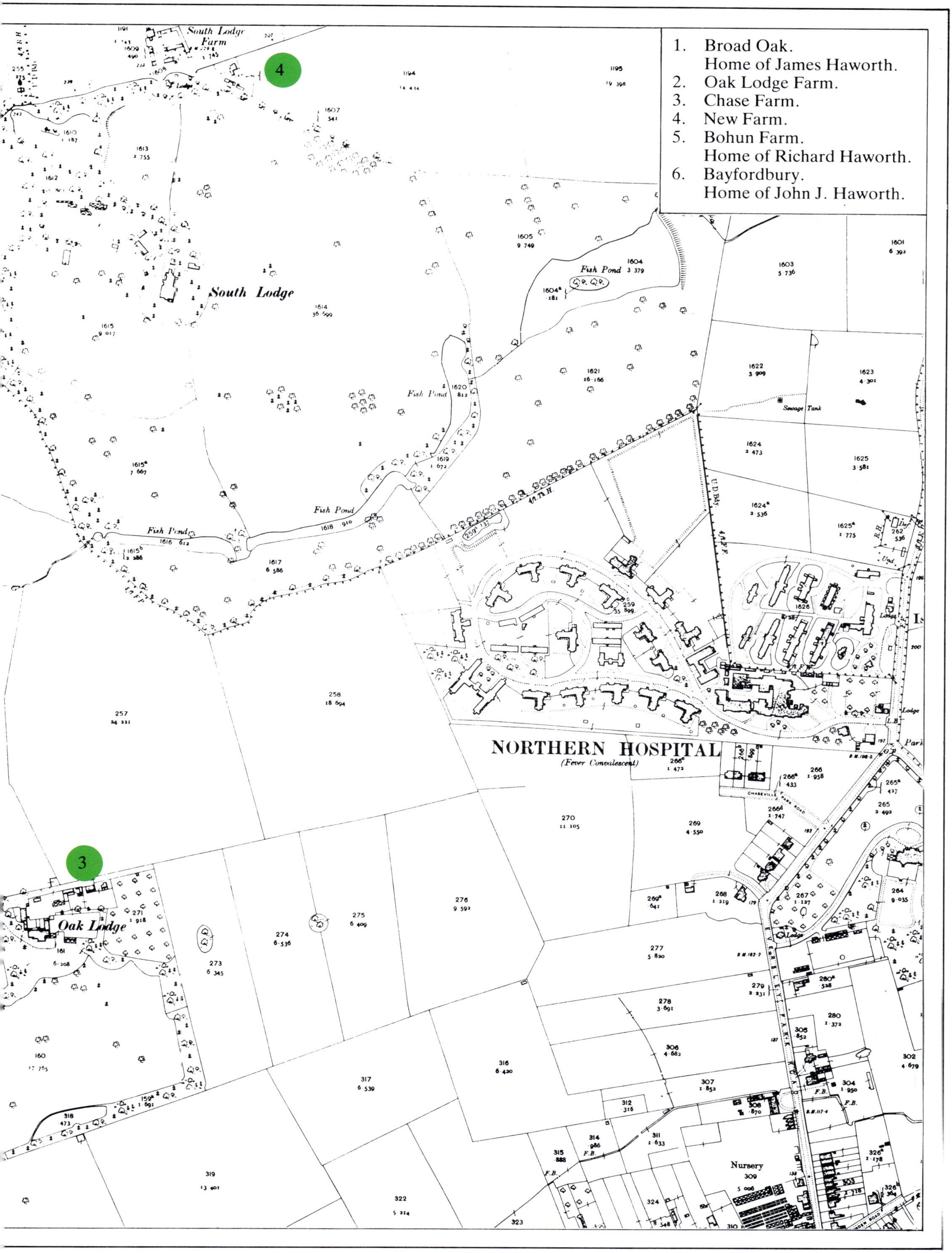
1. Broad Oak.
Home of James Haworth.
2. Oak Lodge Farm.
3. Chase Farm.
4. New Farm.
5. Bohun Farm.
Home of Richard Haworth.
6. Bayfordbury.
Home of John J. Haworth.
4
3
South Lodge Farm
South Lodge
Fish Pond
Oak Lodge
NORTHERN HOSPITAL
(Fever Convalescent)
Sewage Tank
Nursery
Lodge
Park

1920 Motorcyclists at New Farm, Enfield Road
First right - Harry Haworth on a Rudge Multi-Special shortly to die in an accident with this machine 4th July 1921.
Second right - John J. Haworth.

Sporty lady friends of Harry and John J.

Ann Haworth – 1920 – "Avondale".

John J. Haworth on XB3937 Rudge Multi-Special.

Southgate – still quiet in 1920's.

Tragedy had struck the family some two years earlier with the death of younger son Harry in a motorbike accident, reported in the Palmers Green and Southgate Gazette as illustrated.

The last sentence showed that young Harry was in the printing company and perhaps destined to inherit the business, leaving John J. with the farms.

Harry's death and the sale of the farms meant that John J. aged 24 was to join the business at last, having perhaps left behind his wide open space days on motorbikes and horses.

Bacup, July 1921.
A last photograph taken by Harry Haworth.

Above left: Trip to Lancashire, Sunday July 3rd 1921
John J. took photograph of Harry - far left - and cousins.

TTE, SATURDAY, JULY 9, 1921.

YOUTH'S TRAGIC DEATH.

SAD ENDING TO HOLIDAY TOUR.

A well-known Southgate youth, Harry Unwin Haworth, younger son of Mr. and Mrs. James Haworth, of 84 The Mall, met his death as the result of a motor cycle accident near Hinckley, Lancs., on Monday.

Deceased, with his brother, left home a fortnight ago for a tour in Lancashire, and were returning via Bacup at the time of the fatality. Death took place in Leicester Royal Infirmary at 11.30 on Monday evening.

The brother, John James Haworth, told the tragic story of the youth's death to Mr. E. G. B. Fowler, City coroner, at the inquest in the Infirmary on Tuesday.

"About 3.30 on Monday afternoon," said witness, "we were riding on the Watling Street main road, and when we got near Burrage, about four miles from Hinckley, we had to pass over a river bridge where there was a steep incline. My brother took the bridge at about 20 miles an hour. I followed. When he was descending the other side he looked back towards me, and the front wheel of his bicycle hit some loose stones in the roadway. His machine wobbled and he lost control, and fell head first on to the roadway." Witness vaulted from his own machine and went over to his brother, who was unconscious. Having obtained assistance, witness rode on to Hinckley and brought a doctor back on his carrier. His brother was removed to Leicester Royal Infirmary, where he died the same night without regaining consciousness.

Dr. Beyers, house surgeon, said deceased was in a dazed and delirious condition when brought in, and was suffering from injuries to the head. Death was due to a fractured skull.

The body was conveyed to 84 The Mall on Tuesday, and the interment will take place to-day (Saturday) in Southgate Cemetery at 3 p.m.

Harry Unwin Haworth, who was but 17 years old, was an old Wood Green County School boy, and was in business with his father as a printer's clerk.

Harry Unwin Haworth
Born 22nd February 1904. Died 4th July 1921.

With the sale of the farms, James, as well as John J., felt cramped at "Avondale". Early in 1924 "Avondale" was sold for £1,105 and Broad Oak (nearly opposite where Monkfrith Avenue meets Chase Side) with some 2 acres of ground running between Chase Side and Trent Gardens was purchased for £2,500.

Motorbikes were banned on Harry's death but John J. was able to keep a horse in a stable at Broad Oak and for further company bought an alsatian called Wolf. A cow for milking also arrived in the orchard end of the garden by Trent Gardens.

Broad Oak, demolished in 1985, and now the site of De Bohun Court, was a house of great character when viewed from Chase Side. This view was to disappear in 1960 by building in the front garden a row of maisonettes. Town planners where were you!!

John J. saddled up and father looks on.

In 1924 Broad Oak was the last residence on that side of Chase Side, Southgate, until you reached Potters Bar, some 3½ miles up the road. This is perhaps not true if you counted the original lodge entrance to Trent Park.

Wolf.

The house, Broad Oak, was built by Charles Jacob Newby in 1869 for a Mr Clements, nurseryman. When built it had no frills, such as the turret and first floor verandahs. In the front were rows of greenhouses. There were two wells inside the house and an underground passage led to a very large boiler house some 40 feet north from the house. This boiler house supplied heat both to the greenhouses and Broad Oak.

Seasons at "Broad Oak".

I recall visits to Broad Oak, both as a small boy and teenager. Every time I went it was like entering a time capsule and this was comparing with the 1930s and 1940s. Everything, combining with that not unpleasant "old time smell", reflected very much the late Victorian era that the new occupants James and Annie had known in their young days. They had obviously transferred their liking for such a period by the purchase of old and large pieces of furniture.

James and Annie engaged, almost at once after their move to Broad Oak, a live-in maid called Cissie, whose home was in Cumberland. Her wage was 10s per week. Broad Oak was to become Cissie's home I recall, until James' death in 1948. A more devoted lady to James and Annie would be hard to find, as in later years she had to put up with the difficulties some elderly people could cause those who are close to them. James and Annie were no exception in their tantrums.

1946 – "Broad Oak" Dining Room.

Chase Side, Southgate early 1900's.

1926 – Roadworks outside "Broad Oak".

1928 – Lucy Haworth marries Alan Lord.

"Halcyon Days" 1927 – "Broad Oak" Tennis Party.

Lucy and John J. continued through the 1920s to live at Broad Oak. Lucy was, in 1928, to marry Alan Lord, a cotton representative. They moved into a new house in the recently built De Bohun Avenue, just north of Broad Oak, which ran up to Broad Oak's now side entrance. This entrance, in summer and autumn, would often have a small stall by the gate with excess garden produce for sale. Sales were never great, as the prices always had to match those of the Southgate greengrocers, reported in daily by Broad Oak's full-time gardener. Family were also expected to purchase on visits!

John J. as a representative, quickly set out to overtake his father as the chief obtainer of business. By 1928, he had achieved this situation which he maintained until 1940, when James finally retired from travelling. James was to become increasingly irritated at his son's success and there were long periods of silence between the pair during the 30s. Fortunately, it never seemed to affect the company's performance.

John J., in 1926, was able to buy a Talbot Tourer car thanks to his earnings by commission. No company supplied and maintained cars in those days!

This car, christened "Ginger" by reason of its colour, was to give John J. a standing in the eyes of the young "flappers" of Southgate. Broad Oak, with its grass tennis court was to host many tennis parties with eligible ladies present.

The Talbot car – otherwise known as "Ginger".

However, John J., prior to this time, had in 1925 set his heart on an attractive lady who often travelled on the same train which John J. caught each morning at Palmers Green Station, bound for Moorgate. John J. alighted at York Road, Kings Cross for a tram or bus to High Holborn. It was unusual for a youngish lady to travel 1st class, when there was a 2nd class and even 3rd class, in those days, which most office workers had to use. The problem was, as the winter went by into spring of the new year, how to make contact with her as John J. left the train at York Road, whilst the lady carried on down the smokey tunnels to Moorgate.

May, 1926 saw the General Strike, with John J. enrolling as a Special Constable for guard duties on the trains. Knowing father, I think this enrolment had more to do with the lady on the train, than strike breaking!

The strike being soon over – it only lasted for some 10 days – the problem was still how to make contact, for their social paths did not cross and to "pick a lady up" in the street, or, worse, on the train, would have meant the sternest of rebukes. If a policeman was handy, a quick arrest for molesting and up in front of a magistrate that morning, was something that could not be contemplated.

King's Cross suburban trains, evening 11th May 1926 at the time of the General Strike. Hotel curve platform is on right out of picture. This platform was so named as the then line from Moorgate came out from a tunnel just underneath King's Cross Station Hotel.

There were many thousands of volunteers who replaced public transport workers. Special Constables acted as train guards.

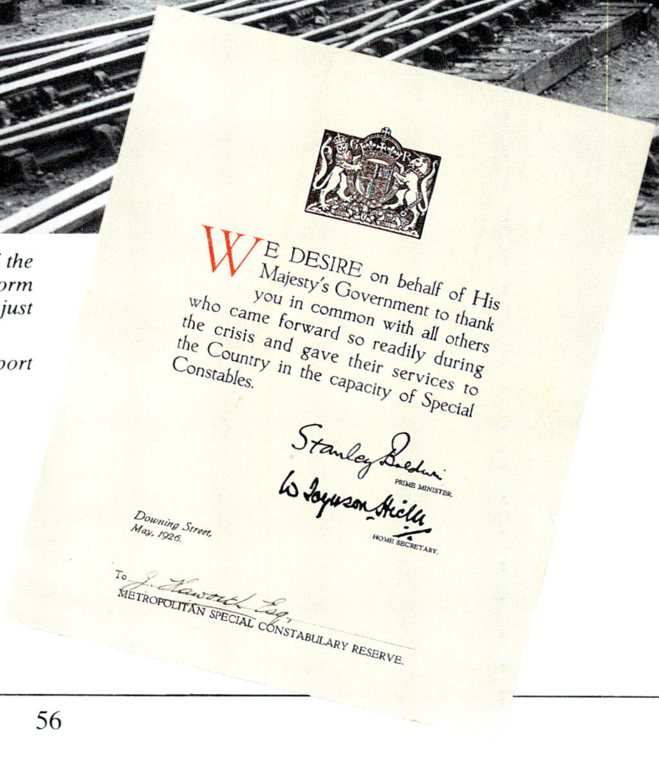

WE DESIRE on behalf of His Majesty's Government to thank you in common with all others who came forward so readily during the crisis and gave their services to the Country in the capacity of Special Constables.

Stanley Baldwin
PRIME MINISTER.

W Joynson-Hicks
HOME SECRETARY.

Downing Street,
May, 1926.

To J. Haworth Esq.
METROPOLITAN SPECIAL CONSTABULARY RESERVE.

Florence Watts, 1926. The sharp-eyed will note that she is in a Southern Railway carriage!

Suburban train in the country between Grange Park and Winchmore Hill, 1920s.

This lady, obviously caught the train further up the line, so there was nothing for it, but to try and see her in her 1st class carriage on her way home. This meant several evenings patiently waiting on Kings Cross Railway Station's Hotel curve platform, as it was known. Here trains from Moorgate would rise out of the murky depths with great noise and volumes of steam and smoke.

At long last the lady was observed in her 1st class corner seat. Unknown to her, John J. was discreetly able to see her alight at Enfield Chase and go to her nearby home "Clyst Hydon", 5 The Villas, Chase Side, Enfield. This row of villas still stands in splendid isolation on Chase Green.

In reality however, John J. was no further forward as far as an introduction was concerned, but at least he knew her address. An enquiry of the local Register of Electors would get her surname, that is if she was not married and had no sisters. There was only one young sounding name at that address – Florence Alice Watts.

Florence Watts was born on 24th August 1895, in a flat over Enfield Police Station, London Road, Enfield where her father, William King Watts, was Station Sergeant.

William Watts was born at Barnstaple in 1860, the youngest of three brothers. The family moved to Clyst Hydon, near Ottery St. Mary and he was accepted as a constable in the Devon Constabulary at Ottery St. Mary in 1880.

The newly formed London Metropolitan Police was seeking very much to expand its numbers and offered 2s 6d a day more than the Devon constabulary. So William transferred to London in 1883 and was stationed at Greenwich. There he met a seamstress, Ellen Eveleigh, whom he married in 1884.

Their first daughter, Annie, born at Greenwich in 1886, died in 1913 at Enfield from amoebic dysentry, having been a buyer at Selfridges for the past five years.

Far left: The Police truncheon of William King Watts.

Above: Florence Watts, aged 13.

Right: Ellen Eveleigh, 1880. Lived in Exeter before moving to Greenwich in 1882.

Clyst Hydon Village, 1987.

The old Police Station (1987) Ottery St. Mary, Devon.

A second daughter, Blanche Ellen, born in 1889 at Clyst Hydon, Devon, was to become a G.P.O. telephonist. She married Gordon Wheaton in 1913. His sister Elsie was to marry Frank Barratt of Barratt's Sweets, Wood Green (factory recently demolished). In 1914 the Barratt's moved to "Ashridge", a large house at the country corner of Chase Road, Southgate and Enfield Road (now Bramley Road). They lived there until 1938 when the house was used as A.T.C. Headquarters and fell into disrepair after 1945. It is now the site of Ashridge Court Flats.

Blanche and Gordon Wheaton lived in a fine house on Windmill Hill, Enfield, where son Geoffrey was born on June 25th, 1921, preceded by Audrey and Pamela.

Back to William and Ellen Watts. William, on promotion to Sergeant, was housed, in 1893, in a flat at Enfield Police Station.

Annie Watts, 1912.

For Florence, from a baby to a 10 year old girl, the Police Station was her home, exciting at times, but a noisy place to reside and there was no garden.

By 1905, father William had reached retiring age after serving 25 years in the force. Only 45 years old, he sought a new occupation to supplement his pension and took over an Off-Licence near the Great Northern Cemetery, New Southgate, the family living in a flat over the shop.

William gave up this tenancy in 1910 and went as Court Warrant Officer to the new Enfield Police Court, situated at the bottom of Windmill Hill.

The family moved into the nearby row of villas on Chase Green and called the house "Clyst Hydon". He was to remain Warrant Officer until 1929, and died of a stroke in November 1933.

With the move back to Enfield in 1910, Florence Watts had to seek a career. She enrolled at Clarke's Secretarial College, Wood Green, leaving after 2 years, aged 16, a very qualified shorthand typist with beautiful handwriting, the latter to be admired until the end of her days.

The Wheaton family, 1922.

1923. Sisters Blanche Wheaton (left). Florence Watts.

Enfield Police Station 1888.

1924. Geoffrey, Audrey and Pamela Wheaton.

"Denholm", Windmill Hill, Enfield.

It was 1912 and looking older than her 16 years, Florence obtained a position with a City of London firm, Charles Pinnock, corn merchants, who maintained a city office near the Corn Exchange.

Florence, in due course, came to the notice of the owner who made her his personal secretary and to a certain extent, assistant in his affairs. This led to a close relationship between them, but divorce was a very unpopular course to take in those days, for anyone of standing in the city.

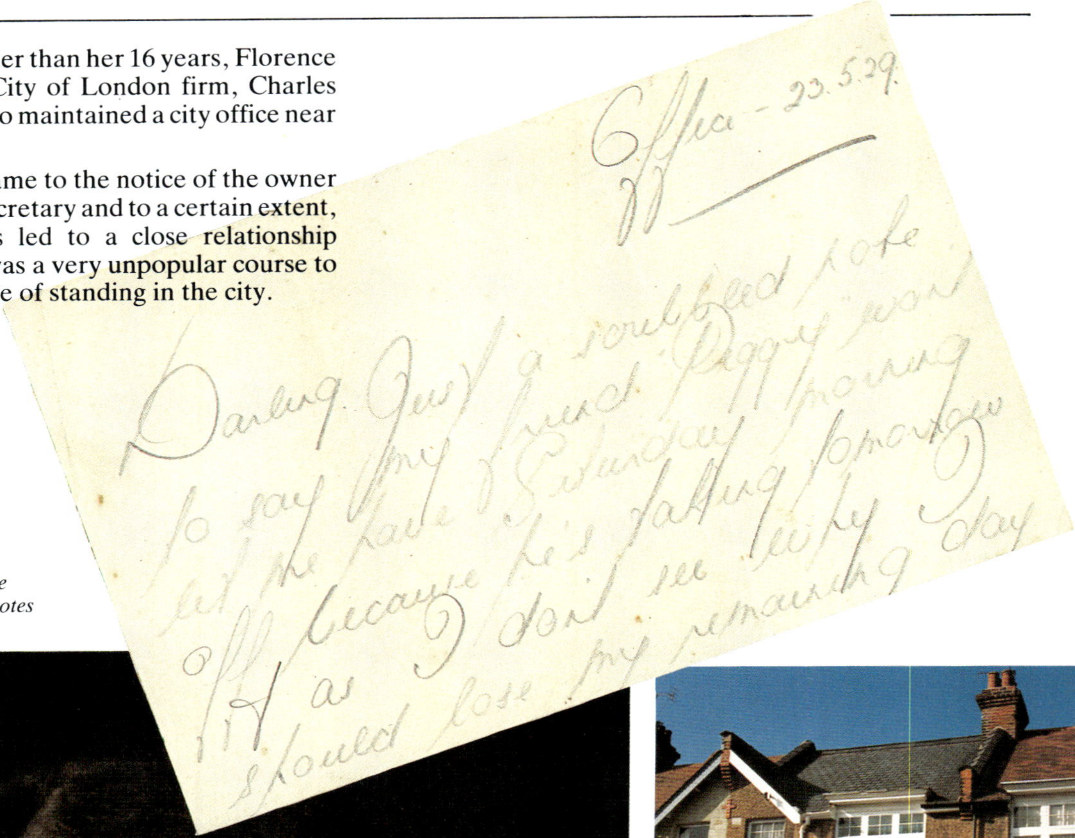
Office – 23.5.29

Darling. Just a scribbled note to say my friend 'Peggy' won't let me have Saturday morning off because he's taking tomorrow & as I don't see why I should lose my remaining day

Florence Watts's handwriting had the admiration of all who received her notes and letters.

5, The Limes, Chase Side, Enfield. 1927. Home of Florence Watts.

Florence Watts, 1927.

It was against this background, unknown to John J., that he had designed and made at considerable cost, a diamond arrow brooch. With its value, he hoped to justify his sincerity and sent the brooch with this letter on March 22nd 1927.

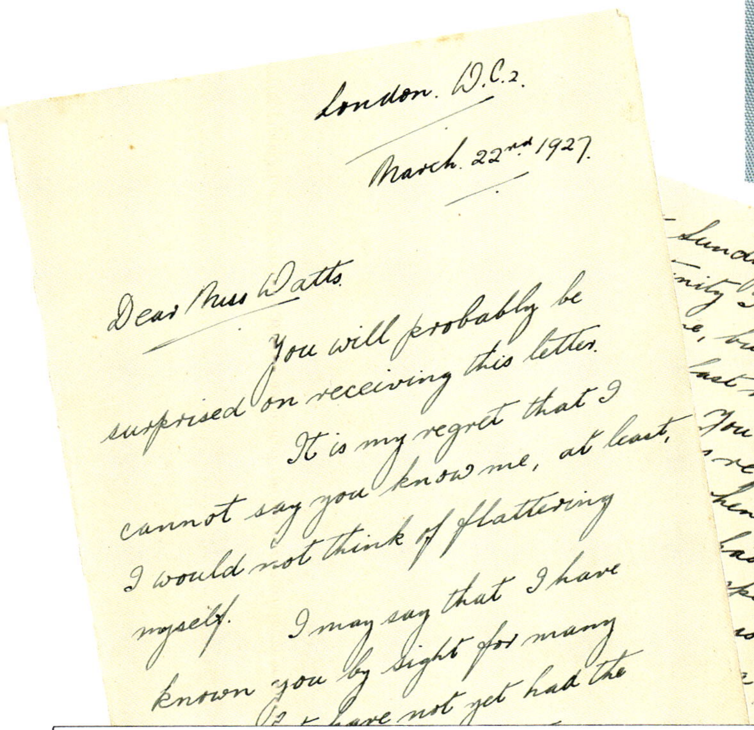

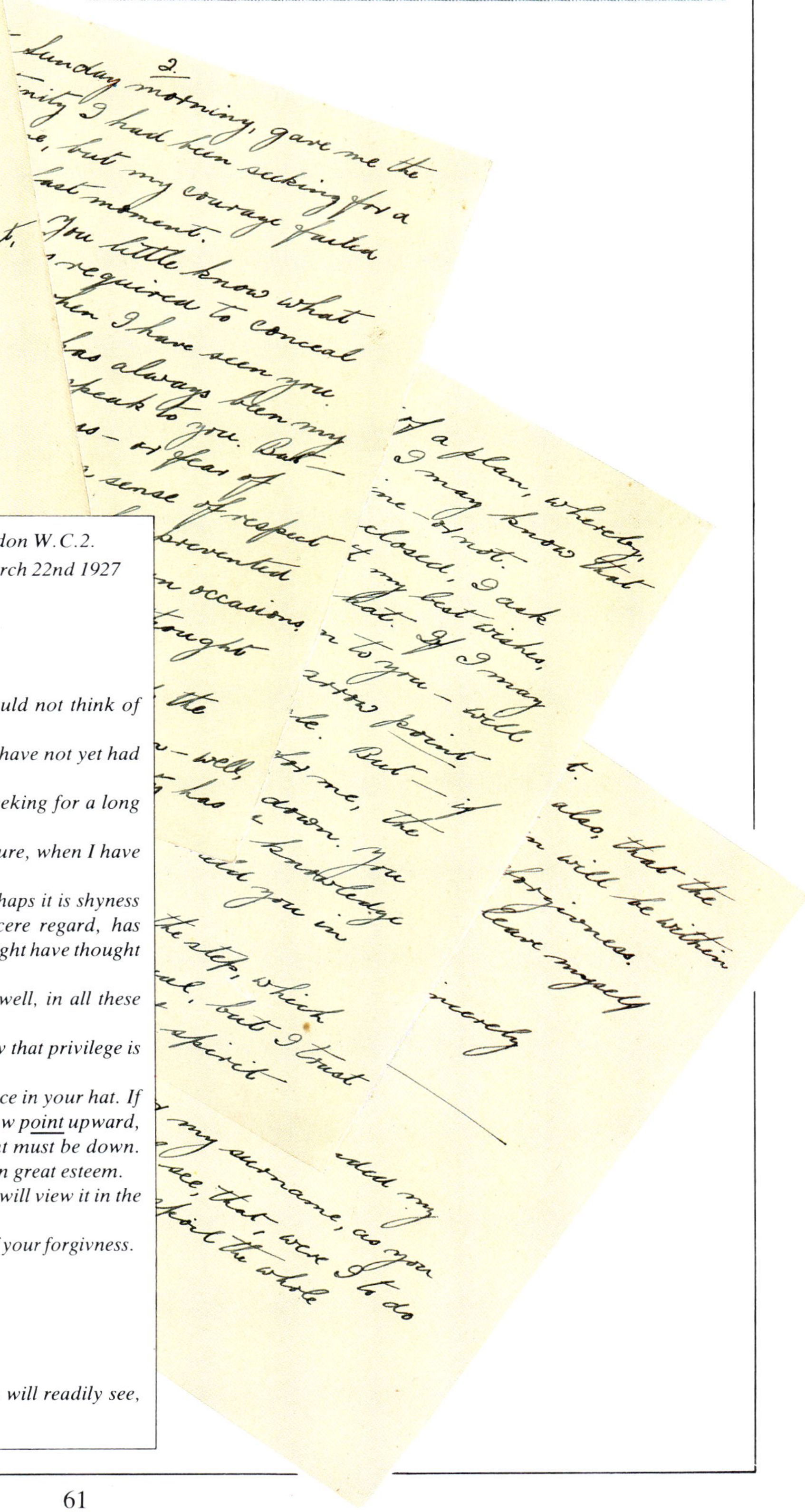

London W.C.2.
March 22nd 1927

Dear Miss Watts,

You will probably be surprised on receiving this letter.

It is my regret that I cannot say you know me, at least, I would not think of flattering myself.

I may say that I have known you by sight for many years, but have not yet had the pleasure of an introduction.

Last Sunday morning, gave me the opportunity I had been seeking for a long time, but my courage failed me at the last moment.

You little know what effort it has required to conceal my pleasure, when I have seen you.

It has always been my greatest wish to speak to you. But – perhaps it is shyness – or fear of rebuff – but more – a sense of respect and sincere regard, has prevented me from speaking to you on occasions, which others might have thought opportune.

To meet you through the ordinary course of introduction – well, in all these years, no opportunity has presented itself.

I have thought of a plan, whereby, with your help, I may know that privilege is to be mine – or not.

The enclosed. I ask you to accept, with my best wishes, and place in your hat. If I may make myself known to you – will you please wear the arrow point upward, at any angle. But – if that honour is not for me, the arrow point must be down. You will at least have the knowledge that someone has held you in great esteem.

I know the step, which I have taken, is unusual, but I trust you will view it in the spirit which prompted it.

I hope, also, that the liberty I have taken will be within the range of your forgivness.

Now, I leave myself in your hands.

Yours very sincerely
John –

p.s. I have not appended my address, or my surname, as you will readily see, that, were I to do so, it would spoil the whole.

No doubt Florence Watts was taken aback by such an unorthodox approach. Suitably flattered, she wore the brooch the next day at the upward angle to signify her interest in meeting this unknown admirer.

Upon sighting the brooch (most likely the next day), John J. was indeed a happy man and introductions were made. They were subsequently to enjoy each others company very much over the next two years. There was many a courting walk, beginning from Bayford Station into Hertford, dinner at the "Salisbury" and return by the last train of the day to Enfield. They also enjoyed many a trip to Devon in the Talbot car.

Florence, meanwhile, for obvious reasons, left the corn merchants and easily obtained a short-term job with another City firm.

Holiday in Looe.

Happy country walks.

The courtship 1927 to 1928
Introduced at "Broad Oak".

Florence Watts "in fashion" for the 1920's.

"Broad Oak" paddock.

Holiday in Looe.

Standing back row (left to right): James Haworth, Reginald Mills (principal artist of the James Haworth & Bro. Ltd's Studio) John J. Haworth, Florence, William Watts, Audrey Wheaton. Front row, Annie Haworth, Pamela Wheaton, Evelyn Watts.

Their marriage was to take place on 10th July, 1929 at Christ Church, Cockfosters, Herts, with a full reception at Broad Oak.

This was the last splendour the happy married couple were to enjoy, as the trade depression was imminent, affecting almost everyone for the next seven years.

Wedding Reception in the grounds of "Broad Oak" 10th July, 1929.

The guest with camera and cigarette is Albert Buck, who as Studio Manager at James Haworth & Bro. was to see nearly 60 years' service.

A newly built house was bought at East Barnet Road, (changed to Bramley Road in 1930) 150 yards up from the junction of Chase Road. This four bedroomed, semi-detached house (still standing in 1988 with the garage as a men's hairdressers) was named "Bayfordbury" as a reminder of their courting walks.

In 1929 the house was very much in a rural setting. On one side a large house with a lovely garden. On the other side, more cottages, an old country pub (now rebuilt as "The Merryhills") and Ashridge House. Opposite there was a nursery and a country vista across to Trent Park.

In this rural setting of Enfield Road (now Bramley Road), "Bayfordbury" was built in 1929 on the land behind shrubs on the right of this photograph.

October 4th 1930. The Airship R.101 flying over Trent Park, towards Southgate and crossing the site of, to be shortly, Enfield West Tube Station. The airship, seemingly low and not flying in a steady manner or direction as it turned from a southerly to a westerly direction over Southgate Village.

That night the R.101, then the largest airship in the world, struck a hill near the French town of Beauvais whilst on a maiden flight to India. It burst into flames and was totally wrecked, with the loss of 46 lives. Among those who died were its designers, Wing Commander Colmore, Lieut. Colonel Richmond and Major G.H. Scott, with distinguished observing passengers Lord Thompson and Sir Sefton Brancken.

These three photographs were taken by John J. from Bramley Road

One can imagine Florence's and John J's shock when within two months of moving in, a sign was to go up at the corner of Chase Road and Enfield Road (now also called Bramley Road), signifying the building of a tube station to be known as Enfield West (Oakwood) to serve the Piccadilly Line which then terminated miles away at Finsbury Park. Such shock would have been compounded by the fact that, John J. had, some 6 years earlier, farmed that very corner and that in front of the house were to be the maintenance and carriage sheds stretching all the way to Cockfosters.

This railway line was to affect so many people and businesses, including James Haworth & Brother Ltd, as we shall see later.

1929. Junction of Enfield Road with Chase Road.

"Bayfordbury"

Southgate Transport 1929.

1932. Building the Piccadilly tube line between Southgate and Enfield West (now Oakwood). Bridge in foreground leads into the, yet to be opened, Oakwood Park. Bridge in background carries Merrivale. 1917 to 1923 this land was the site of Chase Farm, farmed by John J. Haworth.

1930. The end of rural Southgate.

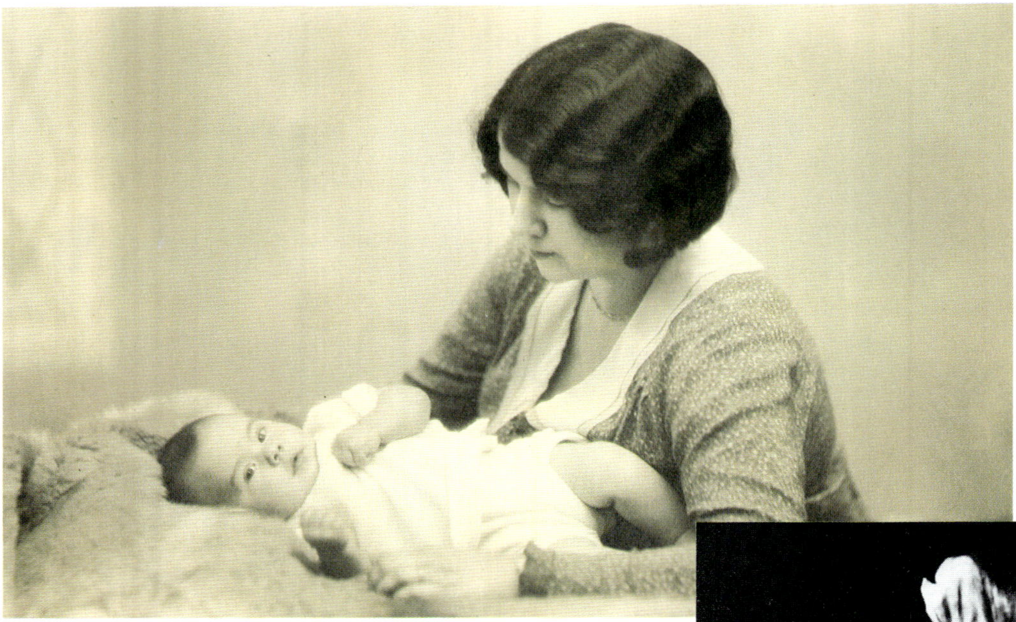

June 23rd, 1930 was to see the birth at home (which in 1930 was the acceptable procedure) of son John. A second name – Stewart – was to come 18 years later in an effort to avoid the confusion of two "Johns" in the same house.

1931 - 1932. "Bayfordbury" and Enfield Road. John Haworth is becoming aware of his surroundings.

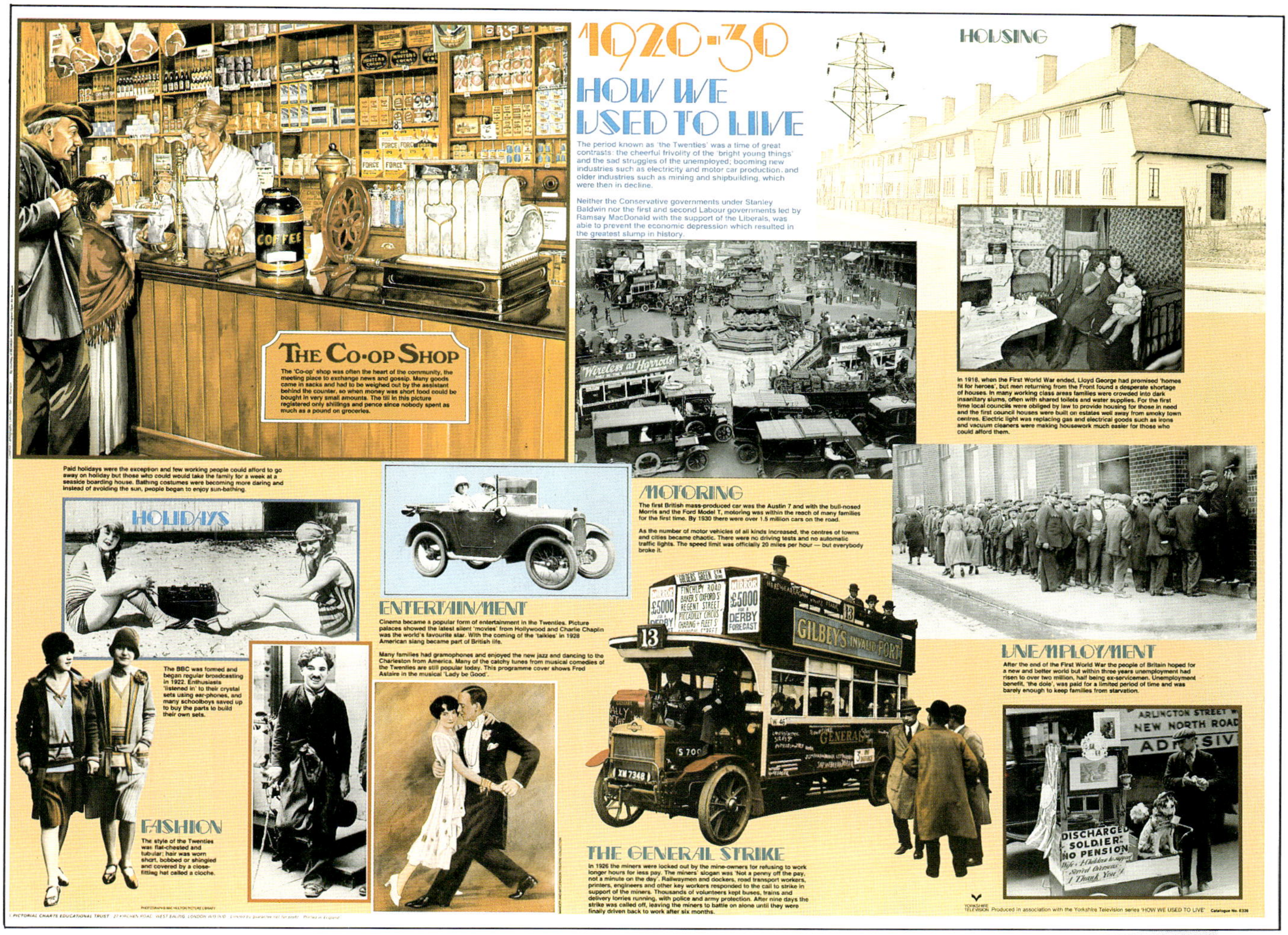

I arrived into a world and a country that was beginning to appreciate what a world trade recession meant. This situation was to last until 1936, when business gradually recovered, aided by Government building programmes for new factories and public works and the need for rearmament to meet a forthcoming, unavoidable war, if we were to remain a free country.

1931. Views across Enfield Road (Bramley Road) from "Bayfordbury".

Top of Page: "Background to the early 1930's". Reproduced by kind permission of the Pictorial Charts Educational Trust, Ealing.

With the marriage of John J and Florence in 1929 followed by years of depression within the country, the Talbot Tourer had gone, replaced by an Austin 7, which in turn was also to go by Christmas 1932. Money was short, made even shorter by the necessity to dig out the entire foundations of "Bayfordbury" because of dry rot. As a result, mother and I, early in 1933 were packed off for four months to her parents home in Chase Side, Enfield. Unfortunately, I only have the vaguest memory of grandfather Watts and the stories he would read me to keep me amused.

"Bayfordbury" 1933. Ravages of dry rot and its cure!

1934. A very quiet Enfield West.

In the summer, we returned to "Bayfordbury" and I have slight recollections of a first day free ride to Southgate on the new railway.

1934. The view is changing!

1934. "Bayfordbury" a rural garden.

My early years seem to constantly require me to spend lengthy periods in bed with repeated bronchitis and bronchial pneumonia, all supposedly brought on by catching whooping cough as a two year old. I recall more than one Christmas spent within the confines of my middle-back bedroom. Bathing took place in the, considered modern bathroom, half-tiled in white, with black lining at the top. A huge iron bath on feet filled this room. A gas water heater with a spout that could swing scolding water into the wash basin or bath. This geyser, as such water heaters were known, would light up with a big "swosh" or a "bang" if too much gas had been allowed to accumulate, before tossing the lighted match into an aperture at the base.

On bedridden occasions, during the festive period, I would be visited by cousins, Pam, Audrey and Geoffrey and aunt Blanche who had come to enjoy Christmas Day with us. Uncle Gordon Wheaton had, unfortunately, fallen on hard times, brought about by the Stock Exchange collapse. The family were now in a flat in Brixton and mother felt she must repay the good times she had enjoyed in better days at Enfield.

The Summer House, "Bayfordbury".

Dining room fireplace "Bayfordbury".

I always enjoyed Christmas, in bed or out, and Father Christmas. I did think however, he must come in a furniture van to carry so many toys for so many children. This shadowy figure would creep into my bedroom on Christmas Eve night, with a pillowcase full of small toys – wind up animals, books, games and sweets. Years later I realise how fortunate I was to have so much in the way of toys. It was however a set plan to keep me amused, for I was to have no brothers or sisters, nor young friends. The latter as a result of going to a nearby children's party, when I was struck on the head with a poker by a fellow four year old. After this unfortunate incident young friends were to be discouraged!

A spell in bed.

I did however, enjoy my young days, despite illness. Through books, comics and toys I learnt very much about the outside world. Mother had taught me to read quite well by the time I was five years old. This reading opened wide my horizons, despite the protective environment imposed by a devoted mother.

Until I was eight, I recall very little of my father John J., grandfather James or grandmother Annie. Grandfather Watts had died at the end of 1933 and grandma Watts, by way of economy, moved into a 1st floor, one bedroomed bedsit at what seemed an endless walk to the end of Ladysmith Road, Enfield.

Father was very industrious. In Bayfordbury's medium sized garden he created almost a small village with a self-made summer house/toy house, lychgate and sheds, using nothing else but handtools. There were raised flower beds and a rockery with flowing water into ponds.

Scenes at "Bayfordbury".

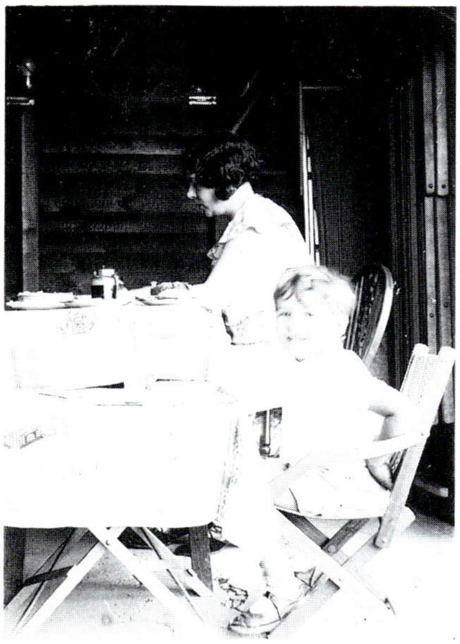

Grandfather and Grandma Watts.

So what with his efforts constructing in the garage in his spare time and long hours at work, I, and even my mother, came to see very little of father. An exception perhaps, was when late holidays, because of business commitments, were spent at Mrs Jacobs oil-lamp-lit terraced cottage by St. Mawes Harbour, Cornwall. Father would show his rowing skill, or lack of it, and would get stranded on a mudbank with an outflowing tide from the creek.

School in 1936 raised its head and meant that the curtain was to be slightly lifted on my current cloistered existence. I was enrolled at the North Middlesex School in Waverley Road, just off Windmill Hill, Enfield.

This school was mainly for girls up to 17 years; cousins Pam and Audrey had attended there in years gone by. The school maintained however a kindergarten for boys and girls. In the short time I was there, I recall very much the kindness of form mistress Miss Singer, and Miss Thorpe, head of the junior section. Both ladies were to live and teach in the Southgate area for much of their future lives.

In the mornings I would be walked down to Enfield West Station and shortly a large car would draw up, filled to capacity with giggly girls, and I would somehow be squeezed in, for the journey to Enfield. Mother would collect me, having come by bus, at 12.30 and we would return home by bus, in those days the 307 (soon to become the 107 route, which in 1987 reverted back to route 307).

1936. Where are they now!
North Middlesex School, Waverley Road, Enfield. Miss Singer and her class.

1936
St. Mawes,
Cornwall.

1936. St. Mawes, Cornwall.

Pause at Marlborough on the way to Cornwall.

1937. Recovery at Broadstairs.

1936
St. Mawe
Cornwall

Early in 1937, around "Bayfordbury", great changes were taking place. The old house and cottages alongside had been knocked down and the foundations for the present block of seven shops and flats had begun. Next door the other semi-detached was made into a café to serve the many construction workers putting up new homes and shops all round Enfield West Station.

Father, not unnaturally, took exception with the owners, to the overnight opening of a café next door, with the noise coming through the thin dividing wall into our sitting room.

Following on this, came the traumatic occasion when, in the short time it took to collect me from school, a Bedford lorry was backed into our garage driveway, the front door forced and the entire, easily moveable contents of the house stolen. Carpets, tables, clothes, toys and all drawers with their contents were loaded onto the lorry, never to be seen again. The next door occupiers and witnesses thought we were moving!

The shock for mother and father was so great, it was to affect their lifestyle for the rest of their lives. "Bayfordbury" and every subsequent house was turned into a fortress and they were most unwilling to leave their house, in future, unoccupied.

At the end of April, 1937, I was to cause mother and father an even greater trauma when I contracted double pneumonia. I really only survived, with the loving care of my mother, combined with the efforts of Dr Shepherd, whose surgery was at 186 Chase Side and was regarded as one of Southgate's most able doctors. Dr Shepherd obtained some of the first sulphonamide drugs, known as M & B tablets (having been made by May & Baker). They were, incidentally given to Winston Churchill during the Second World War and helped to save his life.

I remember hallucinating, imagining seeing live rabbits on my bed and mother in tears as I slowly recovered. I would be dressed each night in a linen jacket, the inside of which would be a coating of hot clay-like kaolin. This went on for four weeks, until I was judged better. Convalescent meant more periods in bed and the world came once again to see me.

Happily, this last illness marked a turning point in health and periods in bed were seldom to be repeated.

Business was obviously better and it was affordable for me and mother to spend four weeks at "Braeside", a large guest house on Broadstairs sea front. Father stayed to guard the house, but came down at weekends in an Austin 12 he had purchased the previous year.

The fine old house makes way for seven shops in Bramley Road.

1936. James and Annie Haworth at "Bayfordbury" and grandson John. Bars at windows after burglary.

1936. Chase Side, Southgate changes. This outfitters is about to close to make way for a new three storey Littlewoods store, which in the 1950's became todays Sainsburys.

I was not to return to North Middlesex School at the end of summer holidays but was despatched to Inglemere, Uplands Park Road, Enfield, an all-boys school, whose pupils wore blue caps with the school's name in white.

The classrooms were in every corner of this damp and dark house. The Headmaster, Mr Kane, frequently lived up to his name when it came to punishment.

Christmas 1937 was a high point. Father replaced the stolen toys with a layout of Hornby trains, which I discovered laid out in the sitting room and, to cap it all, I was in good health.

1938 came with a fine spring and summer. There were lifts to school in father's new Ford V8, with all its 30-horse power. I could now make my own way home by bus and would often buy for a penny, one of the delicious triangular ice sticks from the Wall's Stop-Me-and-Buy-One man on his large tricycle.

Saturdays were relaxed days before 1939. Father would either go in the morning to the "works", or London office and studio at Soho Square. Occasionally I would accompany him. My arrival would signal the artists to relax, forget work for the morning. I would be entertained with indoor rounders, using a cardboard tube and rolled paper ball. Back home for a late lunch at 2.30. Mother and father throughout their lives seemed to specialise in late lunches!

Then, especially in wintertime, we would set forth as dusk was falling, in the V8 Ford, first to Lee's Store in Chase Side, Southgate, where we were able to park outside. Cars, even in 1938, were owned only by very few.

Practically everything bought at Lee's had to be weighed and packed by hand. Butter was cut from a large rectangle by wooden hand bats and beaten and cut again to the required weight, then wrapped in greaseproof paper; bacon sliced on a red machine, wound by hand which started a large flywheel which zipped through a side of bacon as if it was butter. Cheese was cut from a huge piece by a thin wire with a handle at the end. Biscuits were chosen from 7lb tins arranged along the front of the counter, with glass lids so that the contents could be seen. Lee's Store was still the Southgate Post Office, so mailmen, bags on shoulders, had to push their way through the waiting customers, sampling the aroma of coffee, ham, spices and floor sawdust, as they waited their turn.

The V8 Ford.

1937. Chase Side, Southgate. Lee's Stores and Post Office. Wheeler's Newsagents next door.

Interior of a branch of Lee's Stores at the corner of Chase Road and Ivy Road, Southgate, closed in April, 1935. This interior was very similar to their shop in Chase Side.

The Hornby Trains.

Ivinghoe Beacon Bucks 1939.

Afterwards we would continue to Baily's Greengrocers, London Road, Enfield, where Mr Eustance the owner, would always bring the goods to the car.

Then perhaps to Evans and Davies, a large department store by The Triangle, Palmers Green, which sold everything ladies might require for the home or for their kitting out. Leaving father outside, probably to go into Coombes to get his "Passing Cloud" cigarettes, mother and I would, on entering, be met with the comforting smell of fabric. Mother would usually go straight to the wonderful range of sewing silk reels, which had all the colours of the rainbow and more. I meanwhile, would gaze in awe at the overhead, ugly shaped money and bill containers winging their way on wires to a central, glass panelled cash office, manned by several ladies with their hair tied in a bun. They would deftly unscrew the containers, receipt the bill, include any change, screw up the wooden container to the metal truck, pull a lever and away went this aerial miniature cable car from whence it came.

If time permitted, (we always seemed to be the last customers in such places) it was to Howells Cake and Tea Shop on the corner of Aldermans Hill and Lakeside Road, where could be obtained, boiled eggs with bread "soldiers", followed by a Cadbury's long wafer biscuit wrapped in blue and gold foil.

If it was summer, then perhaps across to Broomfield Park model boating pond, with a Hornby clockwork motor boat I just happened to bring in the car. Unfortunately, the motor would run out of power some 30ft out from the side, and father's face would signal not such a perfect end to a perfect day!

We would then go home, perhaps to listen to "In Town Tonight" on the wireless. This was a tallish wooden cabinet with a dial recording romantic places such as Hilversum, Droitwich and Luxembourg, but no sound ever came from them. Then it was bed at 9pm to the warm room above the kitchen, with perhaps a read of Percy F. Westerman.

Developing Westpole Avenue 1938.

1939. My pet dog, unfortunately run over later that year.

Even aged 8, one felt something traumatic was in the air. Grown-ups talk, in particular grandpa James to father and uncle Alan Lord on visits to Broad Oak would mention Czechoslovakia, Austria, Spain, Japan and China, and above all Germany in serious tones.

Pictures in newspapers would show burning buildings, and people with young children pushing their belongings in a small cart; I feared even then not to be one of those children with the cart.

Business was obviously good; mother has new clothes and father would buy even more tools from Grouts at Enfield.

Ominously, gas masks were to be collected from the new school in Green Road. At the bottom of the garden a construction by Newbys began on a room-sized concrete air raid shelter, only to be filled in temporarily as a result of Premier Chamberlain's "Peace in our time" speech. Holidays were out, other than a day train trip to Hastings.

War was on its way, The Meccano Magazine, which I would eagerly await each month, would have more and more articles on the British Armed Forces, with the advertisements promoting war-like toys.

Christmas 1938 came and went with its usual speed. Little did I know, along with almost every other inhabitant, that this was to be the end of all the colourful displays of toys, groceries, Christmas crackers, sweets etc, that seemed to symbolise the wonder of Christmas as portrayed in Southgate or London's Oxford and Regent Streets.

Many of these wonders were never to return, as the lights gradually went out throughout Europe in the New Year of 1939.

A small selection of wartime publications 1940-1945.

1939. The shelter - soil mound. War on the way.

1939. John J. Haworth.

I was growing up fast. No more periods of illness, now riding a 20″ bike, school work getting hard. Homework to be done, something called Latin had to be mastered, along with unintelligible French which seemed to consist of nothing but verbs, which had to be learnt by heart.

The view from the window of the classroom at Inglemere was made more interesting by the erection of a fixed battery of 4.7 inch A.A. guns in the fields at the bottom of Slades Hill, Enfield. To retain our interest in form matters, desks were re-arranged with backs to the window. With open windows that fine summer, we could not help but hear the shouted orders and the clang of shell cases falling to the ground during practice drill.

White and black painted stripes appeared round items of street furniture, sticky tape in bizarre patterns appeared on windows in homes, including ours. Sandbags round the Police box at Enfield West Station, with its siren on a column (a siren still there in 1988).

War was indeed on its way. It was something that seemed both exciting and fearful, in that order. I, along with other 9-year-olds in big cities, were to grow up fast.

I recall vividly the lines of hundreds of London Transport buses that assembled all round Enfield West (now Oakwood) tube station in the last days of August and first two in September 1939, to take evacuee children from inner London to the safety of the Home Counties, as London was expected to be pulverised from the start, by bombing.

My exodus was discussed; Canada, unheard of relations in the north of England, a farmer acquaintance of father's near Royston. All these prospects seemed far more daunting in outlook to me, than air raids (no one ever thought then that England would be in danger of invasion one year later). So I stayed at home.

Economy of expenditure was the order of the day! Father quite rightly thought business would rapidly decline, along with his income.

The concrete shelter was dug out again and finished by Newby's in double quick time. Mrs Mills who came to help Mother most mornings, for 2s 6d a morning, stopped coming, amidst tears all round. Father acquired some 7lb sweet jars from Dipples of The Parade, Southgate, in which to place "iron rations" so to speak, of butter, lard, eggs, sugar and tea. He built a special high shelf for the jars in the cold, unused bedroom (no fridges in those days) above the garage. After a couple of months, only the tea and sugar remained, the rest either eaten or rancid.

Father acquired, for £60, a brand new Ford Prefect 10 H.P. car from an American who was not inclined to linger at his American film company's office in Soho Square. The V.8 was confined to be under a dust-sheet at the company's factory, Rossendale Works, Southgate as this car travelled 12 miles or less to the gallon. Petrol was to be one of the first items to be rationed.

Father and mother had much to worry about, this fine first weekend of September. The previous Sunday had seen half of Rossendale Works destroyed in Southgate's largest fire to date. Print and display orders were already being cancelled if not started and stopped, at the request of customers, when midway to completion. This in turn meant that the James Haworth factories and studio would be coming to a halt within weeks. No work would mean closure and the end for a company that was not essential to the war effort. But survive, just, we did. How, is related later.

1988. A pillbox from the original 'Defence Ring' remaining on tube railway embankment.

1947. Winter - Bramley Road from "Bayfordbury". The pillbox has just gone from gap in hedge, together with the tank blocks by fence.

School continued at Inglemere. The Headmaster did not seem to have heart in his school. Class numbers had fallen dramatically, partly because parents could not afford the fees and a number of pupils were evacuated as the war worsened. The school was to close towards the end of 1940.

Dunkirk, like so many other disasters dressed up as victories, came and went. Winston Churchill was now in charge and father felt there was now hope, though grandfather James felt Lloyd George would do better.

A pillbox appeared almost opposite "Bayfordbury". A line of 5ft high x 4ft square concrete blocks started along the fence by the "Merryhills" and went via the pillbox in a wide semi-circle, across the tube line and back to Bramley Road by Prince George Avenue. Slots were placed in the road to take old railway lines bent triangular to form a tank stop. If the Germans came "Bayfordbury" was going to be in trouble!

Going still to school that fine autumn, was enlivened on two occasions seeing shot-down German airmen in flying gear, with pale blue uniform visible, coming off the tube handcuffed to Military Police. There they would wait for transport to take them to the prison camp at Trent Park House, having first been interrogated at Kensington.

Apart from the above incident, the Battle of Britain did not really touch Southgate. We had no nearby airfields and only once did we have a dogfight over "Bayfordbury", when about 12 Dorniers, after bombing Hatfield Aerodrome, were engaged by two Spitfires, and bullets were pumped into their "tail end Charlie" which crashed, I think, at Edmonton. A great search was then made to find spent cartridges, with some success.

The night Blitz that followed in late September and October 1940 was a different matter. Air raids would last 10 hours or more, before the all clear sounded.

The north part of Southgate was lucky. Incendiaries set fire to some old tube carriages between Enfield West and Cockfosters. Some small bombs fitted with special loud whistles fell in and around Westpole Avenue, one of which took the side of a house out. These whistles sounded terrifying. The guns at Slades Hill would occasionally open fire if they had something at which to aim.

CAPTURED German airmen under guard in London. They are both quite young. The one with a growth of beard, on the right, is wearing an Iron Cross.

BATTLE ABOVE THE CLOUDS

1940. Captured German airmen under guard in London.

1944. Mucking-out the chickens.

We were treated, for quite a few nights, to a morale booster, in the arrival on the open ground opposite the house, of a Bofors gun and ammunition truck. It was quite usual for one or two of the gunners to be in our kitchen to prepare pots of tea for the crew, but they supplied their own tea. Then on to father's garage to discuss the merits of his tools, as these chaps all seemed to have been carpenters in civvy street.

If there was a raid during the night, they would loose off a few rounds in the general direction of any aircraft sound and by early morning depart.

Early in 1941, we began to keep chickens on the spare ground behind the flats. To obtain feed for the chickens, eggs in sufficient quantity had to be ready to hand over to the egg packing station van on its weekly call. Eggs became our staple diet and supplemented our food rations, which always seemed adequate and made for a healthy diet.

My pocket money went to half a crown per week if I fed the chickens each night on my return home from school; that meant mixing hot water with meal to form a mash, corn being non-existent.

The raids diminished in intensity during Spring 1941 as Germany prepared to attack Russia and as a consequence we tended, when the siren sounded, not now to go to the shelter. We had grandma Watts living with us, as her room in Enfield was required by the owner. She was now getting very frail and unable to look after herself.

I recall one night the sound of a lone plane, a few bursts of gunfire and the plane faded into the distance. As it did so, there was a peculiar rustling sound, the world seemed to go upside down. The lights went out and there was a kind of soot-filled whirlpool of comparative silence. The curtains and windows were sucked out in a roar of wind, then silence again.

A parachute mine had landed in Chase Road, just down from the station. Houses had been completely destroyed in Chase Road with deaths of occupants. Next morning showed that we had lost every window at the rear of the house and the roof tiles had shifted into waves. All of course repairable – Lady Luck had been with us again.

Grandma Watts died living at Auntie Blanche's home in Streatham, in 1943. During this time, because of the closing of Inglemere, I really had no school to go to. A lady came twice a week to set work and would check my efforts the following week. This arrangement was both costly and unsatisfactory, for my educational intake was minimum and playtime maximum.

1941 – May. Landmines, Chase Road, Southgate.

De Bohun Avenue, Southgate.

Bomb near "Broad Oak".

High Street, Southgate.

Dec. 1940. Bombs Addison Avenue, Southgate.

Devonshire Road, Palmers Green.
Blast damage from V.2 rocket on nearby railway line.

Come September 1941, I joined Mr Gilpin's establishment, Beaufort Lodge, Station Road, Barnet. His job was to get me through what was called Common Entrance, necessary to get into Highgate School, where it had been decided I must attend because they played football. Barnet and Enfield Grammar played rugger - all far too rough in my parents eyes!

Mr Gilpin was, at times, of uncertain temper and his lack of accuracy of aim, with any handy object to bring any committed misdemeanour to an end, meant that those both guilty and not guilty could be hit with flying objects from books to flower pots.

Not a very happy school for me, but thanks to Mr Hardwick, Second Master's patience and efforts, I passed the coveted exam and entered Highgate Public School in April 1944, much to my relief and probably father and mother's as well, for with money short, they must have made many sacrifices to get me there.

Highgate was a complete change of atmosphere, masters treated you as grown up. The school was in two sections – one, the larger, down at Westward Ho! North Devon. The London end in two houses near the original school which in 1944 now housed the Royal Navy Writers' School.

Attendance was six full days a week; this was to fall into line with the few boarders, games being on Saturday afternoon. To get there on time I would leave home at 7.30am and return about 6pm.

"D-Day" came and we knew the war would soon be over. A few days later we boys knew we were back in the firing line. A doodle bug, V1, exploded during breaktime 100 yards from our classrooms and eleven boys were taken to hospital badly cut with flying glass.

Mother was appalled when I arrived home carrying as many pieces of flying bomb as I could cram into my case and pockets.

School closed for the rest of the term.

Caps of experience!

Fargate House, Highgate School. July 1945.

Flying bombs were not to finish for some time and mother and I, on bicycles were very near to the one that fell on the Girl's Home at the top of Avenue Road, Southgate.

Father also had a bicycle. Sundays would be spent putting us and the bikes on a train at New Barnet, alighting at Hatfield or Stevenage and cycling through the very peaceful Hertfordshire countryside to Hertford, whence back by train to Enfield Chase.

Father was just too old to be called up for wartime service with the forces, and I often wonder how he would have got on if he had been, but I know he felt very keenly the deaths of any people he knew, as a result of wartime action.

It is a very sorry thing for me to say, but family life seemed to me to be at its best throughout these six years. We all worked together, there were no disagreements and if there were any, it did not warrant any argument to settle.

Perhaps by reason there was a shortage of print work, mother and I saw more of father, he could give us his time, rather than his customers.

September 1944, as a result of the flying bomb damage and the end of the war in sight, Highgate School regained its buildings. Boys at Westward Ho! returned. Evacuees returned from America and Canada, and as we had space, there was a big general intake of pupils.

The school sponsored a very large Army Junior Training Corps section which was to reach some 800 boys strong in due course.

There was a House system, divided roughly into, as far as day boys were concerned, where one lived. For Enfield West and Southgate the house was named appropriately, Fargate.

A Southgate resident, Mr Ray, was always very kind to pick us up if he saw boys waiting for a bus at Bounds Green or Muswell Hill. It was some time before we realised it was Ted Ray the comedian, a Southgate resident for a long time.

The World War during 1945 ground to a halt. To us 15-year-olds, perhaps rather mature for our years, war's end was an anti-climax. The majority had survived quite well, both as individuals and families, despite all predictions to the contrary. In our diaries we had recorded victories and tragedies, bought books on the war issued by the Stationery Office. We would miss this extra dimension to our lives and upbringing.

Snow and sunshine.

"The General inspects"
Highgate School Junior Training Corps.

Last days at "Bayfordbury"
1947-48.

Warrant Officer Geoffrey Wheaton.

Joined the Royal Air Force at Uxbridge 11th March 1941 becoming a Signaller at Headquarters 11 Group November 1941, as a Leading Aircraftman. Transferred to aircrew as a Sergeant Wireless Operator/Air Gunner November 1942. Posted May 1943 to No. 1 Torpedo Training Unit. Joining No. 38 Maritime Squadron, Middle East October 1943 and promoted Flight Sergeant Wireless Operator.

Prisoner of War April 1944 - May 1945, being appointed Warrant Officer November 1944. Discharged as a result of war wounds December 1945.

The family's two near relations, serving in the Armed Forces during World War II had survived.

Geoffrey Robert Wheaton, born 25th June, 1921, only son of Blanche (my mother's sister). Geoffrey was born at the family's large home "Denholm" on Windmill Hill, Enfield and sharing the family's misfortunes, moved to Brixton and Streatham. Whilst still at school, he became a very enthusiastic Scout.

His story from then on is best recounted by his widow Kathleen, whom Geoffrey married in July 1959, and from R.A.F. records.

"Geoffrey was working for a small firm of wholesale grocers at the outbreak of war in 1939.

He became one of the youngest air raid wardens and saw much of the "Blitz" in South London.

Volunteering for the Royal Air Force, after nearly a year's training he became a Sergeant Wireless Operator Air Gunner and was posted to No. 38 Squadron based at Shalluva, Egypt. His Squadron was equipped with Wellington Bombers, adapted to carry torpedoes as well as bombs. Their targets were mainly ships and submarines still supplying the Germans and Italians, as they retreated in front of General Montgomery's 8th Army advancing through Libya to Tunisia. The Squadron followed this advance by being based in Malta and Tunisia.

With Africa won, Geoffrey promoted to Flight Sergeant, returned to Egypt. It is recorded that in December, 1943 the Squadron flew a record number of 210 sorties, of which 128 were anti-submarine patrols, 64 offensive strikes in the Aegean Sea on German ships supplying their bases in the Greek Islands and 18 sorties laying mines.

The pattern was to continue off Greece into the early months of 1944, with about two aircraft being lost each month.

Geoffrey's flying luck ran out on the night of April 8th 1944, when his Wellington blew up some 100 feet above the water, caused most likely by one of their own mines exploding on contact with the sea. The pilot Jack Normandale, one other crew member and Geoffrey were the only survivors out of six crew. The German Air Force Sea Rescue Launch came out to investigate the crash and picked up any survivors. Quickly picking up the pilot and the other crew member, they missed Geoffrey in the dark, who, though badly wounded, managed to blow on his whistle attached to his Mae West. This attracted the Germans who returned to pick him up from certain death.

Geoffrey was taken to the local German Air Force Doctor, who realised his injuries were very serious and that he must be flown to their main hospital in Athens for the treatment of his broken back, broken left shoulder and foot, and bad wounds in his cheek and neck. This latter wound caused an empyema infection to enter his left lung. This meant a tube had to be pushed through his back to this lung to drain the infection away. This operation was carried out without anaesthetic, due to lack of medical supplies.

Geoffrey remained under the care of the German Air Force doctors and nurses until 24th September 1944. He always spoke highly of the senior German doctor, who did so much to help him recover and said that Geoffrey must have been an extremely fit young man to have survived his injuries.

The Germans were beginning to leave Greece and Geoffrey, still barely able to walk, made a slow train and lorry journey through Yugoslavia, Hungary and Austria to a Prisoner of War Camp near Munich, by December 1944. There he remained, suffering shortages of food and medicines, until his release by the American Army in May, 1945".

It should be recorded that it was nearly 4 months after Geoffrey's crash that the family knew he had survived. One can imagine the joy and relief of the entire family on his letter from Athens and the Red Cross. However, because of Geoffrey's move to Germany from Greece, there was no further news, causing much anxiety until nearly the end of the war.

Wellington Bombers of 38 Squadron over the Mediterranean in 1944.

Geoffrey (standing left) and Wellington crew.
Skipper, Jack Normandale (seated right).

Geoffrey with sisters Audrey and Pamela in father's garden, August 1979.

Geoffrey was invalided out, with a small pension, from the Royal Air Force at the end of 1946 as a Warrant Officer. He went back to his wholesale grocery firm and resumed, as best he could, his cycling activities with the Rover Scouts. Later he was able to join a cricket club and after playing for a few seasons, became an umpire, until ill health finally overtook him.

In 1954 he joined the well-known American grocery firm of Armour as a Representative, covering South London. In 1966 he decided on a complete change of occupation, by passing the exam set by The Society of Hearing Aid Audiologists, becoming a Hearing Aid Dispenser.

In 1980 Geoffrey had an operation for cancer of the right lung. This combined with his left lung injury, left him very breathless and weak. For a little while he resumed work, but needed further treatment for cancer during 1981, but this was of no avail and he left this life on the 17th February, 1982, aged 62 years.

Geoffrey throughout his life had had to face more than his fair share of adversities, yet he was never heard to complain or grumble about his lot.

Cousin Geoffrey Wheaton was a very brave man and one of Nature's gentlemen.

Heartache memories of Geoffrey as a prisoner of war, including top left his prisoners I. D. card.

Geoffrey Haworth was to return, without injury, in 1945. He had joined James Haworth & Bro. Ltd in September 1931, aged 18, whereupon he was given a bag of samples and, to quote his words, told to "Get on with it!" So he became a print representative, covering the whole of the north of England and Scotland seeking business, and without a car until 1938.

The Thomas Haworth family, 1930.
Geoffrey (first left) about to join James Haworth & Bro. Ltd.

Geoffrey married Margaret Pierson, whom he had known all his school days, on 4th March 1939, with war clouds gathering. A daughter, Susan, was born in February 1941 at 323 Walkden Road, Worsley, Manchester.

In March, 1941 Geoffrey was to be "called up" to fight the Germans now supreme across all Europe. Russia and America were yet to be involved, whereby we could see a winning end to the conflict.

He volunteered for the Navy and became an Ordinary Seaman, training at Tor Point and H.M.S. Drake, Plymouth, during which time Plymouth was almost obliterated as a town by German bombers.

His first ship was H.M.S. Pytchley, a Hunt Class destroyer, but she had hit a mine whilst he was on the way to join her. She had limped in to West Hartlepool and was towed to the Tyne for major repairs. Most of the crew, including Geoffrey, were sent back to Plymouth.

He was then sent, in June, to Scapa Flow Naval Base in the Orkneys to join the aircraft carrier, H.M.S. Furious which then sailed to the Mediterranean to fly R.A.F. Hurricanes off at sea to relieve the defences of beleaguered Malta, being battered day in and day out by German and Italian bombers.

H.M.S. Furious then sailed to Bermuda, Jamaica and Philadelphia. Here many of the crew were to join the famous aircraft carrier H.M.S. Illustrious which, after surviving many bomb hits, was being refitted, thanks to a friendly America, in Newport Mews Dockyard, Norfolk, Virginia. After sea trials, it was back to England.

During the sea voyage, Pearl Harbour was bombed by the fanatical Japanese, thus bringing America into the war. Everyone, including the writer, aged 11½, knew from that moment the end of this world holocaust was in sight, though many would yet have to die in reaching that end.

Unfortunately, the Illustrious suffered considerable damage, resulting from a collision at sea with another carrier, a frightening experience one would think for Geoffrey Haworth. And so back to Cammel Laird for yet more repairs, but at least it was Christmas 1941. Home to see baby Susan, before back to Plymouth for yet another posting.

Geoffrey was given an opportunity to train for a commission, and after an eight week course at H.M.S. King Alfred (this "ship" in fact was based on a large public house and various small hotels on the sea front between Hove and Brighton), he became a sub-Lieutenant R.N.V.R. There followed 14 days at Greenwich Naval College to become an officer and a gentleman.

Aircraft Carrier H.M.S. Illustrious.

Perhaps Geoffrey was getting wary of big ships, as he was able to get on a Light Coastal Forces course at Fort William and when spring came in 1942 he went to join a wooden built motor gun boat ML 286 as the 1st Lieutenant, based at Scapa Flow.

There he and the boat remained for two years, as one of the guard ships to the naval base, with the weather being the enemy and providing the excitement. During this time, he was promoted to Lieutenant and C.O. of ML 286.

Geoffrey moved down to Dover for the Normandy invasion of Europe in June 1944 by British and American troops. The boat's task was laying smoke screens between the Goodwin Sands and Dungeness, so that the long distance German guns, firing from Cap Gris Nez, could not see the many ships feeding supplies into the Normandy beaches, plus keeping the Germans guessing that a further invasion could take place in the Calais/Boulogne area.

The war moved fast and by the autumn Geoffrey had a group of ML's under his command. He had moved to Ostend and their job was to hunt German midget submarines off the Dutch and German coasts, throughout the winter.

The war in Europe finished on 5th May, 1945 and Geoffrey's boats went to show the flag in Rotterdam for a few weeks. Then it was back to Poole where his boat ML286 was paid off in the autumn, heading to be sold for scrap or, as some were to become, a pleasure boat.

His final posting was as a Commander Assistant at the Rossmouth Clyde Demobilisation Centre and he himself became a civilian again in February 1946.

H.M.S. M.L.286. Skipper, 1st Lieutenant Geoffrey Haworth R.N.V.R. (From a painting by Walter Thomas).

A son, Roger, was born on 4th February that year. Roger was destined to seek a separate career away from the family business and became Chief Planning Officer for the Outer Hebrides.

Geoffrey, like so many others, perhaps found it hard to readjust to civilian life and picking up business again after so long. His father Thomas had attended to many of his customers during the war but was now thinking of finally retiring. Geoffrey looked after our northern business interests until 1987, when he finally laid up his samples after 56 years of service. His life span to date almost equals the Company's existence and sadly it is the "end of the family print line" from one of the two founders of the company, way back in 1913.

Geoffrey, at the time of this narrative, lives at his original home of his marriage, enjoying good health and retirement with Margaret. He is an enthusiastic member of the R.S.P.B., enjoying birdwatching throughout England. Cricket is perhaps his first love as a hobby, being a player well into his 50's and for 19 years Chairman of Worsley Cricket Club. He remains a Group Company Director.

In peace, Highgate continued as a full time school occupation. I saw less of father as customers came back to the fold, which took up once again a great deal of his time.

Obtaining the essential School Certificate, I went into the Modern VIth form for Higher School Certificate. It was 1947 and if I was to take this exam I would have to get my call-up postponed, for war-time call-up regulations were in force. I did not fancy postponing what was regarded as an unpleasant period in one's life, so never sat the higher certificate.

Geoffrey in retirement 1987 with youngest granddaughter Frances.

Hunt 32 R.A.F. Bridgnorth. "In the centre of things".

I recall the disbelief of an army recruiting Major when I told him that, despite corp prize, etc. in the school's Junior Training Corps, I preferred to be an Aircraftman 2nd Class in the Royal Air Force to a possible 2nd Lieutenant in the Middlesex Regiment.

I left Highgate on Saturday and on the Monday I was in the R.A.F. at Padgate, Warrington, Lancashire.

Ships' sirens sounded on the fog-shrouded Manchester Ship Canal, adding to the melancholy and uncertainty as the thirty of us assembled in this cold, fog-bound hut, on behalf of King and Country, pondering upon our fate in such an unpleasant place.

Fate was kind, I was duly kitted out after eight days of processing, into an Airman 2nd Class. Then it was the train to Bridgnorth, which looked like heaven with its rosebeds and winter sunlit countryside.

We were not disappointed in this camp, as the weather became the coldest for a decade. Square bashing became non-existent, for we had sensible N.C.O.'s and Officers who realised that outdoor training was impractical. As a consequence, they got the very best of us. In all my time in the R.A.F., I only once heard a complaint about R.A.F. discipline.

Bridgnorth Town.

R.A.F. Credenhill, Hereford.
Middle row, left: Learning to be a clerk - with distractions!

Passing Out parade came amongst the snow, with seven days leave, but then a good dose of 'flu was already on the way, so ten days in bed at home. Then back to Bridgnorth to find that a posting to Wilmslow had been missed.

The choice of trades available at that time were clerk, butcher and fireman, as the R.A.F. did not really want any new servicemen, for they still had many from wartime service on their hands.

Clerk it was to be, but the next group would not be going for this particular trade training for another seven weeks. So to Pool Flight with a job in the dental centre. This meant that I was assigned to a particular dental officer. My job was to keep his surgery clean. As he was short of a dental assistant, I was promoted to holding the kidney dish to catch the teeth he deftly extracted, often in large numbers, from a mouth.

This was a good section, with 48 hour passes to home every weekend and a lift from the officer to catch a train from Wolverhampton on Friday afternoon.

Thence to Credenhill, Hereford, for a concentrated course on R.A.F. administration, where I was somewhat outnumbered by W.A.A.F's. – my first experience of world-wise ladies en masse!

R.A.F. Hornchurch, Essex.

"Orderly Room" 1st floor left.

Home on leave.

Passed the trade test with sufficient marks to have a slight choice of a station.
Then a posting to Hornchurch, former Battle of Britain Fighter Station. I had asked for Hong Kong, but someone's writing was at fault!

However, this was a good station. Plenty of work in the orderly room, with endless records to be kept up. Passing excitements, like the Berlin Airlift and two London dock strikes, when the aerodrome looked like something from the Boer War, with tents to house some 5,000 Airforce and Navy personnel to work in the docks.

R.A.F. Hornchurch, Essex.

Wellington Bomber at R.A.F. Hornchurch.

The N.A.A.F.I. Break.

Dai Davis in the Orderly Room, with a James Haworth calendar.

Growing up in the Royal Air Force.

"My boss" W. O. Williams and staff.
Ron Hampshire (second from left) was to join the James Haworth Studio for a period in the 1950's.

Night in the Barrack Room.

Promotion came my way, but by June 1950 I was due to become a civilian again, any thoughts of staying on being firmly resisted by father, as he considered I was enjoying the Airforce too much and there was no lifetime future in such a career.

He was probably right. I compromised by carrying on in the R.A.F.V.R. as a weekender at Hornchurch, until it disbanded in 1962.

If I am asked which university I went to, I always reply, the R.A.F. It was certainly a university of life and taught me a great deal about one's fellow human beings from all over the country and all walks of life. A most welcome experience, which has always helped me greatly in work and understanding others who may have different opinions and may not have had the best of fortune as they passed through life.

Tiger Moth of R.A.F.V.R.

A German V.1 bomb on the premises!

"Off duty".

"The way out".

C.O.'s Parade.

Friends at Hornchurch.

In June 1949, mother and father moved into 187 Chase Side, Southgate (on the corner of Osidge Lane). They turned it into a very attractive house with lovely, though small, landscaped gardens. They never really settled in, mainly because of the noise of the traffic throughout the day and night.

Chase Side then was the route all vehicles took from the north and midlands to reach the then vast London Docks.

London was being rebuilt after the bombing. Brick lorries from the brick works of Bedfordshire would pass in constant numbers. Their noise was worse when returning empty, as their tailboards had a nerve and ear piercing rattle as they passed over the uneven road surface that formed the junction with Avenue Road and Osidge Lane.

Traffic lights had yet to be installed and hardly a week went by without a vehicle accident. Rather than go to the doctor's surgery on our opposite corner, the walking wounded, as it were, of such accidents, dripping with blood, would appear needing succour, which was always given. The plain blue carpet seemed to develop a pattern of, what looked like, red wine stains – and our house was supposed to be teetotal!

I am sure that particular part of Chase Side is much quieter today in comparison, though today's residents might not think so.

"In the firm" 1950.

Garden, 187 Chase Road.

The Chase Side/Avenue Road crossroads from No. 187.

Chelsea Flower Show.
John J. Haworth with Thomas Haworth.
Behind Geoffrey and Margaret Haworth, 1951.

Thomas Haworth, 1954.

"Broad Oak" dining room. James and Annie Haworth's Golden Wedding Anniversary, 11th June, 1946.

Lucy Lord with Annie Haworth, Mr and Mrs Christopher Lord. Garden – Beech Hill, 1955.

Having left the R.A.F., the end of June 1950 saw me in residence at 187 Chase Side, returning to a cloistered atmosphere and immediately down to the firm at Rossendale Works where father was now in charge.

Grandpa James had died in October 1948. The family quickly sold "Broad Oak" to Mr Herbert Brooks, whose son Roy Brooks was to live there until its demolition for flats in 1982.

Grandma Annie Haworth moved into a bungalow at 27 De Bohun Avenue, Southgate, next to Lucy and Alan Lord until she died in 1955. She was buried alongside James and son Harry in the Southgate Cemetery, Waterfall Road.

Aunt Lucy (my father's sister) was to continue to live at "Levens", De Bohun Avenue, until her husband Alan retired from James Haworth in 1968. They went to live at Winton, Westmorland in a bungalow on their son, Christopher Lord's farm. Sadly, Lucy died shortly after moving in, but Alan continued to live there until his death in 1978. Older cousin Gary Lord, was to become a research chemist and live in Loughborough.

This period of the early 1950s saw the death of James Haworth's two brothers: Thomas, who married Florence Lord (no relation to Alan) on 14th February 1912, and went to live at 30 Queen's Road, Urmston, Manchester and, as we have seen, became a joint founder, with James, of the family printing company. Thomas was to remain always in Manchester looking after the northern customers. When his son Geoffrey returned from the Navy, Thomas retired from active business and died in September 1955.

"Broad Oak" - 1950's.

James Haworth grave at Southgate Cemetery, Waterfall Road, Southgate.

Richard Haworth, 1948.

Dick continued to work in the mill until October 1914 when his elder brother James, now a man of considerable means, sent for Dick and the family to work on one of his farms, and leaving mill life and the steep streets of Bacup, Dick, Annie and their by now 5 children made the long journey to New Farm, part of Southlodge to once again resume life as farmers. During the following 10 years Dick worked and lived both at New and Chase Farms, but the two brothers and their wives had little in common and relationships between the families became more and more strained until in 1924, with the farms sold and finding his situation as his brother's employee untenable, Dick went into considerable debt and purchased De Bohun Farm in Bramley Road.

James Haworth's second brother Richard with his family were very much connected with Southgate. Their life is best described by Richard Haworth's granddaughter Vera, now living in Oxfordshire, who writes:-

"George Richard Haworth was born at the Slip Inn, Bacup on 16th June 1874, the 6th child and 2nd son of James and Ellen. There is little recorded of the young "Dick" as he was always known, except that around the age of 10 years he contracted the severe children's disease, infantile paralysis, now known as poliomyelitis. This must have been devastating for him as for the rest of his life he was condemned to wear an iron brace on his leg.

This was such an ugly contraption that when he eventually died aged 78, the brace, at his own insistence was buried with him 'so that others never have to look at it'.

Like the rest of the family, Dick was brought up a Methodist and as a young man he played the church organ, a skill that was later to entertain his family and friends when he transferred it to the piano. However, unlike his brother James he was not a strict Wesleyan, and certainly when I knew him as an elderly man, he always enjoyed smoking his pipe and taking the occasional pint of beer in the Robin Hood on the Ridgeway at Enfield.

Although Dick began his working life on the farm, with the death of his father and the consequent sale of the Slip Inn, he was forced to take work in the mill at Stacksteads, and it was here that he met, and in 1907 married, Annie Mary Reed, the daughter of a brick works manager. The couple lived at No. 40 Acre Mill Road, Stacksteads where on St. Valentine's Day 1909 their first child Winston was born. Like his parents before him, Dick was to have 8 children, 3 sons and 5 daughters. The family included two sets of twins, Florence and Lillian, and Amelia and Dennis, but sadly Dennis died at birth. Of the remaining seven, only one daughter, Vera failed to reach middle age, dying of meningitis, aged 21.

Richard Haworth with wife Annie Mary, De Bohun Farm, 1926.

His eldest son Winston was by now 15 years old and on the road to fulfilling his life's ambition to become a jockey. But Dick, no longer a young man, and crippled with his iron, had a farm to run and 8 mouths to feed – not a task to accomplish single-handed. So Winston had to leave his ambitions in the stables at Lambourne, Berkshire and return to help his father.

Dick and the family turned builders and the fields were turned into tennis courts, pig stys into catering facilities, and cow sheds into a ballroom, and by 1928 the "De Bohun Sports Club" was in full swing with County players on the list of members. The whole family worked long hours to make the business a success and in the early 1930s when a licence was granted for bar facilities it seemed that life may be taking an upturn. However, all hopes were dashed when in 1939 and the onset of World War II the Club was taken over first by the Coldstream Guards and finally the Home Guard.

Vera Brown, granddaughter of Richard Haworth.

De Bohun Farm, Bramley Road.

The family like many others, turned their attention towards the war effort, and Dick, though well into his 60s spent many a long night mounting fire watch over Rossendale Works in Southgate. However, when eventually the war ended in 1945, none of the family were in a position to take up where they left off; most were by this time married and making lives for themselves. In the early 1950s Mrs Rene Read rented the land from Winston and turned the De Bohun Club into the Oakwood Sports and Social Club, making extensive alterations. Mrs Read purchased the lease in the early 60s, shortly after which the land was sold to a local estate agent for private building development.

Life was very hard for the family, the bailiffs never far from the doorstep, and the situation was only worsened when within a few years a compulsory purchase order was put on a large piece of their land (now the area on which stands De Bohun School and the Fairway Houses). Nothing daunted, the decision was taken to turn the remaining acres into a sports' facility, maybe the first of its kind in north London.

Dick died in 1952 and his son (my father), Winston in 1978, but 3 of Richard Haworth's daughters, Lillian, Amelia and Margaret and one son, Arnold, are still living and he is succeeded by 6 grandchildren and 10 great-grandchildren and it is lovely to be able to record, as this part of the story is told, the birth of his great-great-grandson, Samuel Thomas on St. Valentine's Day 1988, at Chase Farm Hospital, Enfield".

Father, always in his trilby.

Sleepy Hadley Wood, 1960.

John J. Haworth and family were not to stay long at Chase Side in view of all the noise and by autumn 1951, No. 11 Beech Hill, Hadley Wood was purchased for some £8,000. We named the house "Fairlawn".

Hadley Wood was then very much a rural and not too popular outer suburb of London, with half completed roads and houses left over from 1939. Such an area was not popular with housewives, for unless they could drive (in those days very few did and there were no such luxury as the second car) they were marooned in the house for much of the time.

Mother could not drive and really did not have the temperament to learn. A chauffeur was engaged to look after father's new acquisition, the Mulliner-bodied sports saloon Bentley, with a Ford V.8 Pilot as a runabout. The original Ford V.8 was kept for a while and, if lucky, I was allowed to take it out at weekends, but despite my pleas to keep it, it was sold for a very small sum in 1954.

Business was still good and mother enjoyed the luxuries and father the distractions of owning a prosperous company.

By 1954 I had progressed to earning a reasonable income by sales effort within the company.

Ladies of that period all seemed very much to want to get married and in November 1955 I married Pat, whom I had met at the Y.C.'s and took out a mortgage for 82 Lancaster Avenue, Hadley Wood, costing £4,750.

Paul was to join us in 1960 and Anne in 1963 and we were to enjoy all the family events and outings that business commitments would allow. In 1965 we moved to a larger house, 48 Lancaster Avenue.

Paul and Annie Haworth, 1964.

Off to a wedding, 1955.

Trent Park, Cockfosters, a favourite place for John J's walks.

Meanwhile, mother and father at 11 Beech Hill, where they were to spend the rest of their lives, cultivated the garden to the highest of standards, with the garden being tended, until the end, by Thomas Cadwallader who lived in Potters Bar. This garden became, in due course, the only interest of John and Florence Haworth.

Father in 1951 had already indulged himself in purchasing a Bentley, which in 1962 he was going to exchange for a Silver Cloud Rolls Royce, but as Jack Barclay's would offer more for father's runabout, a 3-litre Rover, this went in exchange rather than the Bentley. I retained the Bentley, which has now been in the family for 37 years.

Somehow, such mechanical possessions of quality never enabled father to recapture his early days, even with the purchase of a Land Rover!

"Fairlawn", 11 Beech Hill.

Thomas Cadwallader - Gardener.

John J. Haworth - a would-be farmer again.

"Fairlawn's" garden.

He expected his instructions to be obeyed without question. A firm but benign paternalism would be exercised over family and workforce. Anyone, including myself, would be in for some harsh criticism if a contrary view was proposed or, even worse, carried out.

"Fairlawn" became father's haven from the outside world, from which he would not travel far. Rossendale Works for short visits, usually about lunchtime, meant that staff to whom he might wish to have a chat would themselves miss lunch.

When mother was well, there were trips to Fortnum and Mason and occasionally car outings in the summer to the Hertfordshire countryside.

Holidays away from home were, from the early-1960s, far too much of an effort and trouble to be contemplated.

Mother had few friends, even from her earliest days at "Bayfordbury" and together with father, never seemed to have any real social friends outside the family circle. Mother did however have one very loyal friend, Dorothy Cawkwell of Sheringham Avenue, Southgate, who was always a great conversationalist and companion to mother for the last 35 years of her life. Dorothy was to survive mother by quite a few years and was very much a well-known lady of Southgate.

Mother, in 1965, was to have a mild heart attack, but the drugs she took in its aftermath never seemed to agree with her. She became more and more housebound and although tended with skill by Dr Hyman, she suffered two strokes and quietly slipped away at home on 12th October 1979, aged 86, having celebrated 50 years of marriage the previous July.

Mother was to see me remarry in April 1978 to Janet, who had first been the young secretary to Mr Shaw at Rossendale Works in the early 1950s. Janet was to give mother much companionship in her last days.

In 1980, Janet, Simon and I moved to Braughing, a very pleasant and unspoilt village in North East Hertfordshire, where the improved quality of life, near in journey time to Southgate, is so much to be enjoyed.

Paul had already joined the company in 1978, followed by Simon in 1981.

They, now being the fourth generation, will have to see the company of James Haworth reach the 21st century and beyond.

Braughing - "A quiet place".

John Stewart Haworth, married to Janet Allen 12th April, 1978.
Below - Left to right: Tony Scheck, Studio Director, James Haworth Ltd, Doris Stephenson, secretary to both John J. and John S. Haworth, Paul Haworth, John and Janet, son Simon, Shelagh Brown, John Bowden, Director James Haworth Ltd., Marion Bowden.

By the mid-1960s father began to withdraw within himself and his own thoughts, which were not always in keeping with the changing times. Churchill and Montgomery were his idols. He would write letters galore, typed by his devoted secretary, Doris Stephenson, who would have to go to "Fairlawn" to take dictation.

Father would write endless letters to politicians and newspapers, stating his viewpoint on various issues of the day, his major target being the Common Market to which he was vehemently opposed. He would write notes by the dozen at a time, by way of complaint, praise or reminder, to all with whom he came in contact.

The change in the business climate, causing the reduced need for display material, was a situation with which he was never going to come to understand nor come to terms with.

It was always very difficult to understand his attitude to so many matters. He could be a kind, angry, generous, mean man, show compassion and intolerance all within the same hour, depending on the situation or subject that had come under his scrutiny. In many ways not a man of the mid-20th century, but of the late Victorian era, when life for those in reasonable circumstances was very ordered and they could set their own pace.

Father, on mother's death, was left on his own and still enjoyed good health, aged 80. The effort in maintaining mother's comfort during her last years, with the coming and going of day and night nurses, home helps and frequent visits by Janet and myself kept him going, with their and our presence.

But now, without the effort of looking after mother, father became rather lost, with now no permanent interest and died suddenly in his sleep from a heart attack early on Sunday 22nd March 1981.

I had seen father twice the previous day, accompanied by Simon, when father was in good spirits and due also to see him on Sunday, but Stanley Prime, who had chauffeured father and mother and looked after their wants in previous years, 'phoned Braughing to say he could get no reply to his 'phoning Mr John. I tried to call as well, with the same result.

Although I had the keys to "Fairlawn" I knew that the doors would be heavily bolted. I 'phoned for the police to be present. Accompanied by Janet and son, Simon, we arrived at "Fairlawn" with a sledgehammer, fearing the worst, to break open the front door.

Janet, Simon and I were met at "Fairlawn" by a policeman and policewoman, and after forcing entry, discovered father lying peacefully in bed, no longer of this world. End of an era. Father now at peace ending his days overlooking the garden he loved so much. He was buried with Florence in the Watts family grave at Enfield's Lavender Hill Cemetery.

I was never close to father, which I deeply regretted. I now felt very lonely with his passing, so soon after mother.

"Fairlawn" was sold that summer to meet death duties and the lovely garden passed away to wilderness as well, perhaps in sympathy with father and mother.

A last photograph.
John J. Haworth in his garden.

Father at peace.
Lavender Hill Cemetery.

James Haworth & Brother

THE STUDIO, CHANCERY LANE, 1914 – 1929

Chancery Lane 1913.

A cold, damp and raw January 1st 1914 would see the first gathering of the 4 artists, led by Edwin Byatt, 3 travellers and 3 office staff headed by Office Manager William "Digger" Shaw. The name "Digger" derived from his liking of the pipe tobacco of that name.

The office had been in use by James Haworth and brother Thomas, with a typist since mid December.

The first task of one of the artists that morning would be to paint slowly, letter by letter, the title JAMES HAWORTH & BROTHER, DESIGNERS AND PRINTERS on the glass of the front door. Thereby proclaiming to the outside world, the company was now very much in business from their London address of 55 Chancery Lane, W.C. on the edge of that famous square mile that constitutes the City of London.

This glass door on the third floor of an early Victorian building, would lead to a suite of rather dingy rooms, each heated by a coal fire or paraffin stove.

Two of the rooms at the back would be given over to the artists. Edwin Byatt, not only because of his importance, but to accommodate his poster designs which he would paint to the actual size, would have a room to himself. Mr Bertram, Mr North and a young trainee artist Mr Buck, doubling as tea boy and pallet washer, would be crowded together in the remaining room.

James would have a room overlooking the street, with its companion room housing Mr Shaw, a typist and a young man to help with the estimating.

Artists, office staff, travellers and Thomas Haworth had forsaken the comparative safety of their previous employer Alf Cooke, to better themselves, they hoped, by following the tenacity and enthusiasm of this little man, James Haworth, into the unknown.

Edwin Byatt by the Studio Entrance room.

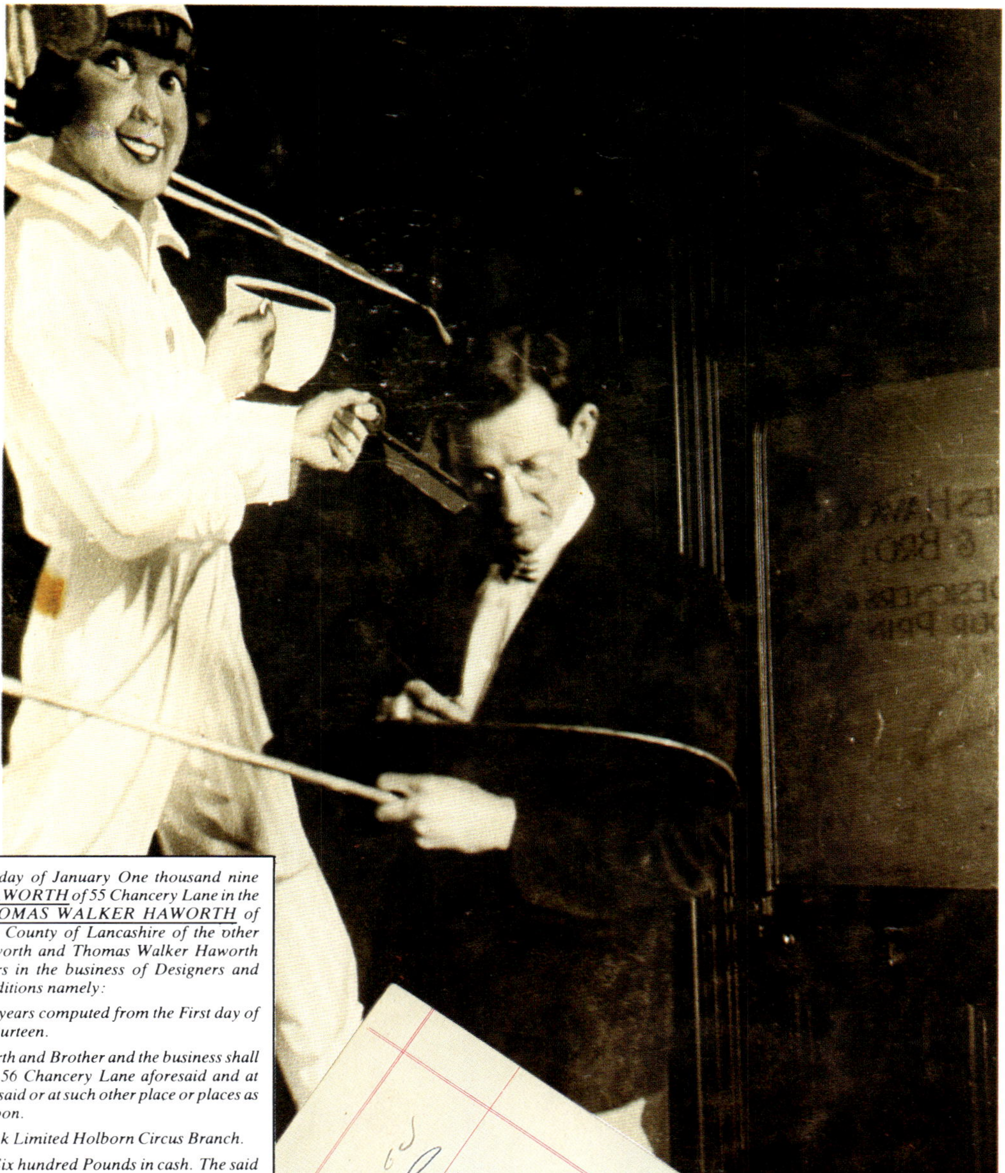

Transcript of original agreement.

THIS AGREEMENT made the Thirty first day of January One thousand nine hundred and fourteen BETWEEN JAMES HAWORTH of 55 Chancery Lane in the County of London of the one part and THOMAS WALKER HAWORTH of 38 Queens Road Urmston Manchester in the County of Lancashire of the other part WITNESSETH that the said James Haworth and Thomas Walker Haworth hereby mutually covenant to become partners in the business of Designers and Printers upon and subject to the following conditions namely:

1. The partnership shall be for a term of Ten years computed from the First day of January One thousand nine hundred and fourteen.
2. The name of the firm shall be James Haworth and Brother and the business shall be carried on at the premises Nos. 55 and 56 Chancery Lane aforesaid and at 38 Queens Road Urmston Manchester aforesaid or at such other place or places as the partners shall from time to time agree upon.
3. The bankers of the firm shall be Lloyds Bank Limited Holborn Circus Branch.
4. The capital of the firm shall be the sum of Six hundred Pounds in cash. The said capital shall be provided by and belong to the partners in equal shares. Each partner shall be entitled to interest at the rate of Fifteen Pounds per centum per annum upon the amount of capital for the time being standing to his credit in the books of the firm and such interest shall be paid or credited before any division of profits is made.
5. The profits and losses of the business shall be divided between the partners as follows:- An account of the gross takings at each of the two aforesaid places of business of the firm shall be separately taken and each Partner's share of the profits shall be based upon and proportionate to the gross takings actually received at each of the said places of business.
6. Proper accounts shall be kept of all partnership transactions and on the Thirtyfirst day of December in every year or as soon afterwards as possible a balance sheet shall be made out showing the assets and liabilities of the firm and what belongs and is due to each partner for capital and share of profits and the same shall be signed by both partners and when so signed shall be conclusive except that if a manifest error shall be discovered therein within three calendar months after the signature thereof such error shall be rectified.
7. James Haworth may draw each calendar month the sum of Twentyfive Pounds and the said Thomas Walker Haworth may draw each calendar month the sum of Seventeen Pounds out of the partnership cash on account of his share of profits for the current year but if on taking the yearly account it shall appear that the monthly sums drawn out by either partner exceed his share of profits he shall forthwith refund the excess.
8. All matters in difference in relation to the partnership affairs shall be referred to two arbitrators one to be appointed by each party according and subject to the provisions of the Arbitration Act 1889.

AS WITNESS the hands of the parties the day and year first above written.

SIGNED by the above named JAMES HAWORTH in the presence of Solicitor

SIGNED by the above named THOMAS WALKER HAWORTH in the presence of Solicitor

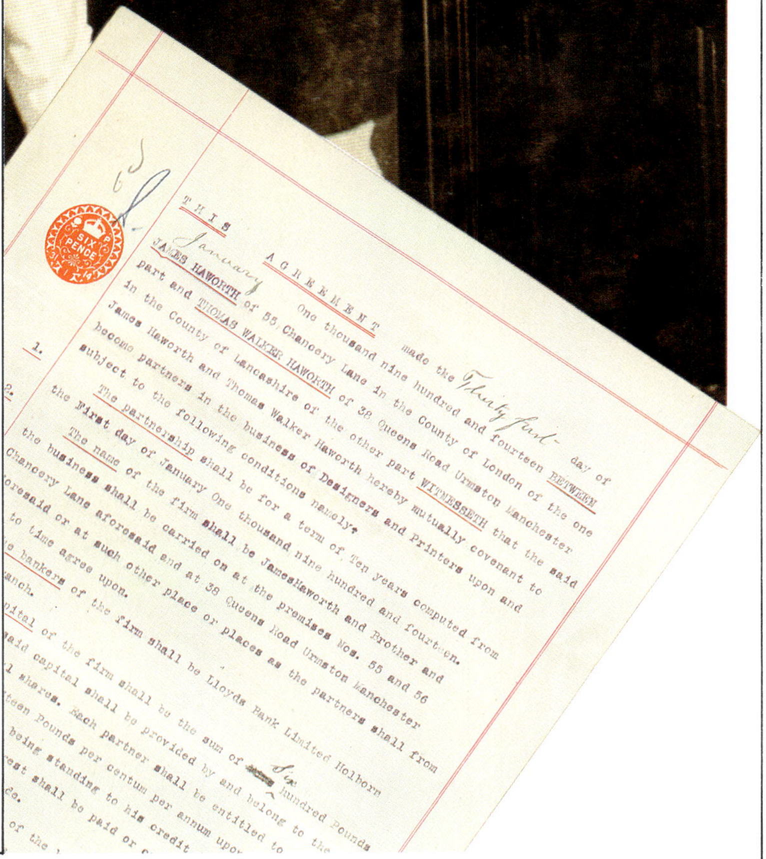

Studio Artists at Chancery Lane 1925.
1. *Edwin Byatt in a cowboy role.*
2. *Reginald Mills framing "Edwin".*
3. *The artists with John J. Haworth (Bottom left).*

1.

2.

3.

A similar range of buildings to those of 55 & 56 Chancery Lane still exist in 1988, at 67 Chancery Lane.

James and Thomas had no doubt canvassed their regular customers as to the business support they might receive if they branched out on their own. Many buyers, it would seem from correspondence at the time, gave active encouragement to their endeavours.

From the start both brothers were held in their highest esteem by the senior buyers at such important firms as Cadbury's, Oxo, J & J Colman, Rowntree and many others. Therefore, they could rely on enquiries, followed by orders coming to them, if their designs, quality of print, and, above all, service were equal, if not better than Alf Cooke Ltd.

Buyers were not disappointed, for successful designs flowed from the brushes of the artists who had joined this embryo company.

As Spring 1914 came, two more artists were engaged and the office busied itself in processing print orders being carried out by P.P. Press of Liverpool with whom James had an arrangement to produce print on behalf of the new company called James Haworth & Brother.

Shortly a retarding to this success was to appear – the outbreak of war, 14th August 1914, with the German Empire. Fortunately, from the business point of view, the impact, initially was not so immediate as in 1939. Economies had to be made in staff, in the face of falling demand for advertising. The war had begun to bite on Home Front consumption, in order to sustain a war economy.

'Oxo' World War I Advertising.

World War I influence in print subjects.

In mid 1915, Albert Buck volunteered for the Artist Rifles Regiment and survived, by some miracle, three and a half continuous years in the infamous trenches of Northern France. Albert was to become a sergeant and served as a Military Policeman with the British Army that occupied Cologne in 1919.

Artists Byatt and Bertram remained throughout the war at Chancery Lane. "Digger" Shaw and two of the travellers engaged in 1914 were also called to the colours. James and brother Thomas had therefore to do most of the necessary travelling and office work.

They kept the firm in business, supported by the farms at Southgate, operating profitably as a result of the demand for home-produced food. German submarines, in the sinking of our merchant ships, had meanwhile reduced imports of food to a minimum.

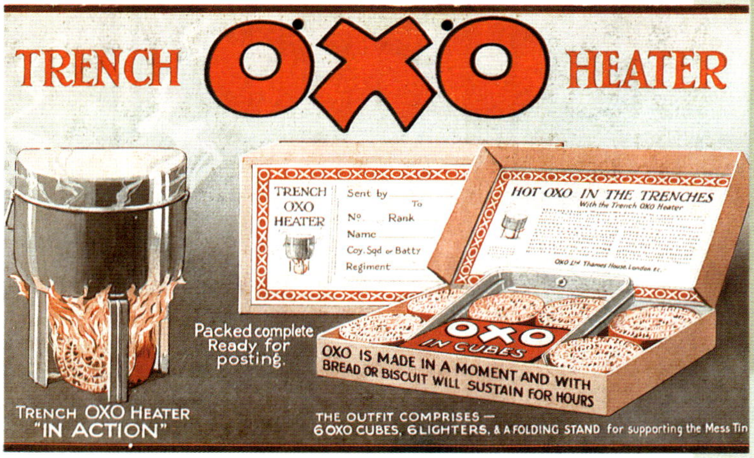

Cartons designed by the Studio 1913-1920.

Peace came thankfully on 11th November 1918, leaving a great proportion of the young men, who went so unknowingly to their deaths in the mud of the Western front.

The war was to cause a fundamental change in the lifestyles of all, both rich and poor. It speeded up, for civilian use, such items as dry batteries, cars and labour-saving devices in homes. Female servants had gone to do war work for good salaries and would not go back to the low pay of doing household drudgery for a demanding lady of the house.

As a consequence, home labour-saving devices, electrical goods, vacuum cleaners, wireless sets, refrigerators, etc., became new products to advertise. New foods, like cornflakes, shredded wheat, tinned foods and many others were to appear alongside the traditional items on grocers' shelves.

These new products were the result of American companies opening up production plants in the British Isles, to meet the demand, for the time being, of people who had money to spend on enjoying these new luxuries.

1920. A design reflecting War Campaign Medals.

In the early 1920's the James Haworth studio, strengthened by additional artists, met the demand, from both old and new customers, to supply label and showcard designs of new originality, required to advertise these 20th century innovations.

The question of originality, coupled with artistic quality, was of the highest importance. The ground rules imposed then by print buyers being — he who puts up the best idea and sketch, obtains the business.

In the period between the two world wars, competition between printers with design studios was great. Buyers, if they knew it would not cost their company money to consider submitted designs, would be always willing to accept on a speculative and competitive basis, designs to promote their products.

It was commonplace, even if only one item of display material was required, for up to a dozen printers and designers to submit full size, highly finished by way of artwork and construction, ideas for consideration. Some printers, James Haworth included, would hedge their bets by submitting 2 or 3 competing alternatives.

1924. New products to make life easier for the housewife.

1925. "Art Deco" in Display Design.

The waste in artists' wages, expertise and materials in unsuccessful submissions was astronomical. To avoid waste, disappointment and financial loss, the submitted design in its impact and originality had, at all costs, to be a winner.

James Haworth and Company fortunately had many and continuous winners, from single labels through to complete full window displays, made up of different print items to promote a complete sales theme.

In the period 1920 - 1940, it was the practise of cigarette, food, cosmetic and dry battery producers, along with breweries, to pay a fee to the shopkeeper for the exclusive right to dress a whole window for an agreed period. This arrangement usually made for a public eye-catching solo display of the company's products with its advertising material, to the mutual benefit of the manufacturer and seller.

John J. Haworth 1924.
About to start his Print career at 55 Chancery Lane.

1920-1930.
A selection of designs produced by the James Haworth Studio.

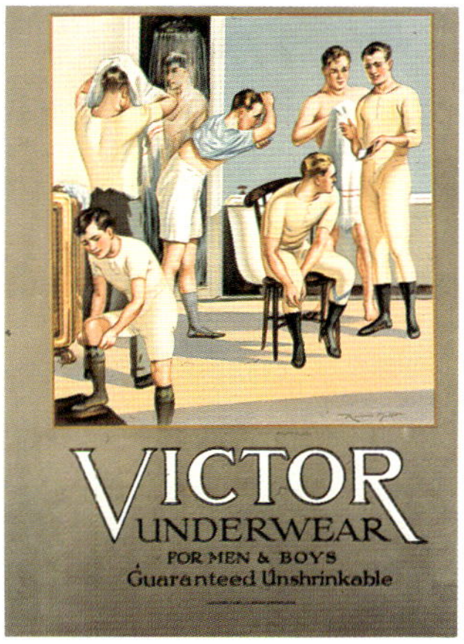

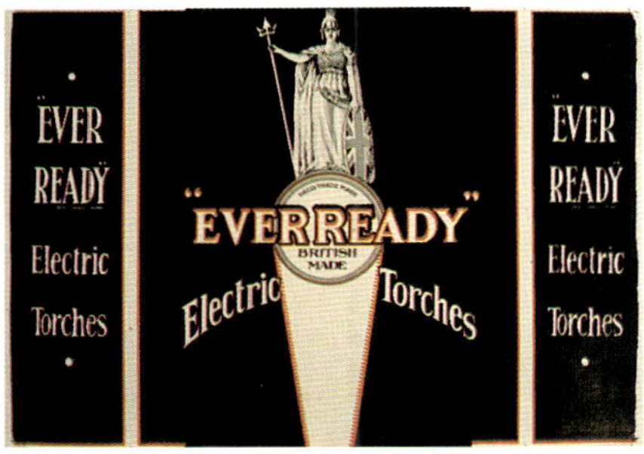

1925. The first showcard for the Ever Ready torch and dry battery company.

1924. James Haworth Studio have always claimed they were the originators of this Design and Slogan.

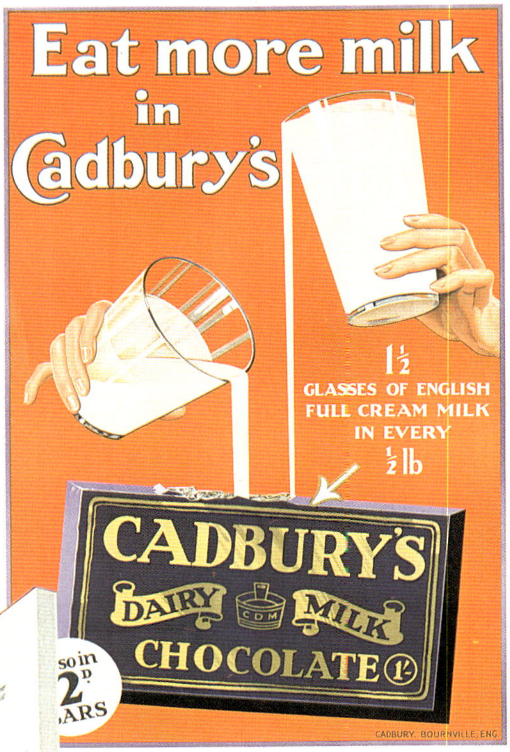

1929. A design and construction unique for its time as a complete Shop Window Display. This display could be packed flat but when stood upright would automatically become three dimensional.

James Haworth's son John J., joining the company in 1923, was, in due course, to exploit to the full his expertise and enthusiasm to obtain these valuable orders for complete window displays. In particular for Ever Ready, Exide, J & J Colman, Peek Frean etc., John J. was to retain this business consistently until 1940.

John J's brother-in-law, Alan Lord, joined as a salesman in 1929, together with another salesman. Servicing these new arrivals meant more artists and office staff and 55 Chancery Lane was becoming far too cramped and crowded.

1929. Some last designs from the James Haworth's Studio in Chancery Lane.

THE STUDIO, 21 SOHO SQUARE, 1930 – 1970.
SOUTHGATE, 1970 – 1988.

Early in 1930, the 2nd and 3rd floors of 21 Soho Square, W1 were leased. Allsop & Co the estate agents had the ground floor, with its prestigious entrance. Our entrance was down the side in Sutton Row.

Soho Square, just behind Oxford Street and Charing Cross Road, could be regarded as a reasonably prestigious London address in the "West End".

In 1930, Oxford Street, at its junction with Tottenham Court Road and Charing Cross Road was lined with fashionable shops. Senior staff and visitors could go for lunch or tea to Frascatti's, Buzzard's, Fleming's or Lyon's Corner House in Oxford Street. The Horseshoe in Tottenham Court Road, with its several restaurants, next to the Dominion cinema, was also a favourite. Sadly, all these attractive eating places have gone, together with the interesting shops, which sold everything one could possibly want. All of which abounded within a short distance of the leafy Square.

21 Soho Square was a unique building, having been the home, in the late 18th and early 19th centuries of Mr Crosse, who with Mr Blackwell, were to found the famous food firm of Crosse and Blackwell.

Once a pickles factory

Soho Preserved

A PLEASANT change from the remorseless destruction of London's old buildings is that one of the most interesting places in Soho Square, the Manor House, has been renovated. Since 1935 the building, seen in my Geoffrey Fletcher drawing, has been the offices of the estate agents Allsop and Co.

For many years from 1839 it was occupied by Edmund Crosse and Thomas Blackwell. Originally built as a shop with a residence above, it was also used as a factory for pickles and other foods.

An earlier occupant of a house on this site was Adml. Sir Cloudesley Shovel, who was drowned off the Isles of Scilly in 1707 with 2,000 men and nearly the entire British fleet returning from the siege of Toulon.

A London newspaper cutting describing 21 Soho Square's past.

1930. James Haworth occupies the top two floors of 21 Soho Square, (seen between the trees in the illustration below), as their Studio and Head Office. Their office entrance was always down Sutton Row to the right.

Mr Crosse, at the rear of his home, built factory buildings down Sutton Row out to Charing Cross Road. It was basically the top two floors of this old pickle factory, immediately behind Mr Crosse's home, that James Haworth & Brother Ltd., took as their studios and head office. I recall as a boy seeing grandfather's book-lined office, overlooking the Square. This office could easily have been Mr Crosse's bedroom.

The third floor, at the rear with its factory glass roof, was ideal as an art studio.

The second floor, which had been some form of night club, complete with stage and drapes, made for a good showroom to display the fine art reproductions, calendars, Christmas cards and of course the great range of showcards. On this floor, Mr Byatt was to install his studio, rather than be with the noisy, twenty or more artists upstairs.

1933. Artist's humour reflecting the rise of Nazi Germany.

Soho Square still a quiet oasis in 1988. 21 Soho Square hidden behind scaffolding being completely rebuilt but retaining Mr Crosse's original home facade.

The view from 21 Soho Square.

The move to become wholesalers of fine art prints, calendars, birthday and Christmas cards was very fortunate, for on having moved to these new premises, the world-wide trade depression arrived. Artists who would normally be engaged on display work turned to Christmas card designing. These cards could be printed at the Leicester factory (partly acquired in 1918) and, hopefully sold by our representatives to stationers.

Thanks to John J's and his father James' efforts, there was no laying off of staff, despite little or no profit from the business.

Depressing conditions lasted for nearly five years, but by 1936 the Western World began to shake itself out of economic depression, helped, one is sorry to say, by the impetus to British industry in making ready to meet yet another threat of war with Germany.

In the second half of the 1930's, James Haworth had one of the, if not the, largest advertising printer's studios in the country, with row upon row of artists preparing designs and hand-lettering the finished drawings.

Edwin Byatt, the longest serving and principal artist, remained supreme.

Albert Buck became Studio Manager and was able to combine the role of administrator with being a fine food artist.

1937. The Power House of the James Haworth Studio.
Standing (left) - Edwin Byatt, John J. Haworth.
Seated left to right - Louis Johnstone, Albert Buck and Reginald Mills.

Left:
1937. The combination of Albert Buck's artwork and our early studio photography.

Second floor 21 Soho Square. The Greeting Card and "Fine Art" Display Room.

Reginald Mills, joining in 1921, was to be a past-master in being able to reproduce in watercolour, paintings of pageantry and scenes from history, for which their was great demand as a result of the George V Jubilee and in 1937 the Coronation of George VI.

Louis Johnstone, joining in 1932, was a brilliant cardboard engineer. A versatile figure artist of the greatest ability, in designing the most intricate and eye-catching cardboard window displays ever produced.

These four artists' work in 1988, is very much sought after by museums, galleries and ephemera collectors.

Close behind these four supreme craftsmen, were another four artists.

Alan Cameron, an artist of extreme neatness and fine work, drew and painted the biscuit and chocolate illustrations printed in sales catalogues. The studio produced such catalogues for at least a dozen different principal biscuit and chocolate manufacturers.

Lyn Harding, a cardboard construction and food illustration artist of the highest order.

Bill Taylor, the senior lettering artist and typographer. It must be remembered that all lettering on display material had to be hand-drawn and painted in the correct colour on the finished design; a very tedious job demanding extreme accuracy, there being no such thing as Letraset.

Ernest Mills (no relation to Reginald) was responsible for fine art design in the realm of calendars and greetings cards.

To support these eight seniors were twelve or more junior and student artists, who prepared speculative designs and carried out many of the lesser, but no less important, artistic requirements within a busy studio. Many of these juniors were to make their name with other studios and advertising agencies in later years.

Self portrait Reginald Mills, Senior Artist James Haworth Studio 1924-1953.

1937. The versatile work of Reginald Mills.

Left: 1937. Reginald Mills' interpretation of the reputation enjoyed by James Haworth as headmaster and founder of The James Haworth Studio Academy. Showing round Mr Alan Palmer of Huntley and Palmers Biscuits on a "state" visit to discuss display material.

A lady artist in the Haworth studio.

John J. relaxing with ladies from the office on the roof of 21 Soho Square.

An example of lettering artist "Bill" Taylor's work.

(photo right)
"Bill" Taylor

1937. John J. Haworth. "Top Traveller" on his way with displays for Oxo.

There was no such thing as colour photography prior to the late 1940's with which to capture the realism of the product, or live figures. Anything by way of illustrations in colour had to be hand-drawn and painted.

Black and white photos could be hand-coloured by our artists but were very expensive, because of the skill and time required by the colourer.

From the very first days, James Haworth's studio had always maintained a black and white photographic capability. On moving to Soho Square, a fully equipped studio was created in a large room off the main artists' studio on the 3rd floor. This studio was to pose models and products. The resulting photographs acted as accurate references for the artists when it came to preparing the finished coloured artwork. Such photography would be directed by the artist and representative responsible for the account. A small dark room was available to produce the resulting black and white prints.

The four year period prior to 1939, was the peak in the production, within the British Isles, of display advertising using cardboard. Every window and spare shelf in a shop, large or small, would be filled with cardboard advertising in colourful designs of the highest artistic quality.

The display material in a shop was king in attracting a would-be purchaser. Newspapers, magazines and cinema advertising had, in most cases, only supporting roles.

1938. Designed at the studio a selection of the Ever Ready selling fortnight shop window display material produced in great quantity by the James Haworth factories at Leicester and Southgate.

1938. A James Haworth studio photograph is transformed into a "Fine Art" advertising subject.

1938. A small selection illustrating the variety of advertising produced by James Haworth artists.

Despite the hard and exacting work, long hours – 9a.m. to 6p.m. and 1p.m. on Saturdays – there was a camaraderie among the senior artists. This would take them on fine Saturday afternoons, first for a drink in a Soho bar, followed by sketching sessions down by the Thames, lasting usually until opening time at an attractive Thameside pub in Chelsea or Chiswick. I recall our artist group had a collection of metal brass plates joined by one string and when alighting from one of London's old taxis, one of the artists would slam the door, whilst simultaneously, another would drop the plates, which sounded like smashing glass. The gruff cabby would rush round to see the expected damage, only to retire mystified. The plates having been collected up during his journey round the cab!

1939. "End of an Era" for large "Life Size" window displays. These displays would be produced in quantities up to 60,000 copies at a time in a range of various sizes.

1939 marked the height of the display manufacturers art. The imminent World War II was to eliminate to a great extent such large and elaborate displays.

14 Ewell House Grove
Ewell, Surrey.
27th October 1939

Dear Mr Haworth

I am enclosing account for the Robertson's and Stephens Ink Sketches, the Palmolive can wait for a week or two.

It is difficult for me to find anything to write you about, for while there is so much going on of a distructive nature, we with constructive minds find ourselves for the time being at a loose end.

It is my earnest hope that business will return if only in some reasonable measure just to keep the staff together.

Speaking for the artists I still consider them to be some of the most efficient in the business I feel certain that you will help them to carry through.

The reward will be worth it.

Kindest Regards
Yours faithfully
Edwin Byatt.

Studio and Staff Rossendale Works January 1941.

Staff at Peace and War.

However, all pranks were to come to an end when on 3rd September 1939, the inevitable war came with Germany, with a far greater and immediate cancellation of advertising than had occurred at the outbreak of war in August 1914.

As a consequence, the junior staff had all left by Christmas. There was precious little work for the remaining artists, except to produce straight-forward showcards and a few catalogues to go with products for export, – exports so necessary to pay for the war effort.

As the war worsened, to the detriment of Britain, it was felt wise to leave 21 Soho Square before it was laid flat by the blitzkrieg, expected any moment, after the retreat from Dunkirk of British forces.

In June 1940, the studio and offices closed and the remaining artists worked from their homes.

Albert Buck went to Rossendale Works and set up his desk and base there. "Digger" Shaw and Doris Stephenson, secretary to James Haworth and John J. were the only office staff to go to Southgate.

Of the artists, Edwin Byatt went to his home in South London and was to die suddenly in 1942.

Reginald Mills was to join the London Fire Service as a fireman. He served in London throughout the blitz and became in effect official war artist to the Auxiliary Fire Service and, in turn, the National Fire Service. His pictures and sketches record vividly the fire and destruction of London during the war years.

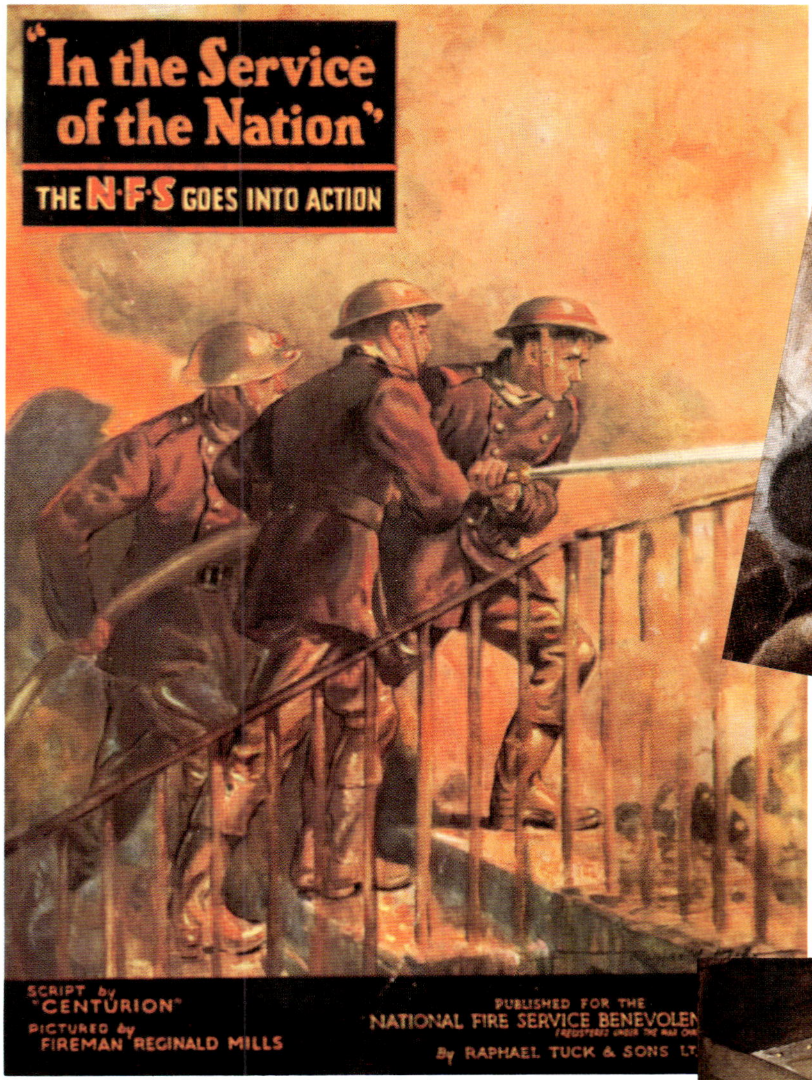

Reginald Mills.
A portrait by Paul Dessau.

On this and following page:- A small selection of the many illustrations by Reginald Mills depicting the Blitz on London and the work of the National Fire Service.

Louis Johnstone was drafted for war work with Vickers Aircraft Ltd where his design and engineering expertise were soon recognised. He became a member of Professor Barnes Wallis' team in the design of aircraft and weapons of war.

Lyn Harding joined the Royal Air Force and perhaps could have had an easy war as a camouflage expert. Instead, he became an engineer fitter and was sent to Burma in 1942 when the Japanese were at the gates of India. Promoted to Sergeant, he was to suffer during these war years, many privations. Serving in forward airfields, encircled by Japanese troops, sniper fire would try and pick off the aircraft maintenance crew. Lyn Harding had many a lucky escape.

Alan Cameron joined London's Civil Defence Service and was drafted into the "heavy rescue section". He was to see at first hand the death and destruction in South London caused by bombs and mines and later V.1. flying bombs and V.2. rockets.

Ernest Mills joined the Army and served all his time in England.

Bill Taylor, centre.

Bill Taylor went to a munition factory and through his interest in music became a leading member of a dance band, touring war factories.

The artists' desks, equipment, sketches – both successful and unsuccessful – which amounted to thousands, were taken to empty shop spaces in the row of shops built next to "Bayfordbury" in Bramley Road, Southgate. These items were to remain there until 1946.

21 Soho Square bore a charmed life throughout the war, with hardly a window broken. After we left in the summer of 1940, Rank Films took over our floors as their Publicity Department and created a large black and white studio with good processing facilities.

War ended finally in August 1945, it was hoped to reach once again the amount of business that had been going through the Studio in 1939. The seven senior artists came back and were soon fully engaged. There was little extra work for new artists and, as I recall, there was now never to be more than three juniors, when in the past there had been fifteen.

Due to Rank Films' occupancy, James Haworth were able to acquire, for a modest sum, all their photographic processing equipment. To manage this new acquisition and to offer a new service to customers as photographers, a fully qualified photographer and technician, Geoff Moat, joined the team in 1948. He was to take us into colour photography, together with its then complicated hand-processing and printing.

The "Head Office" was to remain at Rossendale Works and our lease option on the 2nd floor was relinquished.

James Haworth died in October 1948. John J. became Managing Director with now a free hand to create a new powerful studio, to work once again on the principle – "He who puts up the best sketch, obtains the order".

Louis Shabner, Portrait Artist,
James Haworth Studio 1947-1965.

HM the Queen, portrait in full colour by Louis Shabner. 20,000 of these displays supplied to multiple shops to mark the Coronation, 1953.

John J. engaged the services of Louis Shabner, a wonderful portrait and figure artist. His technique in painting faces has, in my opinion, never been surpassed.

With Louis Shabner filling the gap left by the death of Edwin Byatt, the team was now complete.

In John J's direction enquiries and orders came. Requirements for designs were however not on such a grand scale as pre-war. Austerity was still about, in regard to supply of materials. Though consumer goods were soon in the shops, they needed very little advertising because of demand.

James Haworth's productions enlivening a small electrical shop window.

The work of Louis Shabner.

Exide Battery.
Calendar illustrations.

1948-1958.
The combination of Louis Shabner portraits and Albert Buck's still life, resulting in some of the last hand painted artwork originals. After 1958 colour photography supplanted their skill by reason of cheapness and speed of preparation.

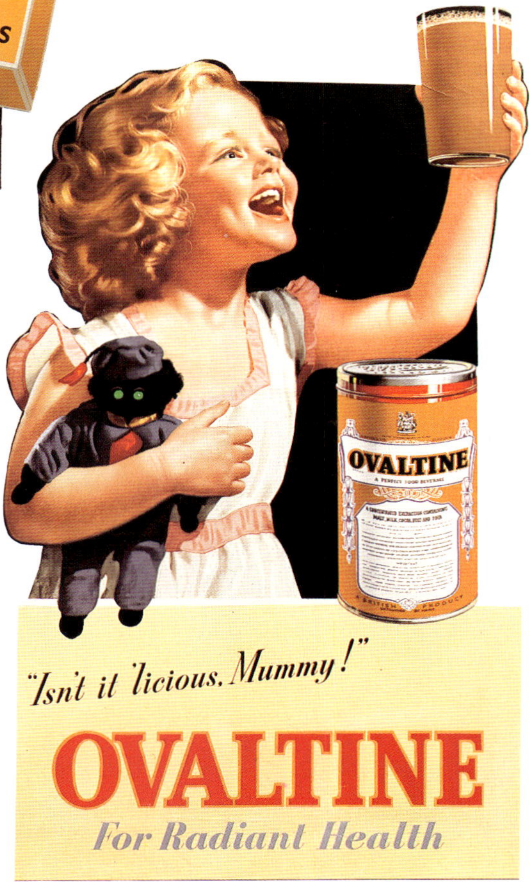

Louis Johnstone. James Haworth studio 1937-1980.

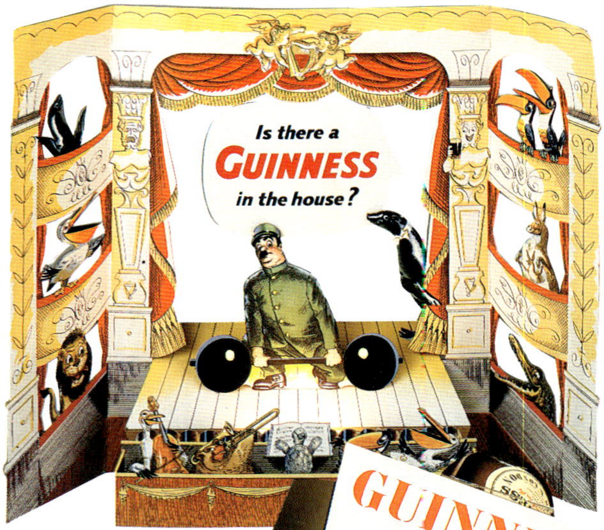

Louis Johnstone was to reach his peak in skill and ingenuity in producing designs for Oxo, Ovaltine and, a little later, Guinness. Charles Moore had joined Guinness in 1950 as Advertising Buyer, having been an artist pre-war in Waddington's studio, Leeds. Louis Johnstone had also been in that same studio before joining us in 1937.

On leaving the Air Force in 1950, one of my first calls was to Guinness, meeting Charles Moore, who was pleased and surprised to learn that his artist friend Louis Johnstone of long ago was still in our Studio.

Louis, in adapting and creating ideas of his own from Guinness advertising themes, was to be responsible for some twenty-five years, in producing the majority of Guinness display material.

"Last of the old school", 1951 left to right:- Geoff Moat (Photography Manager), Albert Buck (Studio Manager), Louis Johnstone, Lyn Harding.

Reginald Mills died, before his time, from cancer in 1954. His many ceremonial pictures for calendars and boxtops, leave a lasting epitaph to his skill.

Lyn Harding was to take his own life in 1961, his invalid wife having died shortly before. This was a tragedy, deeply felt by all in the company.

The 1950s saw Ken Hammerton, Jack Winstanley and Tony Scheck from Switzerland, join us as additions and replacements. Ernest Mills had retired in 1955. Albert Buck was, of course, still Studio Manager and became increasingly responsible for servicing Oxo's requirements.

Albert Buck, a lifetime with James Haworth Studio and his work for Oxo.

The designs of Louis Johnstone
whilst at 21 Soho Square
1947-1970.

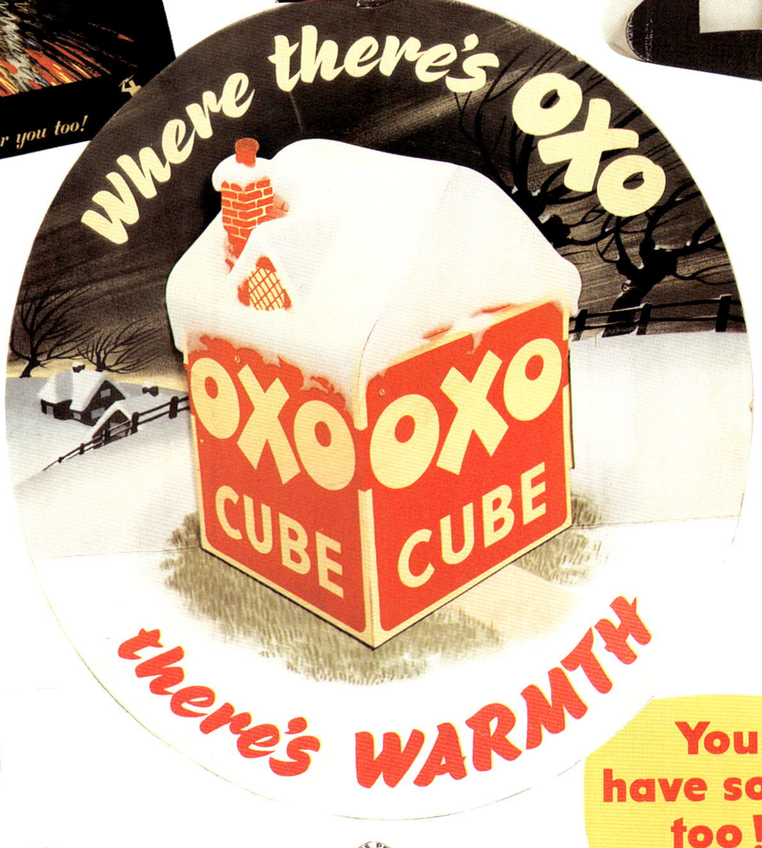

Soho Square. Above - standing, Harold Jones. seated, Alan Cameron.

Albert Buck making a point with Louis Johnstone.

In 1956 an event came about that was to have more long-term effect than any world war on our business.

Commercial television arrived. This expensive medium of advertising had to be funded by raiding every budget in previous advertising appropriations. This included, very much, "point-of-sale material", – now the new advertising jargon for showcards and cut-out displays.

Even worse, the design and production of any remaining point-of-sale material was, from now, under the control of the advertising agency. Naturally, they wished to present a conforming image based on their T. V. commercials, for the product advertised.

Loyal buyers to James Haworth's years of service on their behalf, did all they could to mitigate our loss of business by giving us design requirements falling outside the scope of T. V.

This science of marketing, by 1988, is indeed a science necessary to promote successfully a product. It has made it almost impossible to win orders ever again, on the principle of the best sketch on its own obtains the order.

A further blow in the 1960s was the arrival of the supermarket, so constructed to leave no room for cardboard display advertising.

High Street multiples were also to replace the individually owned shop. Such shops were the last stronghold for the acceptance for the attractive clutter of showcards and cut-outs.

By late 1968, the writing was on the wall for the continuance of the Art Studio in its present size and location. The prospect of renewing the lease of 21 Soho Square at the end of 1971, being prohibitive by way of cost.

My father, as mentioned earlier, could not come to terms with this fundamental change affecting our business.

I felt, however, there was still very much a need for a Studio service, which could sell to customers, separate from any print requirements.

In this respect, the Photographic Department at Soho Square had already achieved success, especially on behalf of Eastern Electricity Board.

The die was cast to build a purpose-built 4½ thousand square feet Studio on spare land at Rossendale Works at Southgate. Two-thirds of this new building was given over to house a large 30ft high ceiling Studio, with colour processing laboratories for prints and transparencies.

Albert Buck had retired, aged 70 years, in 1968, after 54 years of service. A more loyal and devoted servant to the Company would be hard to find. Albert was to pass peacefully away in 1975.

John J. Haworth celebrates 50 years of Albert Buck's service.

Ken Hammerton's view of James Haworth's Studio Staff and Company Representatives:- Back row - left to right:- John S. Haworth, Frank Lovelock, Harold Jones, Tony Pearce, Ken Hammerton, Kevin Atfield, Louis Johnstone, Michael Fawcett, Geoff Moat and John J. Haworth.
Front row:- Keith Smart, Alan Cameron, Tony Scheck, Albert Buck, Bill Taylor and Jack Winstanley (girls in hats wishful thinking).

We moved in 1970, with Geoff Moat in charge of Photography and Tony Scheck the Art Studio.

This move signalled the end of an era and the beginning, we hoped, of a new era in our studio operations.

Of the artists at Soho Square, only Tony Scheck, as Studio Manager, Louis Johnstone and Bill Taylor came to Southgate.

Geoff Moat retired soon after our arrival at Southgate, to take up fruit farming in Kent. His assistant, Miles Winter, took over the reins and over the years to date as Deputy Managing Director, he has moulded the photographic side of our business into one of the best creative and technically excellent photographic studios in England.

In 1979, an additional studio was created within the "old forge" at Rossendale Works. The Photographic Studio is now able to process all its own photography and produce colour prints up to 30″ x 40″; a service that is used very much by other photographers who appreciate our personal service and quality.

The Art Studio, from 1970 to date, was never to be as large as when at Soho Square.

Bill Taylor, who lived in Southgate, still a bachelor, died suddenly in 1975.

Louis Johnstone carried on with us, producing excellent work until his death "in harness" in 1980. Lou Johnstone was an inventor as well as an artist. The Patent Office has records of his many ideas, including a man-powered flying machine! His designs and brilliant flair for originality, combined with high artistic standard of finished work obtained, for us, many orders in a much reduced market during the period 1960 to 1980. His work for Guinness and other companies have become collectors' items, for those interested in recording the art of advertising in the mid-twentieth century.

Miles Winter and a selection of the varied work undertaken by the photographic studio.

George Lyles joined the company in 1973 and became manager of the small team that is still kept busy on producing display items.

Eric Latham, cardboard construction engineer, joined the company in 1939. We shall read later of his early experiences and transfer from the factory in 1970 to take charge of cutter-drawing and sample-making.

Eric, an important member of that present team, is, unfortunately shortly to retire in the summer of 1988.

Tony Scheck, now an Executive Director, heads our art operations and small exhibition department. The latter, designs, builds and erects individual stands for national advertisers at the Birmingham National Exhibition Centre, Earls Court and Harrogate Halls. This department undertakes the installation of permanent stands within shops, as well as stands required for one or two-day exhibitions at fairs, county shows and hotels throughout the British Isles.

As a result of Tony Scheck's work, exhibitors have won a number of awards for the excellence of their stands.

The studio, though changed in its emphasis to major on creative photography, maintains still a creative design team. A lasting tribute to all past company artists, who gave so much of their skill to keeping the company in business, especially in difficult times.

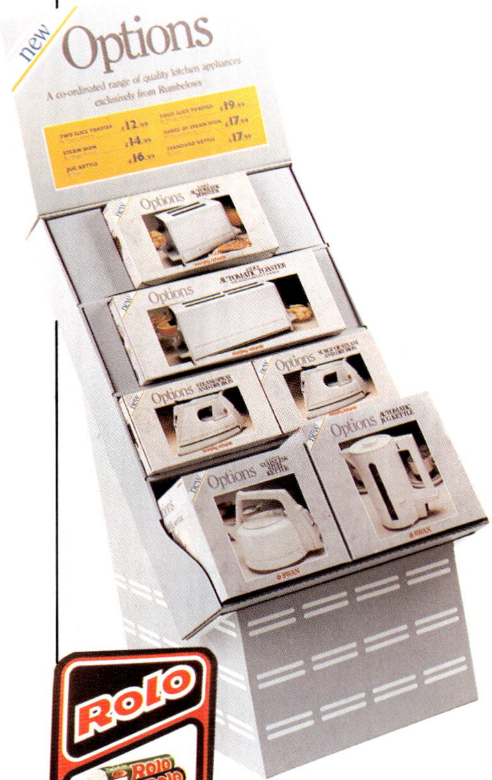

A range of designs produced by the studio.

Left: Final preparations for a still-life study.
Below: Miles Winter directs a studio 'shot'.

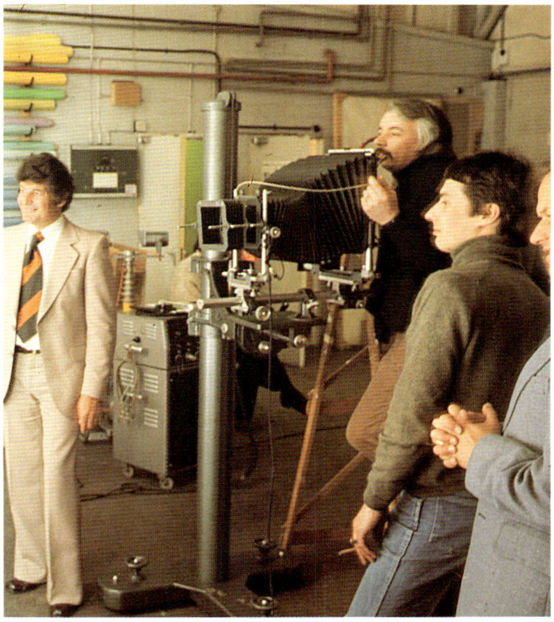

James Haworth

FLEET STREET, LEICESTER

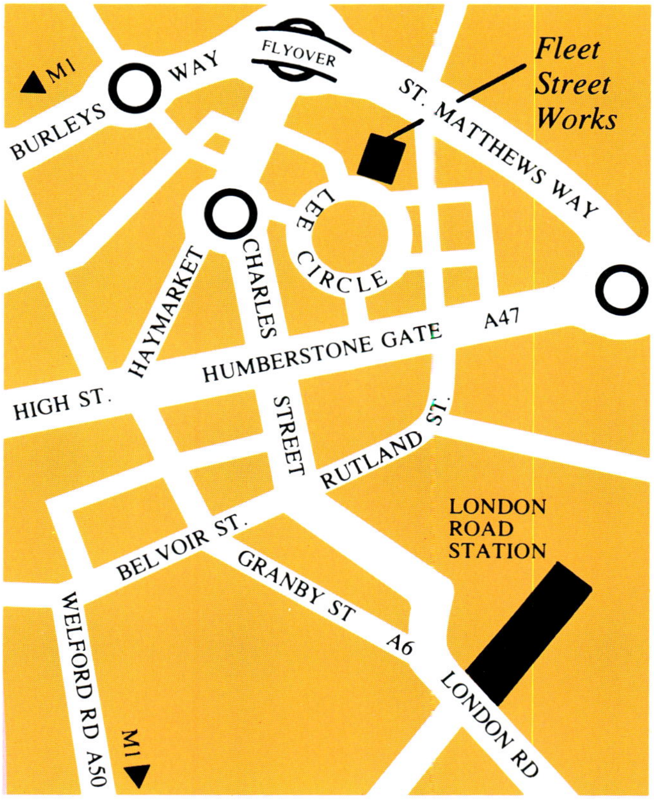

By 1918 and the ending of the First World War, James Haworth & Brother's arrangement with the P. P. Press of Liverpool to undertake all their printing was under strain from both points of view. For James Haworth there was the distance from London, excess profit-taking by P. P. Press with a captive customer, combined with bad delivery time-keeping and complaints on quality. In return, P. P. Press were getting very disenchanted with our delayed payments.

A. H. Skinner & Co had been small general printers in Leicester from the early 1900s having been founded by two printers – Mr A. H. Skinner and W. E. Bunney. They had rented from Wacks & Company, Clothing Manufacturers, part of the site known as Burlington Works, built in 1889 and situated between Milton Street and Fleet Street, Leicester.

Early 1919 Mr Skinner and Mr Bunney decided to purchase for £4,000 the now vacant 'L' shaped block on Mr Wack's site. However, additional capital was required and this fact was probably made known by an advertisement which caught the eye of James Haworth and by December 1919 he was a director with a £3,960 shareholding, on the understanding he introduced business.

By 1930, Mr A. H. Skinner had ceased to have a shareholding, leaving W. E. Bunney of 18 Knighton Church Road the majority shareholder with 7,440 shares and James Haworth still with 3,960. It is perhaps worth noting that at this time the James Haworth studio was moving to Soho Square and the trade depression was beginning to bite, which one imagined left no spare capital to be invested in buying A. H. Skinner's personal shares. At this time Mr F. S. King of 31 Chesterfield Road, Leicester became secretary and director with 150 shares.

WELFORD ROAD, LEICESTER.

Left: A first type of rotary lithographic printer, installed Fleet Street 1936.

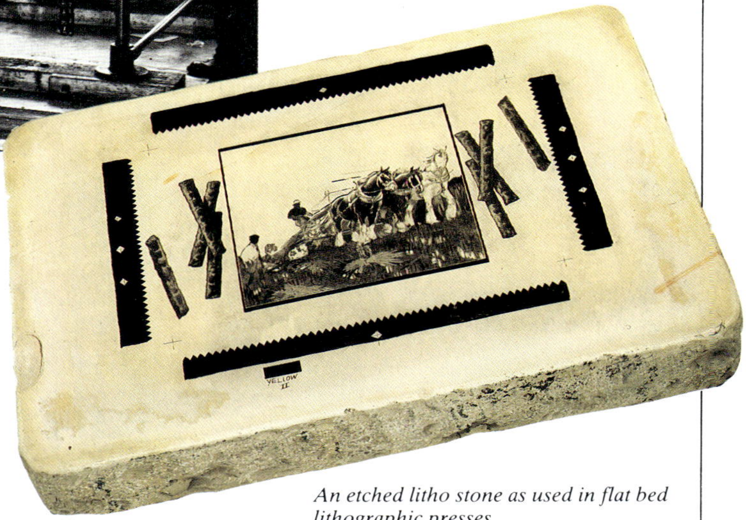

An etched litho stone as used in flat bed lithographic presses.

James Haworth, because of his early experience with lithographic printing at Alf Cooke, soon converted A. H. Skinner's printing to the lithographic process, if only to print the showcards and posters impractical by letterpress because of size. This change-over was certainly made by the mid-1920s the litho machines being flat beds which held a great litho printing stone of a size up to 42″ x 32″ x 3″, weighing 2 or 3 cwt and etched with the appropriate colour image that had to be printed. There could be up to 12 printings required and as the machines were not rotary (they were somewhat similar to today's litho proofing presses in operation), the work was slow to produce, but the quality was excellent.

However, colour letterpress printing was still maintained for biscuit catalogues and all forms of brochures.

In 1935, the first rotary litho machines were purchased. At the same time a plate department was established which refurbished the zinc flexible litho plates. This was by way of thousands of small glass balls shunted back and forth over the plates enabling the plates to be used for forthcoming printing of a new image.

Right: Regraining litho printing plates.

James Haworth 1922.
Portrait by Edwin Byatt, principal studio artist with James Haworth & Bro. Ltd., London.

By June, 1940 W. E. Bunney was perhaps getting to an age where he wished to retire and because of wartime uncertainties (it being Britain's darkest hour as far as the war was concerned), he wished to sell. Once again, because of trading conditions, money was short within James Haworth and Brother to buy his shares outright. Tillotsons Printers of Bolton whom John J. Haworth had got to know well in the 1930s for printing our carton orders, came in to help with the purchase and the shareholding became as follows:-

JAMES HAWORTH	5,470 SHARES
F. S. KING	1,380 SHARES
JOHN J. HAWORTH	500 SHARES
ALAN LORD (married Lucy Haworth)	500 SHARES
TILLOTSON & SONS LTD	2,600 SHARES
R. BROWN (Director Tillotson & Sons Ltd)	1,000 SHARES

When Holland was overrun by German forces in May 1940, a Dutch government in exile was formed in Britain. James Haworth were fortunate to win many print orders for distribution overseas and for their countrymen in the armed forces.

The company name was changed officially to James Haworth (Leicester) Ltd but was not a subsidiary of James Haworth & Brother in London.

Business during the rest of the war years continued in a satisfactory manner, thanks to Government requirements and printing in connection with exports and being more or less the official printers to the Dutch Government in exile.

A small selection of the many print items produced for many government departments during World War II.

Surprisingly the end of the war saw a downturn in printing turnover, there being shortages of paper and ink and little advertising print being required as almost everything produced could be sold without special effort to advertise.

The death in October, 1948 of James Haworth made John J. Haworth the main shareholder. He set about revitalising the Leicester works, making them more competitive, increasing sales and disposing of the letterpress plant. This latter move proved to be very fortuitous, as by 1960 letterpress had almost ceased to be a colour printing medium for advertising.

As a result of these changes, Tillotson & Sons, Mr F. S. King and Mr R. Brown were bought out in 1950.

Mr E. Reeve, Print Room Manager and Mr Leslie Green, Sales Manager both became General Managers in control of day-to-day management, but tight policy and monetary control was exercised by the directors and management at Rossendale Works.

THIS INDENTURE WITNESSETH THAT William Sharp, son of James Sharp, of his own free will and with his father's consent, doth put himself Apprentice to A.H. Skinner & Co. Ltd. Lithographic and Letterpress Printers of Fleet Street in the City of Leicester

to learn their Art trade or business and with them after the Manner of an Apprentice to serve from the twelfth day of June One Thousand Nine Hundred and Twenty until the twelfth day of June One Thousand Nine Hundred and Twenty Seven until the full End and Term of Seven Years and from thence next following to be fully complete and ended. During which Term the said Apprentice his Masters faithfully shall serve their secrets keep their lawful commands everywhere gladly do he shall do no damage to his said Masters nor so to be done of others but to the best of his power shall prevent or forthwith give warning to his said Masters of the same he shall not waste the Goods of his said Masters nor lend them unlawfully to any he shall not do any act whereby his said Masters may have any loss with their own goods or others during the said Term without Licence of his said Masters shall neither buy nor sell nor absent himself from his said Masters service day or night unlawfully But in all things as a faithful Apprentice he shall behave himself towards his said Masters and all theirs during the said Term AND the said A.H. Skinner & Company Limited in consideration of the Services of the said Apprentice agree to pay the following weekly wage viz. from the date of this Indenture until the Twelfth day of June One Thousand Nine Hundred and Twenty One being the first year the sum of fifteen shillings. The second year nineteen shillings. The Third Year Twenty Three Shillings. The Fourth Year Twenty Eight Shillings. The Fifth Year Thirty Three Shillings. The Sixth Year Thirty Eight Shillings. And during the Seventh and last year Forty Five Shillings to their said Apprentice in the Art trade or business of Lithographic Printing which they use by the best means that they can shall teach and Instruct or cause to be taught and instructed. The said James Sharp the father finding unto the said Apprentice sufficient Meat, Drink Lodging and all other Necessaries during the said Term of Seven Years provided always that no wages shall be payable under this Indenture during so long a time as the said Apprentice shall be absent from his said Masters whether from sickness or any other cause except by his said Masters permission.
AND for the true performance of all and every the said Covenants and Agreements either of the said Parties bindeth himself unto the other by these Presents IN WITNESS whereof the parties above named have hereunto set their Hands and Seals the Twentieth day of August in the Year of Our Lord One Thousand Nine Hundred and Twenty

William Sharp
James Sharp

Signed sealed and delivered by the above named in the presence of } *Frederick S. King*

p.p. A.H. SKINNER & CO. LIMITED
A.H. Skinner *Director*
W.E. Bunney *Director*

Above: Printing apprentice indenture for William Sharp at Fleet Street Works 1920.
William Sharp's nephew Jim, was in turn to become a printer at James Haworth in 1953, and later to become Sales Manager at Fleet Street in 1984.

Left: Fleet Street Works, 1988.

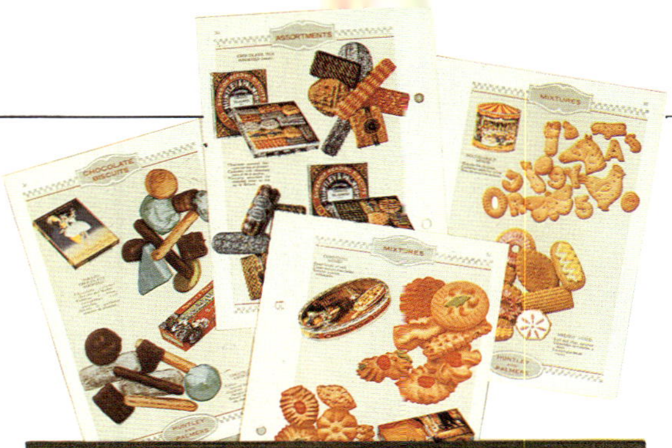

Examples of biscuit and cake catalogues. The original artwork throughout, hand drawn by James Haworth artists at the London studio. Four colour letterpress blocks produced from the artwork for use on letterpress machines both at Fleet Street Works and at L. Bell & Co.

In 1950, James Haworth & Brother was predominant in the field of designing and producing biscuit and chocolate company catalogues by letterpress printing.

Litho was yet to provide the colour detail for small areas of print. Rather than lose this good business, James Haworth & Brother entered into a most happy relationship with long-established printers L. Bell & Co of Guildhall Lane, Leicester, by which they undertook all our letterpress production and we in turn produced their litho requirements.

Letterpress printing requirements gradually declined and by 1970 had become non-existent. L. Bell & Co led by Horace Bell and Derek Hardy, moved their company over to litho, as a result the business connection was severed.

With the death in October 1974 of Horace Bell, together with the inability to cope with fierce competition, L. Bell & Co ceased to trade in 1976, Leicester thereby losing one of its most respected and long-established printers. Derek Hardy was invited to join James Haworth at Fleet Street and in 1987 was appointed a Senior Executive Director.

At Fleet Street, by 1953 all pre-1939 machinery had been replaced, but only with single colour versions, though two and four colour machines were beginning to be produced. However, John J. Haworth was of the opinion that our litho output would always be primarily geared to quality point-of-sale which meant large sheets and relatively short runs of 5 to 10,000 on average. Little did we know at the time that this decision was to cause a lot of financial headache in the 1960s.

Below: 1953. A new single colour 31" x 42½" lithographic print machine. The machine minder is Harold Williams who, in 1980, was appointed Deputy Managing Director within the James Haworth Group; with overall responsibility for operations at Fleet Street.

Below: A selection of paper biscuit tin labels produced from litho stones and early zinc plates.

1956. Colour separation camera.

In 1956 a self-contained repro department, directed by Arthur Almey, was formed. Arthur's skill and dedication was to be the foundation of a repro department with an inhouse reputation second to none. In 1988, led by Michael Ludlow, we are one of the very few printers in the British Isles maintaining its own repro facility as a complete service to its customers. It is equipped with the latest scanner and other repro techniques but can still undertake fine art reproduction by modern technology incorporated within a new direct camera.

1951. Visit to Fort Dunlop.
Second from right: John J. Haworth
First left: Leslie Green
Far right: the author.

James Haworth & Brother, from 1941 at Rossendale Works, Southgate, had established a litho reproduction company known as The Rossendale Photo Offset Company under the direction of Mr F. Crocker. This company was formed by him and some of his staff who had been bombed out of business in May 1941 from Central London — this fact applied to many other London repro houses. In order to safeguard print origination, John J. Haworth formed with Mr Crocker this new company, which existed until 1964, producing excellent work by the old hand re-touching method. But unless it could be re-equipped for more speedy reproduction (minimum time for a proof was 6 to 8 weeks!), its days were numbered. Mr Crocker died in 1961 and the company finally closed in 1964, all production being transferred to the much more up-to-date plant at Fleet Street and although all staff were invited to join the Leicester company — only one took up the offer.

Left and bottom right: Arthur Almey and the Fleet Street Reproduction Staff.

Bottom left: 1948-50. Miniatures used as stickers to company letters, illustrating work produced as showcards and posters. Their reproduction would at this time have been carried out by Rossendale-Photo-Offset at Rossendale Works, Southgate.

At the same time, Rossendale Works litho printing capacity was closed, having started in conjunction with the reproduction formation, and the machinery transferred to Leicester.

This loss of colour printing at Southgate was shortly to be replaced by screen printing, soon to be the vogue for point-of-sale advertising.

Returning to printing at Fleet Street – as indicated in previous chapters, the coming in 1956 of TV advertising, supermarket chains and new merchandising techniques, affected our output of print as a result of our commitment to point-of-sale production.

By instituting great economy of operations, we were still able to maintain a profit and secure print orders that perhaps should have gone to printers with 2 or 4 colour presses.

During the period 1960 - 1963 John J. Haworth retired from active directorship of Leicester and Southgate. Mr Leslie Green became overall executive director with Ray Thornton as deputy and H. W. Hoyland, print manager, Mr Reeve having retired early in 1953.

Above: 1951. Leicester print machine minders at the home of John J. Haworth, Southgate.

Centre left and bottom right: Print finishing, 1953.

Left: First of the four and two colour presses at Fleet Street.

Production efficiency became an increasing concern as we had basically not the right machinery, a complaint at this time which ran right through British industry. The banks would not lend finance even as in our case, to a profitable company, their thoughts being that small and medium printers were not viable and that we should amalgamate and realise our assets for the family. What terrible advice and an indictment of banks' policy of the late 60s which caused the closure of many firms who wished to re-equip to meet competition and buy new technology.

In 1967 Group control within the Company passed on to the grandson of the founder. We had to create a new team and give encouragement throughout the Company, which of course included Leicester. In 1968, changing branches within Lloyds Bank from Tottenham Court Road, London to Cockfosters, Barnet and acquiring a more supportive manager and regional office we were able to enter into 2 and 4 colour press fields. Immediate progress took place and by 1970 we were a very efficient print house once again.

Tribute should be made at this point to Harold Williams who joined us in 1941 as an apprentice. Appointed print manager in 1965 he dedicated himself to seeing that all the new machinery was able to pay for itself within a short time. Leslie Green, who had not enjoyed good health, retired in 1969 after more than 40 years, during which time he had successfully coped with the many problems that beset a printing company.

Above: Derek Hardy, standing, with Harold Williams, 1988.

A fundamental change occurred in 1967 when James Haworth (Leicester) became a wholly owned subsidiary of James Haworth Limited, Southgate, London. This might have meant tighter control from London, but it was decided that Fleet Street Print Works must be autonomous in its operation and be responsible for obtaining and servicing all its own litho printing business. This policy has enabled James Haworth (Leicester) to maintain a continuous success record which in 1988 spans 20 years of ever-increasing addition to plant and replacement of printing machinery.

In 1970 Harold Williams and Ray Thornton became Executive Directors. Ray retired in 1980 and his place was taken by Derek Hardy who is now Senior Executive Director. Harold Williams became Deputy Managing Director in 1980, heading the whole of the Leicester Company's activities and the senior member of the Group's Board of Directors.

With this brief narrative on Leicester, it should be recorded we have always enjoyed the very best of staff and union relations, often in difficult circumstances caused by outside influences beyond our control. We have never lost a day's work through bad industrial relations, a record of which we are extremely proud.

The skill of fine art reproduction.

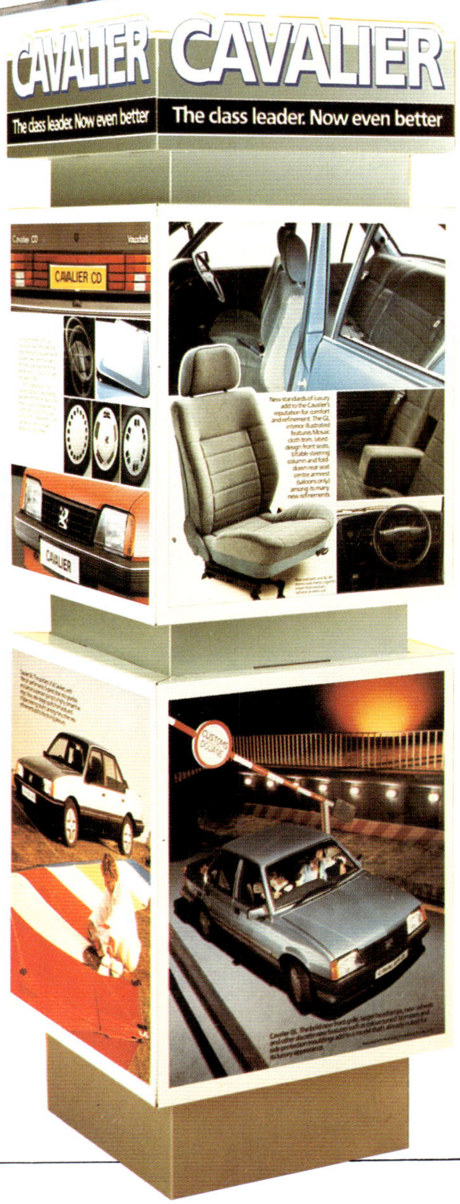

Reproduction and lithographic printing, James Haworth (Leicester) Ltd. Fleet Street Works, Leicester 1988.

James Haworth

ROSSENDALE WORKS

1935. Chase Side, Southgate, about to lose forever the look of a rural village. Entrance to Rossendale Works, centre left.

In two words, the factory's name - Rossendale Works - immediately conjures up Lancashire and its hard industry. This was, of course, the intention by James Haworth and son John J. who, in 1935, bought the various sites and buildings that had become available in the almost overnight transition of the old sleepy village of Southgate into a modern, well-to-do London suburb.

This change, good or bad, was brought about by the building of the tube line from Finsbury Park to Cockfosters, with a station, Southgate, of the latest modern design, right in the middle of the village.

The original landowners, houseowners and shopkeepers, along Chase Side in particular, saw their properties double in value. They became willing sellers to property developers, like Greater London Properties Limited, who bought up many of the old picturesque buildings of Chase Side, Southgate and built the shops for sale or letting. They remain more or less the same today, though with many changes of ownership since they were built in 1938.

1988, Southgate. Last vestiges of a quiet London suburb about to go with the commencement at the base of the picture of a large Asda supermarket. Rossendale works outlined in white.

1930. The entrance of what was to become Rossendale Works.

The site of Rossendale Works, in 1935, lay behind what had been approximately No's 60 to 90 Chase Side. The previous owner, in the main, of this site, including the cottages 60-74 Chase Side, had been Charles Jacob Newby, whose great grandson John is still, in 1988, very much in business as builders in Chase Road, Southgate.

From 1888 parcels of land had been leased and then sold to John Eaton for his expanding stabling, horse carriage building and repair business, and with the progress of the combustion engine, into repair and body building shops for cars.

John Eaton's business had been prosperous in serving all the landed gentry whose fine houses and estates surrounded Southgate up to 1930.

Our small boardroom is housed today in which was John Eaton's, forge, this is one of the oldest buildings still standing from Southgate's past.

John Eaton's family as a result of the increase in land values, were ready to sell to the land developers, who wanted shops and flats on the road frontages only and were not interested in "back land". They would not make the same mistake in 1988!

Southgate at the turn of the century.

James and John J. Haworth had known and used John Eaton's services since they first came to Southgate in 1906. It is perhaps no surprise therefore that they thought the land, with two well-built large repair shops, would make an ideal place in which to produce display material and calendars for which they were now obtaining large orders. Leicester could not cope with these orders and the majority of work was placed with London trade houses.

James Haworth & Brother Limited had already rented a portion of Eaton's as storage from 1930.

With great foresight, the Company purchased between 15th March 1935 and 27th October 1936, 3 parcels of land belonging to John Eaton. They also acquired a large section of land running up to behind No. 90 Chase Side and a portion between the allotments at the rear of Southgate recreation ground. Both portions belonged to Greater London Properties, who could make a quick profit by selling what was to them useless back land!

One section was indeed useless, i.e., that between the allotments. Even in 1937 there were planning restrictions, and building between allotments was certainly not allowed. The land was sold on 31st March 1937 to Southgate Borough Council for £4,000 for additional allotments, a use for which the land remains today, despite the pressures of developers to buy the allotments.

The money was immediately put to good use by James Haworth to build a 4,500 sq. ft. factory building, which was soon to employ some 60 ladies assembling display material and calendars.

The area that had been John Eaton's garage was filled with heavy machinery of two mounters and several platens. These were used for affixing the printed paper sheets to cardboard, then cutting to shape on the platens.

To carry out this manufacture, a wholly-owned subsidiary company was formed called The London Showcard Company, with no mention of the family connection. After 1950 the name was quietly dropped and today it exists only as a company-owned name.

The times, life and work, over nearly a 50 year period at Rossendale Works, are best described by Eric Latham, who joined The London Showcard Company in 1939 and retired in August 1988, after nearly 50 years service! Who writes:-

"I left school in August 1937, at the age of fourteen and started work at a local firm of photographers employed in the picture framing works. My wage was 10/- (50p) per week. I stayed there for nearly two years. On the "fatherly" advice of my older brother (we had no father at home) I looked for a better job.

There were two vacancy advertisements in the local paper; one at the Standard Telephone and Cable Company and one at a showcard company.

On a Saturday afternoon I cycled to S.T.C. but the size of the building scared me away. On the Sunday morning I decided to find The London Showcard Company at Rossendale Works. I was not at all familiar with Old Southgate or the name of the firm.

When I arrived at the closed gates I stood looking for several minutes. I can remember seeing a 3-D showcard on the window ledge. Unlike my visit to S.T.C. I somehow felt this is for me. On the following morning, I ventured down the yard and through the main door. After knocking at the inner door, a small sliding hatch opened, a face appeared from within. After stating the reason for my presence, I was told to wait outside. A few minutes later I was approached by a rather short plump man who gave me a pleasant smile and introduced himself as Mr James Haworth, the proprietor of the firm. He interviewed me and told me he would pay me a better wage than the one I was receiving of 10/-, he would pay me 12/6 pw and asked if I could start work the following day. I was then ushered into the "top factory". This was to let me see the type of work carried out. I was overwhelmed by the number of benches and all the activity of the young girls and women who occupied them. Some of the young girls working nearest to me seemed to find the time to give each other a nudge, to look at the "new boy".

Examples of cardboard shop window displays produced at Rossendale Works, 1937, as illustrated on the company's ink pen blotters.

I accepted the job and started work at "Rossendale Works" the following week (June 1939). I was first employed mainly in the machine rooms loading and unloading the machine tables and stripping.

There was at this time two machine rooms of identical layout. One was always referred to as the "garage", the other machine room was in a more up to date building which was much larger. Both rooms had identical machine layout. Each had a Ratcliffe mounter, one guillotine, two platens and two shear benches. The "garage" also had a tinplate varnishing machine which occupied the full length of the room along one side and there was a long conveyor belt. There were no heated drying ovens, only a long wooden construction consisting of a multitude of narrow shelves. Work was taken from the belt and placed into the shelves to be left to dry.

There were no connecting doors for direct access between these two machine rooms. The chap in charge of the platen, Doug Davies, (recently died aged 73) spent a lot of his time going to and from one room to the other attending to the machines, and with no intercom system it meant an operator requiring assistance would have to walk from one room to the other to ask for assistance and then for both persons to walk back to the other room. One wall of one room consisted entirely of heavy sliding doors, one section of which had to be moved to enter or to leave the room. The "garage" room had a barn door, it must have been at least 10ft high and 4ft wide and had a lift-up latch.

As well as an outer wall of sliding doors this more up to date room also had an inner dividing wall of sliding doors made in the same manner. Within this partitioned area a further small room was partitioned to form the accounts office. Apart from the office, the remaining area was known as the Calendar Room and was managed by a Mr Scott.

There was no mechanical means of conveying the work from the machine rooms to the top factory. There was one trolley which was used for removing loads from the front of the mounting machines. It was not hydraulic, so the load had to be elevated manually by pressing down on a lever which also served as a handle for pulling and steering. A latch which held the load in the elevated position would sometimes slip, causing the load to drop suddenly and the handle would then fly up with enormous force. This "truck" was used to convey loads of work up the yard.

The yard was completely un-made, no surface at all, just rough stones and ruts. We often used this truck to convey full loads of work up this yard. It would take four or five of us to man-handle the load, often using crowbars to ease the wheels out of ruts.

Work commenced sharp at eight o'clock each morning. There was no clocking-in, each department had its own staff book in which we all had to sign our names and the time of our arrival. We worked a 47¾ hour week. Monday to Friday 8am to 6pm with lunchtime from 1.00-2.15pm. In the morning there was a ten minute break but no break in the afternoon period. Saturday hours were 8am-12 noon. We were paid on Saturdays at twelve o'clock and had to queue up at the accounts office where our pay packets were passed through the little sliding hatch. If you were last in the queue it would sometimes be 12.30 before getting away. The morning ten minute break was not a tea break. Tea making only started when members of the studio came from Soho to Southgate in the early days of the war years. However, we were able to have a slice of fruit cake priced at one penny a slice. This cake came direct from Huntley & Palmers in the form of a large square slab which was then cut into slices and was often dry and stale.

Annual summer holidays with pay did not exist and neither did sick pay, and overtime was not allowed except on very rare occasions and without any increase in the hourly rate. James Haworth, the Managing Director was generally referred to as the "old man", not necessarily disrespectfully. During my first few days I was told the "old man is alright but he has tantrums when things were not going right". Looking back with hind-sight this is understandable, for Rossendale Works was no doubt struggling to get established during the period of unrest in Europe and the shadow of war yet again.

Specialised hand work was done in this department carried out by six to eight ladies who produced quality bevelled edged calendars with turn over edges, also covers for the Radio Times, binders for magazines and journals of various kinds. This work demanded the use of nimble hands. For one to be selected from the top factory benches to go and work in Mr Scott's calendar room was always considered to be an honour.

The top factory, built in 1937, was always a hive of activity with approximately 20 benches with women and young girls at each of them. A large percentage of struts in those days had to be corded for hanging, the hole punching for this was done by foot operated machines and the stringing or cording was done on two rather complicated Swiss machines which automatically threaded the cord from a reel through the two holes in the strut, tied a knot and then cut the cord from the reel. These machines were constantly in use and so were the three wire stitching machines and rimmers. Much of the finished work would leave the factory in railway containers which we had to hand load by forming a "human chain".

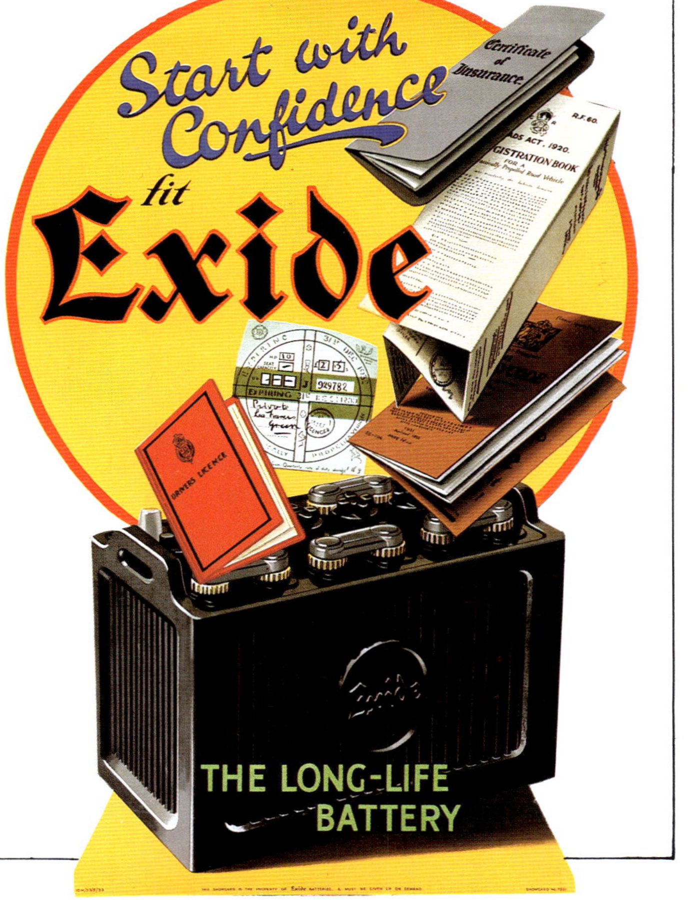

James Haworth had only a small office in the corner of the top factory situated where the Reception is now. He would arrive at about nine o'clock each morning and stay for an hour or so and then after making his presence known in all departments he would depart for Soho Square in his Armstrong Siddeley saloon driven by his chauffeur, Ted Williams. When petrol was in short supply in the war years the Armstrong Siddeley was replaced with an Austin Seven saloon. James Haworth would return again in the late afternoon and usually take another look around before going home to "Broad Oak". His presence in the factory always created a certain amount of tension. He never accepted the fact that people could work hard and talk at the same time. To talk and laugh as we worked would cause him to raise his voice and to tell us to "get on". Consequently if we knew he was still on the premises one felt the need to be constantly looking over one's shoulder. When he departed for Soho everyone became relaxed and the work would go on just the same.

Arnold Haworth was the Works Manager, although a nephew, he always had to address James Haworth as sir, as indeed we all did.

One of the very first things that impressed me was the friendliness of everyone and how well everyone seemed to know each other despite the fact there must have been over 100 employees. As time passed I learned that many of the people knew each other outside of work and many came from the local council housing estate, had grown up together and become related by marriage. There were the Cole brothers, Jim and Jack, Eric and Norman Cobbold, Connie, Gwen and Geoffrey Linnet, Gladys, Marjorie and Elsie Fields and a host of others including cousins and nieces.

I was taught to operate a platen "on the run" during my first few weeks and started straight away to take an interest in the making-ready of them and hoped one day I might be given the opportunity to make-ready on my own. That opportunity was to come sooner than expected. War now seemed inevitable and most of the men were of "military age".

Below: Rossendale Works, top factory, 1939.

Below: An Armstrong Siddeley, similar to that used by James Haworth, driven by his chauffeur. James, despite his desire to do most things himself, never learnt to drive a car.

Above: Rossendale Works staff clearing up after the fire on Sunday 27th August, 1939.

Below: The fire still smouldering and attended by firemen on the Monday.

During the last weeks of August 1939 I was staying at my uncle's house at Oakwood (Enfield West) and from an upstairs window I saw a large column of smoke rising in the direction of Southgate. This happened on Sunday 27th August, and in the morning on my way to work I met one of the young girls from work; she too had seen the smoke and heard there had been a big fire at Southgate. We turned into the yard and saw a group of our people just standing and staring in silence towards the "garage". We both looked at each other and feared the worst. It was a sickening sight. Half the lower factory was completely burned out, a tangled mass of conduit and bare wires, leaving stacks of charred cardboard and the machines barely visible beneath the mass of charred wood and buckled iron work. As I looked closer into the mess I could see the remains of the job I had run on the platen that week. I felt sad, it had been my first printed job, a showcard for Palmolive. The enormous task of clearing the area began a couple of days later and was the topic of conversation for the rest of that week until the following weekend when on Sunday September 3rd, the declaration of war was made. Work had already begun on digging an air-raid shelter and now it was "all hands to the pump" to complete it as well as continuing the clearing work following the fire.

Rebuilding of the "garage" started before the area was completely cleared. Harry 'deafy' Dean did the bricklaying, Mr Vineis manufactured all the angle-iron roof supports and the chauffeur did the re-wiring. Machinery was examined by a Crossland fitter and "blessed" safe to use. Later we had the job of cleaning and painting them. Much of the soiled cardboard was used after the charred edges had been guillotined off, a filthy job which lasted many weeks. We worked in shifts over a longer working day to achieve the repairs.

SOUTHGATE FIRE DAMAGE RUNS INTO THOUSANDS OF POUNDS

Sunday Blaze Ruins Factory Building And Machinery

Fire Fighters Get Full Praise Marks

Mr. James Haworth's Concern For His Employees

Damage to the extent of £5,000 to £6,000 was caused by fire on Sunday afternoon at the Rossendale Works, Chase Side, Southgate, premises of the London Showcard Mounting Company owned by James Haworth and Bro. (Ltd.), Designers and Printers, 21 Soho Square, London.

The site includes three associated buildings, one of which, the machine-room—containing valuable mounting and cutting machinery—was gutted. Each of the others was slightly damaged.

The fire originated in, and was practically confined to, a building which, fifty or more years ago, was used as a place of worship. The structure, originally known as the "tin chapel," formerly stood in Farm Road, Southgate.

When St. Andrew's Church, in Chase Side, was built the old building, which had been purchased by the late Mr. John Eaton, the well-known jobmaster, was rebuilt in Chase Side, where for many years it was used to house his carriages and horse-brakes.

The premises were taken over by the London Showcard Mounting Company about four years ago, when the enterprise was started with a handful of employees.

Today the firm employ over 120 people and efforts are being made to provide them all with work during the rebuilding made necessary by the fire.

The outbreak attracted considerable attention in Southgate, flames shooting sheetlike to a height of many feet while over the area hung a pall of black smoke.

Southgate Fire Brigade (with Mr. A. J. Still, O.B.E., in charge) attended with both pumps and the utility van, and as a precautionary measure Enfield Fire Brigade were summoned.

The local brigade, which had the support of about twenty members of Southgate Auxiliary Fire Service, did excellent work, special appreciation being voiced by competent observers.

The brigade had the fire under control within the hour, though the pumps remained until about six o'clock. The utility van left about two hours later.

The call to the Southgate Brigade was first made by Mr. Herb. W. Newby, of Verandah Cottage, Chase Road, Southgate, who was himself a member of the Brigade before and during the war.

He was in his study at twenty minutes to three when his attention was drawn to a mass of flame and smoke, apparently coming from the yard of Messrs. Newby Bros., Ltd., builders, which adjoins his property and connects with the rear of a strip of property in Chase Side.

His call was received in the watch room of the Fire Brigade at 2.42, a pump and utility van leaving immediately.

In an interview with the "Gazette," Mr. Newby said: "At first I thought the yard was on fire, but after the call was made I found it was not so—although it was perilously near.

"The showcard works abut on our premises. When I first saw it there was a mass of flame with a huge volume of smoke pouring out. Sparks drifted over the yard, one igniting the sun blind over the glass roof of my study and burning the canvas."

BRIGADE WERE SMART.

As an old member of the Brigade, Mr. Newby was especially appreciative of the promptness with which they arrived and the efficiency with which they got to work. One pump operated from Chase Road, a length of hose with a branch pipe and two deliveries being taken through his grounds to play on the flames from the opposite side.

Southgate's second pump was sent for, this also being operated from Chase Side, Southgate. One came under the direction of Chief Officer A. J. Still and the other under Second Officer George Walton.

With the Southgate contingent were a number of A.F.S. men, some of whom had been on duty in the watch room. Others came along to help.

The showcard works are situate in a cul-de-sac behind shops and flats and comprise two factories, one of which is divided into two sections. It was in one of these, in which cutting and mounting machinery is operated, that the outbreak was centred.

TWO-WAY ATTACK.

The fire fighters worked under handicap. While playing on the blaze from the Chase Side angle they were water-swept by their colleagues on the other side! But the double-sided attack was a sound operation.

One fireman told the "Gazette" that the blaze was the fiercest he had ever encountered.

Tons of cardboard were destroyed.

The roof of the building collapsed.

On Monday the "Gazette" interviewed Mr. James Haworth, who said that he estimated the damage at £5,000 to £6,000.

"The cause of the outbreak is a mystery," he said. "I was in the premises at 8.30 on Saturday evening, when everything was in perfect order, and then on Sunday afternoon I was called here again . . ."

Asked whether the fire would mean temporary loss of work by employees, Mr. Haworth said, "I hope not. I am trying to arrange for duplicate work during the day, and to keep employed as many as I can. There may be difficulties, but I want to do what I can to help them. I may put on two shifts daily instead of the usual one."

Mr. Haworth added, "I want to pay special tribute to the officers and the men of Southgate Fire Brigade. They were splendid. When they arrived here the place was one huge flare, but they confined the outbreak to one area and it was not long before they had the flames under control. All praise is due to them."

Two residents in Chase Side state that there was a strong smell of "scorched paper" as early as 7.20 a.m. on Sunday.

So dense was the crowd of people in Chase Side during the early part of the fire that traffic was congested. Neighbouring streets, too, were crowded with people who were brought out of doors by the smell and the volumes of thick smoke.

FROM CRICKET MATCH.

One of the "Gazette" reporters was called from almost somnolent contemplation of a lazy cricket match at Oakthorpe Road to accompany another member of the staff to the scene of the outbreak.

At Chase Side we greeted an old friend, ex-Police-sergeant Fowler, who retired from Winchmore Hill some months ago, but who, responding to the national call, had again put himself into uniform.

It was the first day of his new period of duty, but he looked as neat and smart as ever. During the afternoon we saw other ex-officers on duty again, apparently quite "at home" despite years of retirement.

We were allowed to enter the factory premises and at once was apparent the fine work already accomplished by Southgate Fire Brigade in confining the fire to one building.

This building, by the way, had history. Mr. Ernie Eaton, formerly of Messrs. John Eaton, the well-known garage proprietors of Southgate and Palmers Green, reminded us of the "tin chapel" that used to stand in Farm Road, Southgate, formerly known as Church Road.

THEIR TEACHER.

This was the original St. Andrew's Church, and he and other members of his family, as boys attended Sunday School there under the spiritual instruction of Miss Bonham, who still lives in Southgate.

Mr. John Eaton bought the old chapel and used it as a carriage store. When the church was built in Chase Side, the firm pulled down the chapel in Farm Road and rebuilt it for garage purposes on the site where fire attacked and destroyed it on Sunday afternoon.

To return to the story. In the main factory building we found glass splintered and broken, some damage having been caused by water. Fire fighters were still playing on flames that burst unexpectedly in parts of the now gutted building nearby.

Hoses had been brought into action from three directions, two from Chase Side and one through the grounds of Mr. Herb. W. Newby's house in Chase Road.

Here we were able to climb to the top of a shed in Newby Bros.' yard, adjoining the fire, and from that elevation take a picture or two.

CHARRED BLOCKS.

Considerable piles of valuable paper and card were charred and blackened blocks. The thick wall dividing the factory premises from those of Messrs. Newby had undoubtedly prevented the pread of the fire to what would have been serious proportions.

Second Officer Walton of the Southgate Brigade spoke to us and was warm in praise of the help given by the auxiliary firemen.

Down below, Capt. A. J. Still directed operations which at this stage were mainly concerned with pulling down dangerous posts and removing corrugated iron from places where the fire might still lurk.

CAPT. A. J. STILL (bottom right) directs operations while hoses play. Note the tin-hatted auxiliary in the background.

Collapsed In Tube

It is understood that no inquest will be held into the circumstances of the death of Mr. Albert Thomas Teasell, of 11a Telford Road, New Southgate, who collapsed in a London-bound train on the Piccadilly Railway on Tuesday morning and died shortly afterwards in Turnpike Lane Station.

Mr. Teasell, who was 69 years of age, had complained to other passengers of feeling unwell and they did all they could to assist him.

Southgate ambulance was called to the station at 10.40 a.m., but when they arrived the unfortunate man was dead. It is understood that he died from natural causes.

The Late Dr. Edwin W. Goble

Here is an excerpt from a tribute paid to the late Dr. Edwin W. Goble in the current issue of the St. Paul's, Winchmore Hill, magazine:—

" . . . Dr. Goble lived for his work and his patients, and, as he would have wished, actually died in harness.

"He had a heart of gold, and was always generously kind to those who had not the means of some of their neighbours. Though not having been a patient himself of Dr. Goble, the writer has always understood how greatly appreciated were Dr. Goble's medical services, and with what gentleness and skill he would attend his patients, never sparing himself when duty called or sickness beckoned him to a distant bedside.

"We know that this opportunity may be taken of assuring Mrs. Goble and Miss Marion Goble of the warmest sympathy of all at St. Paul's, Winchmore Hill, in their sudden and tragic bereavement."

THE TROUBLE: WH[...] ON IN SOUT[...]

Latest Developme[...] And Inform[...]

ALL-TOGETHER MOVES AT TOWN HALL

These lines were written on Monday, when the international issue was still very much in the balance, and whatever may be the position at the time of the publication of the "Gazette" following the turn of events on subsequent days, they will serve to show that the municipal authorities and their staffs, together with the members of the splendid voluntary organisations that have been got together, have spared no effort which would help to make Southgate prepared for any eventuality that may have to be faced.

* * *

The first thing that strikes the attention is the entirely different atmosphere that prevails at the Town Hall and in the borough generally compared with that of a year ago.

* * *

Whereas then, however well-intentioned the ideas, matters were literally at "sixes and sevens," the succeeding twelve months have resulted in an organisation and co-ordination of efforts that now prove to have been well worth the while of those men and women, led by the salaried staffs, who have given their time and energies to preparing themselves for A.R.P. service if the need should arise.

* * *

A representative of the "Gazette" paid a visit to the Town Hall this morning and found everybody hard at work, without a moment to spare, but with a calm purpose and organisation behind their comings and goings which gives a heartening indication of the manner in which news of the worst is likely to be received in this borough.

AVOIDING WA[...]

The general idea of the scop[e of the] work that is taking place [may be] gathered from what the Town C[lerk] (Gordon H. Taylor) said to our [represen]tative.

"We are trying to get ready [and we] would go—if it comes," he said. [There] is plenty to do, but we are try[ing to do] nothing that is likely to become [...] We are not blindly optimistic, b[ut on the] other hand we are not unnecessa[rily] ... and we do not want [...] ment" that may subsequently [...] waste expenditure.

"As a matter of fact, most [of the] material that has been purchas[ed up to] this point can be put to use [in other] directions if no emergency shou[ld arise."]

* * *

Our reporter met Councillo[r] Abercromby (chairman of the A.R.P. Committee) who told [him that] since Wednesday of last week [the Con]trol Centre at the Town Hall [has been] manned day and night in ca[se of any] surprise happening.

Councillor Abercromby, [Councillor] George Peverett (chairman of t[he] Health Committee) and Alderm[an] Barber (Chief A.R.P. Warden) [have been] in regular attendance with th[e heads] of their respective organisations.

* * *

Members of the Town Hall [staff, in]cluding the Town Clerk and th[e Medical] Officer of Health, were called [back from] their holidays so that nothing [should be] left undone that could be acc[omplished] in the preliminary stages.

* * *

The public have no doubt be[en able to] notice for themselves that work [has been] proceeding during the week-en[d upon] wardens' posts in various par[ts of the] borough, upon trenches for the [use of the] public, and upon the Decont[amination] Centre in Bowes Road.

* * *

MAYOR'S RET[...]

Various useful conferences [have been] held, and the members of th[e] organisation have met their me[n] and made arrangements for [...] their personnel if the necessity [arises].

Incidentally, it should be [...] that the Mayor of Southgate ([Councillor] Robert Grant) has voluntarily [returned] from holiday to be in touch w[ith every]thing that is happening.

* * *

The Medical Officer of Healt[h (Dr.] Clunie Harvey) is full of thar[...]

THIS LOCAL PICTURE a[...] epitomises the national a[...] preparedness.

staff of the Town Hall and the [members] of the voluntary organisations f[or what] has been achieved during the [...] "They have been at it," he sa[id, "from] early morning until late at ni[ght."]

* * *

From now onwards until furt[her notice,] he told the "Gazette," the us[e of chil]dren's respirators will be demon[strated at] all the Maternity and Child W[elfare Cen]tres in the borough. Owing t[o the fact] that Broomfield House has bee[n taken over] by the R.A.M.C., all clinics [...]

THE SHOW GOES ON!

Calm Counsel Leads to Unanimous Decision: Visit The Horticultural Display In Broomfield Park This Week-end!

Early this week there were doubts as to whether it would be advisable to go with the arrangements for the Southgate and District Horticultural Society's eighth annual show and fete fixed for today (Friday) and Saturday, in Broomfield Park.

On Monday evening the Executive Committee and officers held an emergency meeting, and unanimously agreed to carry on. We congratulate them heartily.

This decision sets an eample to the community; and we hope that a triumph will result from this exhibition of cool, calm judgment.

On with the show!

It is felt that money will be lost (of course considerable expenditure had been incurred before the crisis came), but the society have confidence in their ability to meet liabilities.

So, with the good wishes and backing of His Worship the Mayor (Councillor Robert Grant, J.P.), who is a warm supporter of the "carry on" spirit, the decision was made.

MAYOR WILL HOLD RECEPTION

The gates are open to-day (Friday) at 3 o'clock, and immediately the Mayor will hold a reception, which it is expected will be attended by Mayors of other Boroughs and Chairmen of District Councils.

At 3.30 Cr. Robert Grant will open the show, which on this first day will close at 8.30.

On Saturday, from 11 o'clock till 1, the marquees will be open to members only on production of their membership tickets. The general public will be admitted from 2 o'clock onwards.

A feature of the afternoon will be a mounted gymkhana and there will also be a variety programme presented by pupils of the Morton-Joy School of Dancing.

At 7 the Mayoress will present cups and medals won in the horticultural show, and later there will be public dancing and probably a display of fireworks. If this item is included all noisy pyrotechnics will be excluded. Of course, there will be the usual fun fair.

The Southgate show is well worth a visit. The produce of local horticulturists is invariably of a high standard of excellence, and the trade shows have increased in variety and importance with the years.

The "Gazette" was told on Tuesday that entries were being made steadily, and though they may be down on last year—only because of the circumstances—a comprehensive show of exhibits is assured. A big improvement will be seen in the children's classes, for which there will be at least 200 exhibits.

Mr. W. C. Ludlow, in his first year as hon. secretary, has commanded the respect and appreciation of all who have made contact with him and he speaks gratefully of the loyal co-operation of everyone concerned in the progress of the Society.

As to admittance. A programme (purchasable at newsagent's, price 6d.) will admit free on one or either of the two days. Otherwise the entrance fee is one shilling; after 6 o'clock 6d. No re-admission—unless you pay! Children will be admitted half-price.

Be natural! Visit Southgate's show!

THE LATE MR. ERNEST H. SAUNDERS

Death And Funeral Of Former Southgate Resident

Prior to the burial at Southgate Old Cemetery on Wednesday, a service was held at Christ Church, Southgate, for the late Mr. Ernest Henry Saunders, a former

ham H. Thorp, Mr. Hugh Galbraith, Staff of Thorp, Saunders and Thorp, Mr. H. C. Chambers and Mr. G. W. Drake, Mr. C. W. Carter Page, Mr. R. H. Tellgate, the Harvey Family, Mr. and Mrs. G. P. Welsh and Barbara, and many others.

Mayor's Engagements

Friday.—The Mayor will open the Southgate Horticultural Society Show in

Two-Day [...] and [...]

The first few months of the war seemed uneventful; work continued in much the same way, and then came the first "call-up" of our staff. My foreman, Doug Davies, and the van driver Tom Brand, I think were the first to go. One went into the Kings Royal Rifles, the other into The Rifle Brigade. After Doug's departure, James Haworth told me I must now take over the platens. The opportunity of making-ready had arrived. My wage until now had been £2 p.w; at the end of my first week of being in charge, my wage had risen to £3, the same amount as Doug Davies had earned. I felt highly honoured.

Arnold Haworth was exempted from call-up for a limited period because of his managerial position, but others continued to go and it wasn't long before everyone had gone leaving those of us too young for military service to "carry on in their footsteps".

The air-raid shelter was situated near to where the boiler house yard gates are now and ran parallel to the perimeter wall. It was constructed of steel roller shuttering supported by inverted "U" shaped angle irons and covered with concrete with two thirds of the construction being below ground level. I can recall the very first time we used the shelter, the siren had sounded and we went in. Nobody really knew what to expect. We were all told to keep quiet so that the sound of approaching aircraft could be heard. Arnold Haworth who stayed outside to act as "spotter" thought it a good idea to climb a tall pear tree situated nearby so that he could "observe approaching enemy aircraft coming from the east coast direction". So up the tree went Arnold complete with the helmet and a hand bell. Several of us stood in the shelter entrance watching. Just as Arnold had reached the top of the tree someone said "look out 'ere comes the old man". We all stayed out of his sight but watched. He stood for a while looking skyward, raised his trilby hat to scratch his head and suddenly caught sight of Arnold. He bellowed at the top of his voice "You fool! what are you doing up there?". We stifled our laughter and went further into the shelter followed a few moments later by a red faced Arnold.

Doug Davies 1939.

Previous page: Fire report in the local Palmers Green and Southgate Gazette, Friday 1st September, 1939. World War II was about to start two days later, preparations for which made for most of the remaining news.

During the Blitz of course we were having several air-raid warnings a day and once had a "dog-fight" of aircraft high above the factory. All-night fire watch was manned by all male staff including Mr Shaw and Alfred Buck who by now had joined us from Soho. Mr Richard Haworth (Dick to all of us) did regular night duty every night along with two of us. There were three make-shift beds in the shelter and a small coke fuelled combustion stove. Some nights we had to keep all night vigil because of the incendiary bomb raids on London. This brought about heavy anti-aircraft fire as enemy aircraft passed over, and the following day would start with everyone trying to "spot a new hole" - holes in the asbestos roofing caused by pieces of falling shrapnel. These holes were hastily repaired by a tough little guy named Percy Lack. On one occasion when going about his task on the roof, the siren sounded and in his haste to get off the roof he put a foot wrong and fell through it, still clasping a bucket in each hand, landing on a bench beneath causing alarm and havoc among the ladies. He calmly walked away unhurt.

One night as a result of heavy bombing of the East End of London bus loads of evacuees were brought into East Barnet. They arrived with their only possessions which were the clothes they were wearing and some of these were night clothes. Members of families had separated and did not know if those not present were dead or alive or still buried among the debris of their bombed homes. They were housed in a church hall and local peoples' homes who were kind enough to give them shelter. Later they were moved into empty houses around the district.

Employment was found for them and several came to Rossendale Works, and we were informed in advance they would be coming. There had been some adverse publicity in the press just prior to the war about the East-Enders and the slums, so we were all a little apprehensive when we were told they were joining us.

However, when they arrived, all young girls, we did our best to make them welcome and in a very short time we found them to be altogether different from the impressions we had of them. They were a down to earth bunch, but all so friendly and cheerful in spite of their recent experiences. Several of them came from the one family, "the Tingeys". Many of our young girls and women brought into work articles of their unwanted clothing to give to them which they readily accepted and were so grateful and appreciative.

I had been told in the beginning that James Haworth had a son but was not often seen at Southgate. It was several weeks before I saw him and then I did not at first know who he was. I had passed a smartly dressed man in the yard accompanied by an equally smartly dressed small boy wearing a blue school cap. A little later someone asked me "Had I seen the old man's son and grandson in the yard?".

As the war drew on materials were getting very hard to get, work became scarcer and staff too had diminished as many had gone into munitions and other forms of "war work".

A method was discovered for splitting sheets of cardboard through the centre. This work was carried out at a tanners who were used to splitting cow hides. The finished surface of the board was rough and uneven and the thickness varied and caused endless problems for the mounting machines and platens. However, it helped us to keep the wheels in motion. We also had our own way of re-cycling unused, unwanted showcards by removing their struts and over mounting with lining paper and new prints. These surplus stock showcards came from various customers as the products advertised by the original showcards were no longer available.

Arnold Haworth was eventually called up for war service, exemption was not being granted again. We were told by James Haworth that his son would be taking charge and we were to call him "Mr John". This was to be the beginning of a rather unique "boss and worker" relationship which created a strong sense of loyalty among those of us who worked with him and for him, a loyalty which was to last for many years.

By this time my turn was drawing near for call-up. Mr John was now taking an interest in the work on the factory floor. By the time I went into the army in September 1942 he had already been driving the van on many occasions clad in a boilersuit.

On one occasion I can recall him arriving at his office in the morning wearing a smart suit and bowler hat. There was an urgent delivery to be made; he removed his jacket and donned his boilersuit and climbed hurriedly into the van, still wearing his bowler hat. It wasn't until he spotted us slapping our heads that he realised what he had done. He drove off laughing and waving to us with the bowler.

For the rest of the war years and during my absence, Lily who I married in 1951 has told me Mr John Haworth continued to work with the remaining staff helping with Phil Hall on the mounter (until his call-up) and assisting on the platens but his favourite machine was the tinplate varnishing machine. Although he worked alongside us in this way, no-one ever overlooked the fact that first and foremost he was the boss. He was greatly respected and we always felt he likewise respected us. If he asked for extra effort from us for any reason there would be no hesitation in giving it; everyone seemed to derive pleasure from pleasing him. It was a relationship in absolute contrast to the one we had with his father and it was known that he was aware of it and knew it to be beneficial to all. He had noticed how uneasy people became whenever James Haworth came on the scene.

The top factory was requisitioned for war production and with the little staff now left - including three members from the studio, - had to do the best they could with benches in the lower factory, working alongside the machinery. Peggy Hall (nee Peggy Baker) was called up for munitions work, Phil Hall went into the army, which now left only Lily, Evelyn Mower and Connie Linnet of the original staff, although Connie was later evacuated. They were assisted by one or two boys, school leavers and a few part-time ladies. The loading and unloading of vans was carried out by these folk. Lily and Evelyn Mower were the mainstays during the later period, but they too were eventually twice called-up for war work but exemptions were applied for and granted in each case. On the third call-up exemptions were not at first granted. Both Lily and Evelyn received their documents and travel warrants etc. to go to somewhere in Gloucestershire. On the very morning they were due to leave home, Mr John received further exemption papers in the post. He hurriedly went to their homes just in time to prevent them leaving on their journey. Further exemptions were granted on a six monthly basis after inspections had been made by officials of the type of work done by Lily, Evelyn and Mr John.

My own call-up came exactly one month after my 19th birthday, September 17th 1942. I did my infantry training at Hyderabad Barracks, Colchester with the Gloucestershire Regiment whose officers and N.C.O.'s were veterans of Dunkirk. Whilst there I was selected for the artillery and did my gunnery training at Deepcut, near Aldershot, and then posted to an "Ack-Ack" Regiment serving around the Harwich area, but not for too long.

I was soon posted overseas, to Algiers, North Africa, and then across the water on the invasion of Italy, landing at Salerno beaches with the 56th London Infantry division attached to the American 5th Army. Later in the campaign we made another landing behind the enemy at Anzio. During these times my memories of work at Southgate seemed very distant. So much had gone on, and was going on out there and the future, if there was to be one for me, seemed very obscure, but sometimes when things were less hazardous, I would try to recapture memories of work and wished I could go back to those days.

Lily wrote to me frequently and kept me in touch with events at home and at work. I was still in Italy when the war ended and remained there until my "demob" in early 1947. Lily had written to tell me that Mr Fred Haywood had joined the company and was soon put in charge as Works Manager. The aircraft company had vacated the requisitioned top factory, benches were returned there and more staff were taken on to deal with the increased volume of work and Lily had been made forelady as Mr Haywood's assistant. The increased volume of work came mainly from Raphael Tuck and Valentines whose factories had been damaged or destroyed. We produced their greeting cards and soft cover children's books.

1943. Eric Latham on war service, Algiers.

Mr John Haworth had by 1946 relinquished his factory floor activities and became Managing Director.

Doug Davies was the first to return to the company at the end of the war. He took charge of the platens once again but this return was a shock to Lily who had been told that he had been killed during the war. He and Tom Brand were the only two of the "originals" to return to the company after the war.

There were two fatal war casualties of pre-war staff. One of the Cole brothers, mentioned earlier, Jack, did not return from a bombing raid over Germany. He was reported missing. The other casualty was one of the Cobbold brothers, Eric, he was killed in action at Anzio serving with the Queens Regiment, 56th London Infantry division, The Black Cats. Eric and I were pals prior to call-up. We went cycling and rowing (sculling) together but we lost contact with each other so I had no idea where he was in the "Queens". I too was with the same 56th division and closely associated with his regiment and was at Anzio. We must have crossed paths at times but never actually met. I learned of his death when I came home.

Although the war ended in 1945, I was not demobbed until February 1947. Discharge was based on age and years of service. On discharge I came to meet Fred Haywood regarding my return to work.

June 1945. War over in Europe, stand down parade of Southgate Civil Defence Force, Broomfield Park.

I started work again on the platens but felt unsettled for a while. Life seemed very tame and uneventful after my army experiences so I went to Southgate Police Station to discuss joining the force and came away with the application form. However, Lily and I were contemplating marriage and the unsociable hours and the night duties of serving with the police turned me against the idea.

Mr. H.J. Dean, 1950, responsible for factory maintenance and the coke boilers used for heating. Oil burning boilers were installed in 1955.

Because of the 1939 fire the lower factory had no central heating. The only heating was at first by open brazier coke fires like the old time night watchman's fire. Later small coke combustion fires were installed – and the holes in the wall where the flue-pipes passed through can still be seen. Central heating was not installed until 1950 but in spite of this, this room was always very cold during the winter.

The wartime roofing was unlined and not insulated, it was extremely draughty and snow would often drift in if the wind was from a certain direction. Two or three woollies and scarves were the order of the day during the winter months.

By the end of the 1940s the volume of work was increasing. Frequent board deliveries of 10 and 15 ton loads within a week, were becoming commonplace. So at the close of my first ten eventful years, the way ahead looked prosperous with new machinery, improved buildings and working conditions in the pipeline now the war was over.

1946. Exports again, of calendars for destinations world-wide.

In display manufacture the '50s were our busiest post war years with continuous orders from Oxo, Fray Bentos, Ever Ready, Exide, Kleenex and many more.

The platens, especially the largest one, were showing signs of wear and tear and making ready was becoming difficult. The machine had suffered as a result of the fire and by a certain amount of misuse by inexperienced operators and setters during the war years. In 1951 Croslands produced a new improved design of platen and exhibited one at the I.P.E.X. exhibition, Olympia. This machine was purchased by the company and delivered to us straight from Olympia.

By the mid '50s the volume of work had reached its peak and looked set to stay that way. The orders we had from Oxo for "counter baskets" of various designs will always stay in my mind. On one or two occasions they re-ordered before we had completed the initial order. They were orders for large amounts and involved punching out, Remus bending, backscoring and making-up. Remus bending is a slow operation and because of this an alternative had to be found. "Necessity being the mother of invention", I devised a method of making a similar bend or bends on the platen which speeded up the operation.

Fred Haywood, Factory Manager, 1949 - 1965.

Ladies of the factory, 1951.

In June 1961 Doug Davis handed in his resignation and left the company. Mr John asked me to take charge of the Platen Department.

Rossendale Works unlike pre-war days, was no longer the only place in Southgate to employ people, so it wasn't so easy to employ young people of the right type and to encourage them to stay. The platen room at that time was shabby, cold in winter and very badly lit with outdated enamel lamp shades containing 150 watt bulbs – all of which were widely spaced out and unsuitably situated. I explained to Mr John that if he wanted to have new and younger staff and wanted them to become "permanent staff" we must improve these conditions and make the job more attractive. He agreed and allowed me to put into practice the measures we had discussed including two new 25″ x 35″ platens installed which are still in use today.

Mr John usually paid a visit all-round once a week but during this period of reorganisation he stayed away. Mr John paid us a visit, the first one for several weeks. As he stood watching all four machines, all of which were on the "run". I will never forget the look of joy on his face. He said he had never seen four machines working at the same time, and stood watching for several minutes.

My wife, Lily left the company in October 1961 after twenty-two years service. Although three years short of twenty-five Mr John presented Lily with a gold watch and combined bracelet for her services, awarded prematurely in appreciation of her work during the war years.

During the 1960s there was a further decline in the volume of work compared with previous years. Two platen operators left and were not replaced.

I was presented with my gold watch in 1964 for twenty-five years service. In April 1965, Mr Fred Haywood, Display Manager, resigned to take early retirement. We were all sorry to see him go. He was hard working and worked a twelve hour day for many years. As a result of his leaving, Peggy Hall was appointed overseer to the finishing department, Phil and Ron Hall made jointly responsible for the cutting department. I had overall jurisdiction in the whole factory from the start of the work to the finished product.

Work volume continued to be less than previous years, so when bench workers left they were not always replaced.

June 1966 brought the trade union "recruiting". There were virtually no union sympathisers among us. The general feeling was that if anyone had a grievance, they could approach myself and if necessary for us to discuss the matter with Mr John Bowden, now in overall charge of Rossendale Works.

A.H. Sartain, Accounts Manager, 1946 - 1963.

John Bowden, 1952, Junior Estimator. 1989, the Senior Executive Director of James Haworth.

1958. Mounting Room, Rossendale Works. These machines mounted the colour printed sheets from our Leicester factory, onto cardboard sheets of various thicknesses.

A meeting with union representatives was arranged at the "Waggon and Horses", but only three of the staff attended. The union then insisted on meeting the whole staff on work premises. A meeting was arranged and most of the staff attended, but none were interested in what was being said. The "last straw" was when the union speaker referred to our ladies as "you lot", with this remark everyone walked out and up the yard. The three union representatives for once in their lives were left speechless, Mr J. S. Haworth buying them a recovery drink.

Mr John's visits to us in the early 60s had become less frequent and he seemed less interested in the work in progress. I found this to be more so as time passed. The time he spent at the works became much less and the opportunities to discuss things with him became more difficult for everyone concerned.

We were expected to do a job but were not given the "tools" to do it, the Leicester factory having priority for new equipment. Southgate's output was criticised, and me in particular, for not managing very well. Under different circumstances we could have done better. Mr J. S. Haworth noting my unhappiness, transferred me in the week before Christmas 1971 to the new art studio. I was apprehensive at first but it was to become a complete new chapter in my working-life.

1958. The Platen Room. Here the mounted cardboard sheets were put into a mechanical press, which would cut out various shapes required to form window displays.

In the past I had sometimes been asked to remake or alter a "dummy" or prototype which we had received from the Soho studio, this was my first attempt at cardboard engineering.

There had always been a need for accurate cutter drawings. Often in the past cutter drawings were made from "rough dummies" and "mock-ups" and without the use of a drawing board, consequently cutters were made inaccurately. These inaccuracies were only discovered when the jobs were cut out and their assembly proved difficult or even impossible.

When I was in charge of the platen department, I insisted on examining all cutter drawings before they went to the forme makers, this gave me the opportunity to correct any inaccuracies.

Designing and creating an original product was something entirely new to me and at first I felt I had been "thrown in at the deep end", but it was a challenge which re-kindled my enthusiasm. I strived to design future products in a way which would first and foremost give the customer exactly what they require in the most economical way.

During my time in the studio, 1971-1988 there have been many changes in the company. I have witnessed the continual growth of the photographic section, the introduction of the exhibition section and the introduction and expansion of the silkscreen printing and more recently the distribution activities.

All this has now overshadowed the trade "finishing" section which initially constituted the whole of Rossendale Works. The "finishing", although greatly reduced, still has an important place and has recently had its status improved with the introduction of the Rabollini 60″ x 40″ platen. Oh! how I would have loved to have had that way back in the 1950s and 60s.

At the time of writing I am endeavouring to pass on my practical knowledge to both the personnel of the platen department and to my colleagues in the art studio before I retire in 1988".

Top: Display Assembly, 1972.
Middle: Eric Latham, Cardboard Engineer, 1988.
Right: The Display Design Studio, 1980.

1960's cardboard displays.

1960's cardboard displays.

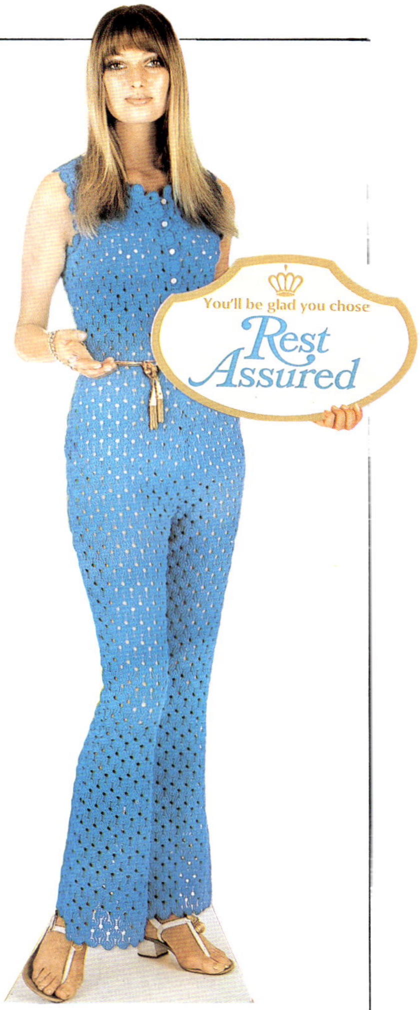

Taking up the story after Eric's narrative —

The fire on the last Sunday of August 1939 was the biggest, to that date Southgate had ever seen. The forensic experts put it down to a pipe smoker who put a still-smoldering pipe in his working jacket at close down on Saturday.

The next weekend, Britain was at war again after only 21 years peace but this time it was expected to be really terrible, with English towns and cities razed to the ground from day one.

Fortunately this was not to happen for a year and life in Britain went back to being more or less normal.

Our customers were not yet into a war economy situation and still needed to advertise, so showcards and displays were required whilst the "phoney war" lasted until after Christmas 1939. Board and other materials began to become scarce. Salvaging board from the fire, then splitting the thicker boards, gave us sufficient boards to meet the declining number of orders.

By Easter 1940 most traces of the fire had gone, the re-building of the lower factory had been completed but lacked central heating. All the machinery had been re-built.

Office staff and artists arrived from Soho Square but by Christmas 1941 Albert Buck was the only artist left along with Mr Shaw and Miss Doris Stephenson of the London office.

John J. Haworth, 1953.

1942 was a difficult year with most staff either called up into the armed forces or directed to essential war work, leaving very few to undertake even our own government work for the Stationery Office and the Central Office of Information.

In 1943, the new factory built in 1937 was requisitioned on behalf of a component aircraft company who were to manufacture among other things bomb bay sections for Lancaster bombers.

This factory was equipped to the highest possible standard with compressed air machine tools driven by a diesel-driven air compressor which could also provide emergency lighting. The reason for this form of power was that should the main electricity supply be bombed, output could be maintained. Also installed was a 10 ton hydraulic press, the machinery being all American and of the latest manufacture.

Despite all this equipment and cost, very little production for the Air Ministry seemed to be achieved and there was talk of items being produced for non-essential civilian use from the aluminium sheets.

John J. Haworth and our staff were very much on the warpath with our uninvited guests and the Ministry of Aircraft Production over the suspicions about the misuse of the war effort within our boundaries.

William Shaw, General Manager, James Haworth & Brother Ltd., 1913 - 1953.

Control of this aircraft firm was tightened, but the end of the war was now in sight both in Europe and Asia and by early 1946 the factory was returned for our own use.

Much of the machinery was left behind, to be broken up for scrap. Our company purchased for £10 the compressor, but could find no real use for it and subsequently sold it in 1949. The web of air lines remain to this day in this part of the factory.

What a waste war achieves!

The remaining area of the factory, during this last period of the war, continued production of simple showcards for export goods, and calendars for the home market.

In Spring 1944, a party of Royal Engineers came for a month to use our two Ratcliffe mounting machines for the mounting of maps, with our staff locked out from this department and all material removed each night. These maps were no doubt needed for the forthcoming invasion of Europe in June.

Rossendale works during the war period saw the formation, as a subsidiary company of James Haworth & Brother Limited, of the Rossendale Photo-Offset Company Limited. The purpose of this company is told elsewhere.

1960. Sam Collins Butchers Shop, Chase Side, directly opposite Rossendale Works. Now demolished to make way for a small office block with the Eastern Electricity Shop underneath.

Also on the factory site from 1937 was a company called M. P. Vineis. It occupied what had been the old forge and machine shop of John Eaton. Mr M. P. Vineis was an Italian subject who was forced to flee from his Italian home town because of his opposition to the local Fascists. He sought refuge in England, came to live in Southgate and married a local lady. He was an expert metal worker and the forge was ideal for him to carry out his business.

Mr Vineis could also make our cutters. These cutters consisted of steel rule, ground with a knife edge uppermost. This steel rule would be inserted to the required shape within an area of block board of up to 30″ x 40″.

These cutters would then be placed into machines, known as platens, which punched to shape the cardboard for our displays. This process is still in use today.

Unfortunately, Mr Vineis kept his Italian nationality and on Italy declaring war on Britain in June 1940 he was interned as an enemy alien on the Isle of Man.

Thanks to the efforts of James Haworth it was not long before he was released to continue his business. It is reputed that he had the sole contract to produce the knives used by our wartime commando forces. In the 1960s, Mr Vineis retired to Porlock, Somerset, and died there some time ago.

The business Mr Vineis founded is still carried on by his manager and is now situated in New Barnet, Herts. This company continues to supply our cutters.

The ground area of Rossendale Works reverted to its original 1936 size of nearly 2 acres, with the purchase in 1954 from Newby Brothers, of land behind No. 46-58 Chase Side. The purchase of this land, ahead of development and purchase by shop owners fronting Chase Side, has resulted in these old shops, in 1988 with their above accommodation, being the only remaining buildings of pre-1914 Chase Side, Southgate, the exception being the Southgate Club.

As local residents know, these shops jut out way beyond today's building line, often to the frustration of pedestrians hemmed in by the narrow pavement and guard rails. One doubts if we shall ever see new buildings there as any new development would result in shops of little depth due to conforming to the building line.

On this land acquired in 1954 stands the Company's large photographic studio and laboratories. This side of our business arriving from 21 Soho Square in 1970.

With the contraction of point of sale manufacturing in the 1960s, screen printing was commenced at Rossendale Works in the early 1970s and by its expansion is scheduled to occupy 25% of the site by the end of 1988.

By way of further diversification, two new warehouses have been constructed in the last four years to accommodate national advertisers' merchandising material which is separated into small quantities for delivery to all destinations in the British Isles, the great majority of which is distributed by our own transport. We are proud of this service, which our would-be competitors seem unable to match because of our personal commitment to our customers – a service commenced in 1976.

Rossendale Works site is by 1989 almost fully occupied with production buildings. A new section for the photographic, art and exhibition side of our business is expected to be complete by 1990.

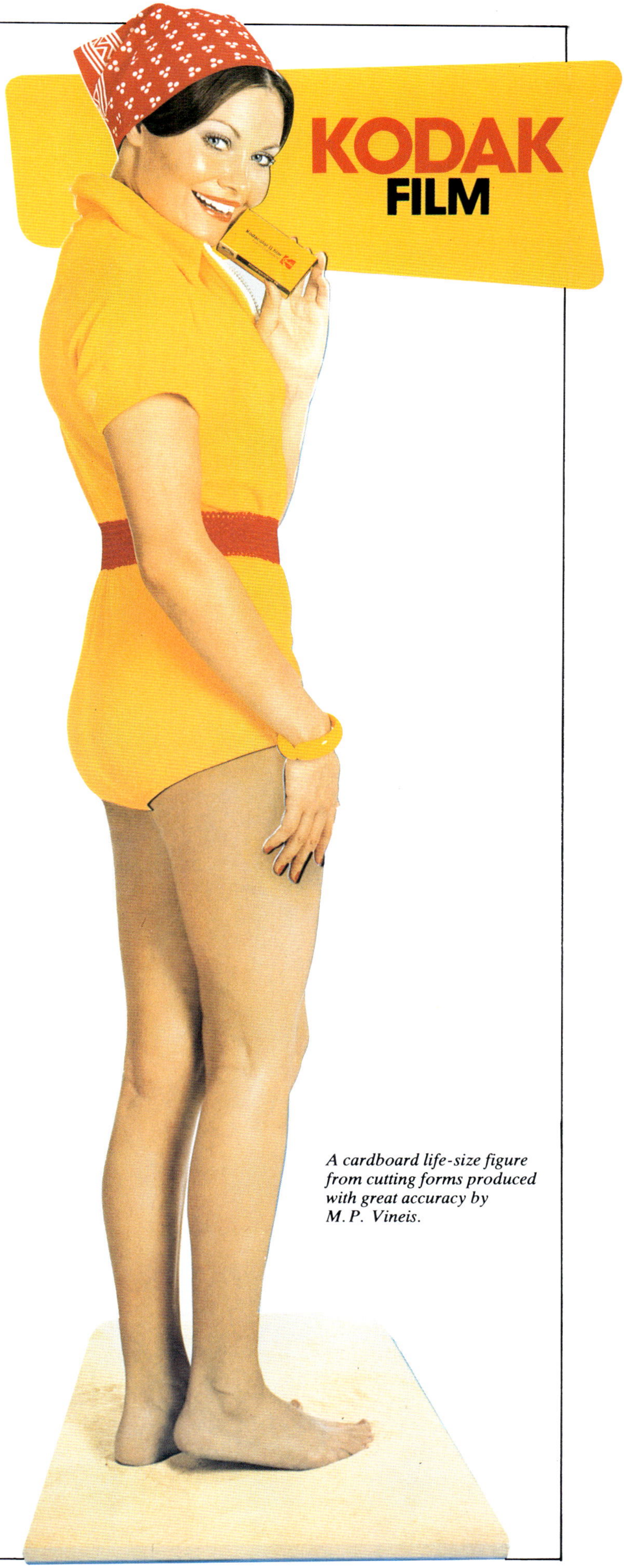

A cardboard life-size figure from cutting forms produced with great accuracy by M. P. Vineis.

Entrance to Rossendale Works, 1980.

The old factory buildings are being refurbished. Laurie Holmes, a longtime resident of Southgate has been responsible for all our internal modernisation, his craftsmanship being appreciated by visitors and staff alike in improving our buildings and surroundings. The "old forge" is used for photographic purposes and for meeting rooms. The horse tethering rail still remains outside the writer's office, as a reminder of the building's use over 100 years ago.

Understandably many local people pass our entrance between the shops in Chase Side, little knowing what exists behind Woolworths, Sainsbury, Boots and all the other shops in that part of Southgate. In 1989 the soon to be completed Asda super store will be our neighbour leaving Rossendale Works at this time the only manufacturing business of any size in what was "Old Southgate".

In conclusion, we trust that through our more than 50 years in Southgate, James Haworth Limited, with its Rossendale Works, has made a rewarding contribution to the life of Southgate and its people.

In town or country, our vans can be seen.

1970 - 1979. Display material from Rossendale Works.

This page and opposite: 1980 - 1989, marketing material produced at Rossendale Works.

From the normal...
From piggy...
To romantic...
To the formal...
To gourmet...
From singles...
From after-dinner ports...
To mixed doubles...
To unforgettable ports...
Every holiday you ever wanted in one...
CANBERRA
THE FIRST RESORT

A HUNDRED CHOICES. A THOUSAND MEMORIES.
CANBERRA
THE FIRST RESORT

PRINCESS VOYAGES
The Caribbean & Mexican Riviera
The Mediterranean & Scandinavia
The Far East & South Pacific
Alaska
Far and away your best decision!
P&O Group

The
eastern
ALL ELECTRIC
Christmas
Show

HEINZ
Noodle Doodles Dominoes
FREE
Back to school maths set
Liptons
Heinz
SAINSBURY'S Gift Voucher
SAVE WITH Heinz SALADS
at Liptons
The May & Baker system for cereal diseases

Inside Rossendale Works 1988.

Rossendale Works and Southgate 1988.

James Haworth

FINE ART

"Fine Art", is a print term emanating from the second half of the Victorian era, when it was discovered how to transfer a full-colour original painting into a full-colour print, matching in colour values, the original.

This discovery, combined with the introduction of large-size, flat-bed printing machines, enabled prints to be produced of a size up to 30″ x 40″, which would be framed. These prints, selling for about 5s. 0d (25p), enabled many homes to hang reproductions of work by famous artists. Previously, their work would only be seen in the homes of the wealthy and perhaps a few museums and galleries, as originals.

The skill of the print reproduction artist, in breaking down the original colours of the painting into up to 14 separate colour values, was almost equal to the skill of the painter. Each colour had to be hand-etched onto a printing plate or stone. The resulting montage of each colour falling in place on the paper after each print run, made, as if by magic, for an almost exact copy of the original.

Alf Cooke of Leeds, in the 1890s were the only printers in the British Isles with a Royal Warrant for colour printing. The granting of the Royal Warrant was very much in recognition for their excellent colour reproductions of Queen Victoria and landscape paintings by renowned artists, the prints of which made for ready sales.

James Haworth, on joining Alf Cooke in 1901, would have been influenced, from his first days, by this "fine art" trade.

Advertisers at the turn of the century, were very quick to give their marketing image a "fine art" approach; this was to convey the quality of both their advertising and their product. This image, then originally applied to James Haworth's printing standards, has, in many ways, lasted through to the present day.

James Haworth & Brother, in the first five years of their existence, as we have learned earlier, had a printing arrangement with P.P. Press, a printing company owned by Joseph Bibby, a large soap manufacturer in Liverpool.

Joseph Bibby himself was a great evangelist and prolific producer of colour prints with a religious and classic theme.

James Haworth, from 1914, undertook to sell these prints through his newly-founded company. He would sell both to picture galleries and to companies, such as Oxo and Cadburys.

These companies had already realised that extra sales could be made by sending a colour print to a buyer of their products, in return for a specified number of labels and/or wrappers from their goods, - a selling technique much favoured by today's manufacturers. Again, nothing new in our world of advertising!

Joseph Bibby's calendars for 1917 and 1918. Overprinted for use as James Haworth's calendar.

"Lady With Fan" by Webster. The first fine art print to be published by James Haworth, 1920.

James Haworth & Brother's connection with its own fine art reproductions came with Edwin Byatt joining the Studio on the formation of the Company.

Byatt, like so many skilled artists at the beginning of the 20th century, could only earn a living by painting advertising subjects. They could only become true artists outside business hours, when they would paint subjects of their own choice.

With Byatt the choice was florals.

Fortunately, on seeing the work Byatt painted for his own pleasure, James Haworth recognised his genius in capturing the beauty of flowers within a painting.

As a result of this recognition, Byatt was asked to prepare floral paintings which the company could reproduce and publish. By 1938, over 40 different floral paintings had been reproduced. The resulting prints were to be seen as pictures, calendars and greeting cards.

Byatt exhibited regularly at The Royal Institute. Queen Mary purchased a beautiful example of his roses, which hangs in Buckingham Palace today.

His paintings are indeed a joy to view and there is no doubt that in due course, his floral works will be regarded as some of the finest paintings emanating from a British artist between the two world wars.

Our reputation for high standard of reproduction of Byatt prints earned us, in turn, print orders from other fine art publishers, who were without their own reproduction and printing facilities.

Edwin Byatt.

The versatility of Byatt.

"Neptune's Bride" by Walter Thomas. A fine art print of 1935 published in the company range.

To balance our own range of prints and greeting cards, reproduction rights were obtained to reproduce the work of other famous artists of the pre-1939 period, such as, Walter Thomas, Norman Wilkinson and Lucy Kemp-Welch, to name but a few.

The outbreak of war in 1939 saw the termination of the wholesaling of our range of prints, with the lack of demand and wartime conditions.

The marketing of our prints, calendars, greeting cards, Radio Times covers, and Rust Craft American greeting card franchise, had, during the 1930s been organised by Phillip Buck, younger brother of Albert, the then Manager of our very large commercial studio at Soho Square.

Phillip Buck was to be badly injured at home in 1944 by a "flying bomb". As a result of this, he was never able to take up full-time work again and thereby possibly resurrecting our fine art department with the end of the war.

In the absence of a fine art sales manager, Byatt prints were to be handled instead by wholesalers, of which Haig's of Twickenham were to be predominant.

Above:
Lucy Kemp-Welch
Pictured with her fondness for animals. Illustrated very much in the excellence of her work featuring farm and horse subjects.
Illustration left used as a leaf for the 1936 Exide Battery calendar.

Above: The Company's fine art and printing stand, British Industries Fair, Olympia, Exhibition Hall 1939.

Below: A reduced reproduction of a "lost" Byatt print issued early 1930. Discovered again in research for this book.

James Haworth & Brother, however, did, during the 1950s and 60s, publish a new selection of prints, which sell regularly today.

The prime seller in this group is "Evening Star" by Terence Cuneo. This painting, of the last British-built steam engine, resulted from a commission by the Company for its 1964 calendar and is regarded as one of Cuneo's finest engine paintings.

Our printing "fine art" tradition has been very much continued in producing the work of some of today's famous artists, such as Terence Cuneo, Frank Wootton and David Weston. These artists set exacting standards in the reproduction of their work as prints and the privilege of satisfying their standards has been ours for over 30 years.

In working with artists like Terence Cuneo, in reproducing as prints his military, train and equestrian subjects, the writer, as the printer, had the privilege of being presented to Her Royal Highness, The Princess Anne (now The Princess Royal) at one of the occasions commemorating the 40th anniversary of D-Day.

This particular occasion was the unveiling, at the National Army Museum, Chelsea, of Terence Cuneo's painting of the British Armies' D-Day landing on the 6th June 1944, the beginning of the ousting of the Germans from Western Europe.

From this painting, the Army Benevolent Fund commissioned a limited edition of prints, the proceeds of their sale going to the Fund.

HRH The Princess Anne and Mr Terence Cuneo

Above: "D-Day" 6th June — a fine art print commissioned by the Army Benevolent Fund from an original by Terence Cuneo.

Left: John J. Haworth (the writer's father) was a great admirer of Montgomery's achievements in North Africa and Western Europe during World War II. He commissioned Terence Cuneo to record, as an oil painting, probably Montgomery's finest hour - the acceptance at Lüneburg Heath on 4th May 1945 of the surrender of the German Forces.

The Field Marshal gave permission for the painting - "The Germans Surrender" - to be done and John Haworth and he became friends, exchanging letters on various topics during the latter days of the Field Marshal's life.

Main picture: Terence Cuneo 'making a point' on his original painting 'Evening Star', one of twelve of his paintings exhibited at the 50th Year Pandrol Ltd Anniversary Dinner held in London October 1987.

Pandrol Ltd are a renowned specialist manufacturer of railway track parts, and for their company calendar, have reproduced many of Cuneo's railway subjects.

Inset: 'Evening Star' commissioned from Terence Cuneo by James Haworth Ltd for their 1964 company calendar. Issued later as a fine art print, it proved to be one of the most successful ever published by our company.

The original painting of this last steam engine built for British Railways, is regarded by many as one of the very best engine subject's ever painted. There is also a story about our 'Evening Star' print and the little mouse, as Cuneo's trademark, which appears in practically every one of his paintings. This story is best told by the artist himself:-

'EVENING STAR'

Or, the mouse that nearly caused an international incident.

Here is the story, and it's a true one.

When this painting was reproduced as an art print by the firm of James Haworth, a copy was purchased by an Officer on a Union Castle liner and was hanging in his cabin when the liner docked at Cape Town. The Captain of the ship happened to bring a friend of his, a member of a famous Cavalry Regiment, to this man's cabin for some reason or other. The soldier immediately noticed the print on the wall. 'That's one of Cuneo's, isn't it?' he asked. 'You know, the feller who always paints a mouse in his pictures'. The other two regarded the soldier in some surprise. Neither of them had ever heard of me, nor had they any knowledge of rodents being inserted into oil paintings. Three able-bodied men then approached the print and searched it thoroughly. Not one of them could find the mouse!

Finally, the Captain said, 'Look here, get a cable off to this chap Haworth and tell him for God's sake to let us know where the bloody thing is!' John Haworth senior duly received this graphic request. He thought for a while and then decided that 'Up telegraph pole first right', constituted both a clear and inexpensive reply. He promptly dispatched this message back to the liner.

It arrived in Cape Town, but instead of being delivered to the ship, it was sent direct to the South African equivalent of MI5, as a highly suspicious message, probably in code.

Whereupon, two members of the Security Force stomped up the gangway of the British ship and demanded to see the Captain. That good man was in his cabin sitting at his desk. The cable was thrust before him. 'Would you kindly explain this, Sir'.

The Captain took the paper. He goggled at it. He had long forgotten the incident and the words meant nothing to him. 'Up telegraph pole first right'. What in hell did that mean? He hadn't a notion. The Captain rose up, his face reddening in anger, when suddenly he caught sight of the word Haworth and he remembered. 'Gentlemen', he announced with great solemnity, 'Follow me'. He led his visitors down through the ship and finally stopped at his officer's cabin. He flung wide the door and with the air of a conjurer producing a rabbit from a hat, pointed dramatically at the print. 'There you are, gentlemen – Up telegraph pole first right - and THERE'S THE MOUSE!'

Right:
Many a mouse in this reproduced Cuneo painting. Any similarity to another famous railway station painting is purely coincidental!

Frank Wootton is an English artist renowned for his Royal Air Force and English countryside subjects. His many limited editions have become collectors' items.

Our Leicester reproduction and printing departments have always enjoyed meeting the standard, which his paintings demand in reaching a faithful reproduction of his skill as an artist in capturing the English landscape, or the grace and power of aircraft in a cloudy sky.

Our skill in this field of print continues to be sought by the publishers of the work by new and excellent young artists, now being reproduced. Their prints are finding a ready market, thanks to the British public's renewed interest in possessing prints of quality to adorn their walls at home.

Examples of Limited Edition prints produced for Wealdown Fine Art Prints, Alfriston, Sussex, from originals by Frank Wootton.

"One Off - Smartly" – from an oil painting by Frank Wootton.

"A Young Fox" – as a print reproduced from an original by Frank Wootton.

"Avocets" – from an original by Raymond C. Watson. As a result of reproducing as a fine art print, this outstanding study, James Haworth Ltd won the 1972 Lithoprinters Award for printing excellence.

"Laid Up" – a print from the work of David Weston. An artist famous for his work in capturing industrial and transport subjects of "days gone by". James Haworth Ltd have been responsible for reproducing many of his subjects as limited edition prints and calendars.

James Haworth

THE COMPANY IMAGE

On the formation of the company, the embracing family name of James Haworth and Brother was registered at Companies House.

In reading the extracts of letters by James to brother Thomas more emotive names like Gainsborough and Ventura for their new company were under consideration.

It is a matter of conjecture if the company would have survived so well the past 75 years of business uncertainties if one of these "stage type" names had been chosen.

A business that carries the family name has a reputation to keep, if the family are in active participation in its direction. It implies, no matter how large the business, there should be a direct and caring interest by the family members in the staff and customers.

I like to think this has been the family image presented as the past 75 years have gone by. If this policy continues, with the family now in their fourth generation of participation of the company's affairs, we should, as a consequence, look forward in due course to a hundred years of trading.

In 1970 coinciding with our departure from Soho Square, the "Brother" was quietly dropped from our title. This action was not without thought and a touch of sadness. Modern communications seem to demand names which are clear and concise and the "and Brother" had become rather an anachronism.

James Haworth, in creating the business, had a quality image fixed in his mind. Working twelve years for Alf Cooke of Leeds, with their high standards and Royal Warrant, James was in no doubt what path to pursue. This, despite the fact he now only had a rented office and studio, compared to the mighty firm he had just left.

The late Victorian and Edwardian period introduced a classical look to almost any decor, product and design. James Haworth's business friend Joseph Bibby, of Bibby's soap empire, had promoted his product and his religious teachings, through a classical style of painting and drawings, as could be found in Bibby's Annual. Despite the title, this was published monthly, along with Joseph Bibby's many other evangelistic publications. Numerous drawings of classical ladies, in a state of semi-undress, seem to be at odds with the message about the "sins of the flesh" conveyed within the text.

However, if nothing else about the new James Haworth company, the business card and letterheading was certainly going to be noticed. The design lasted for 17 years, until the move from Chancery Lane to Soho Square.

1913 - 1929 Business Card.

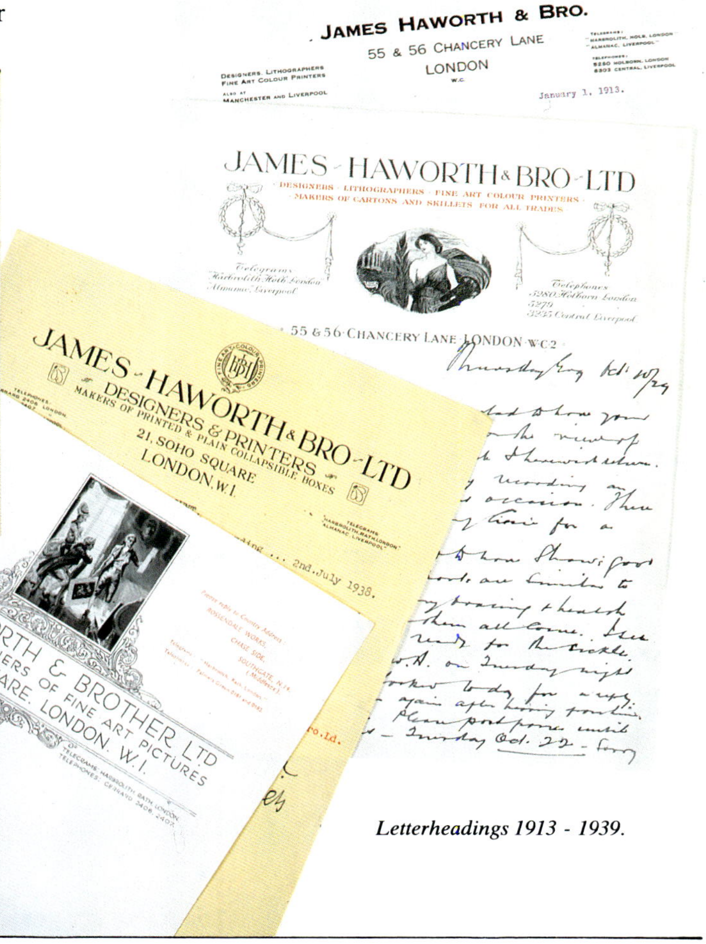

Letterheadings 1913 - 1939.

Letterheadings 1950 - 1980.

The "fine art image" of the company to the outside world, was also a catalyst for James Haworth to publish classical fine art prints, but these were always slow sellers compared to Byatt's florals.

The move in 1930 to Soho Square, signalled a complete redesign of the company's stationery, with even more of a "fine art" letterheading. This used a picture by our artist Reginald Mills, depicting a 17th century artist, placing his desirable pictures before a gentleman and lady of quality, for them to make a choice. This picture did and still does convey the company's image and is retained today by the stationery. There has been many a compliment from customers about our design, both for its uniqueness and thereby ease of location within a pile of correspondence.

Company label designs from 1913 to 1989. 1989 design, bottom left.

Sample company books of 1925-37 period that have become sought after items at ephemeral auctions.

Parcel recognition was a different problem, calling for a quick distinctive recognition. This recognition was essential, as most parcels pre 1950 had to go by rail. Every large main line station would have thousands of parcels at a time. If you were calling to collect, easy recognition of your company's name by the railway staff went a long way to avoiding "It's not here yet".

The American eagle was chosen for this recognition label. This emblem was also to find its way on to the sides of the first 3-ton Ford vans, purchased from 1936. I recall, as a young boy, these looking very smart, with a mid-blue lower half and cream top carrying the outstretched eagle, some eight feet wide, which must have stretched to the limit the signwriter's skill.

Though the vans lasted right through the war, the design did not; the vans reverting to plain dark blue with gold lettering.

Promotion of the company, in the 1930s, to old and would-be new customers, was considerably increased. Two-tone folders of displays produced for a wide range of customers were dispatched at regular intervals.

Phillip Buck, manager of fine art sales, sailed on the Queen Mary's maiden voyage in 1936 to New York.

Arriving after a very stormy voyage, his main purpose had been to finalise with the American Rust Craft Greeting Company, a sole agency for selling their greeting cards in England.

Above: 1931 advertising brochure.
Bottom left: 1935 catalogue issued to show a selection of "Fine Art" calendars available for retail sale.
Bottom right: Rust Craft agency and sample cards.

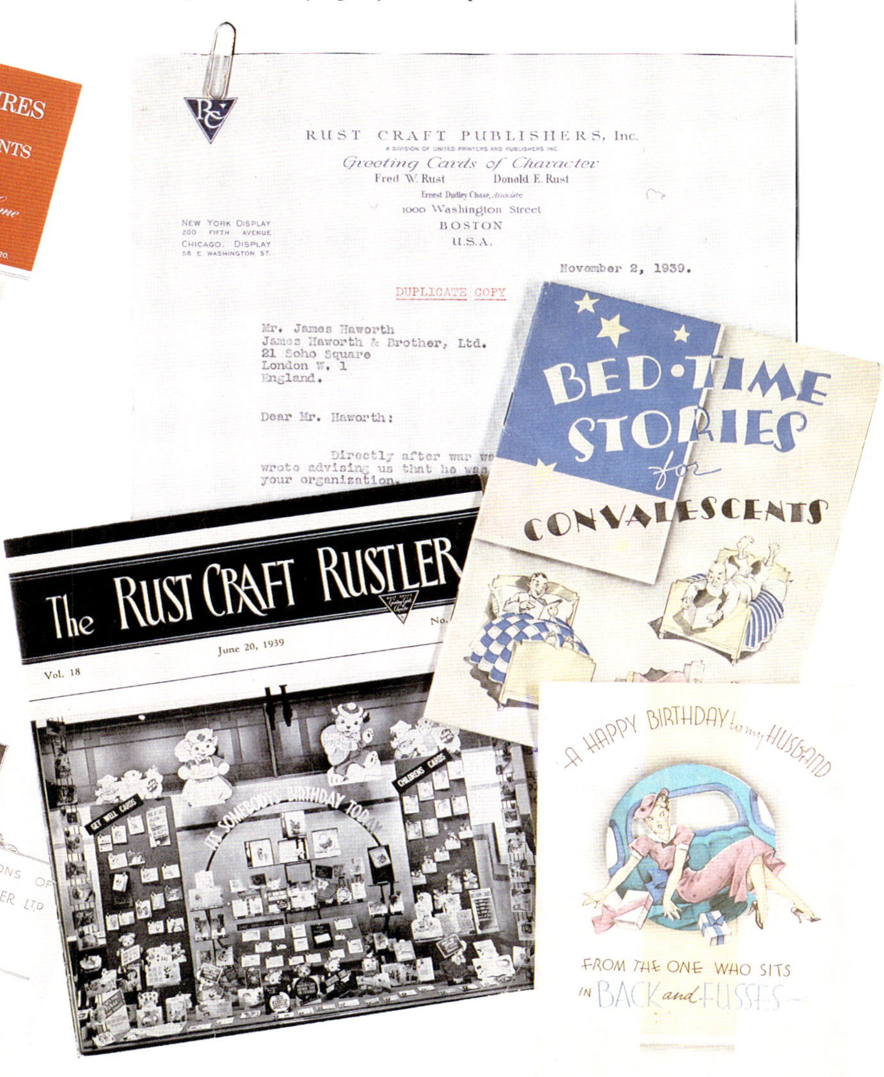

1936 American blotters.

BRITISH INDUSTRIES FAIR, 1938.

Below: 3 of the first blotters 1938.

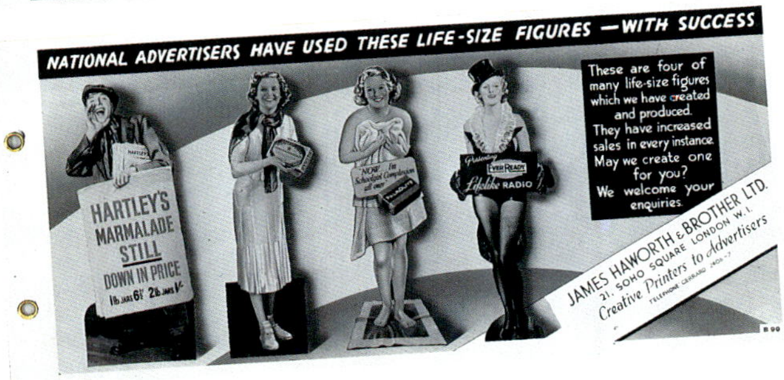

Having successfully achieved this agency, Phillip Buck, on instructions from John J. Haworth was to make contact with similar firms to ours in New York and obtain samples of cardboard displays, then current in America.

One of the contacts was Brett Lithographic Co, Long Island. They produced an advertising ink blotter featuring their printing. We produced similar copies with their permission.

Until the outbreak of World War II, this good relationship, in the exchange of ideas and samples, continued. The war was also to see the end of the Rust Craft business, in the uncertainty of receiving goods across U-boat infested seas.

The advertising blotters, until 1950, were produced by black and white letterpress printing. Due to the improvement of small image litho reproduction, a change was made to full colour.

As far as I recall, James Haworth were the only printers in England ever to use this advertising medium. The blotters would be despatched in the day-to-day mail to customers. The ball point pen arriving in the 1960s, caused the demise of this very successful unique idea.

Range of ink pen blotters issued by the company 1949 to 1965.

Florence Haworth's handwriting can be seen on blotter.

Samples of company print and advertising 1950 - 1960.

James Haworth Limited

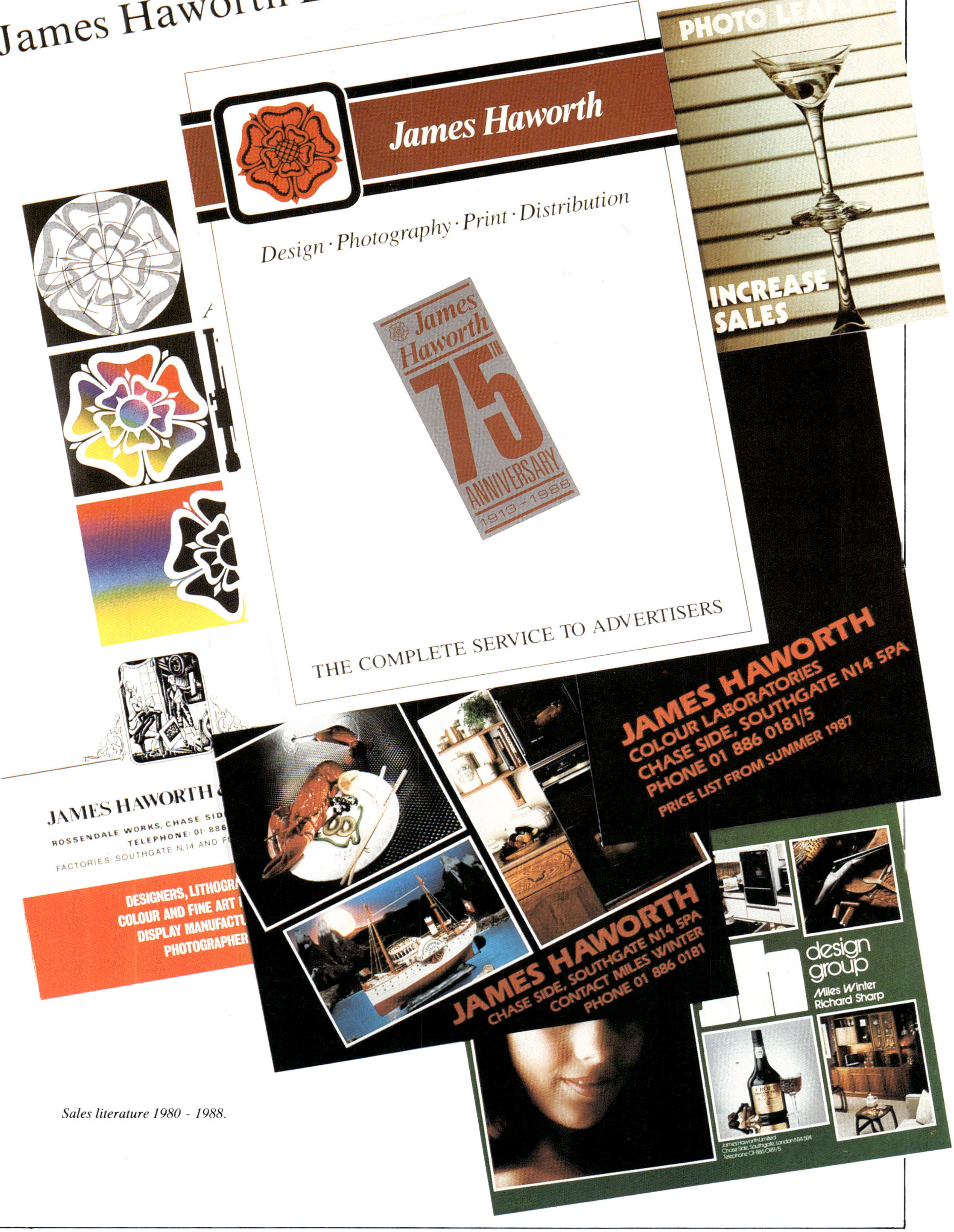

Sales literature 1980 - 1988.

A consistent theme throughout James Haworth's history has been the company calendar. During the first seven years of our existence, use was made of Bibby's annual twelve-leaf calendar illustrations.

The art decor of the 1920s dictated a new approach. Byatt's florals of this period were ideal. Change was made to a single floral subject, printed and mounted onto a thick board of size 20″ x 30″. Hung on a wall, the calendar commanded attention, for striking interest or beauty of its subject.

We have striven to achieve this for every edition to the present day.

By 1953, our calendar's time of issue was changed to March. The thought behind this unusual decision being that, if the calendar proved an improvement on the existing one in the buyer's office, the opposition's subject would find the waste paper basket!

This March timing, more importantly, gave an individual impact, rather than be lost amongst the business gifts of Christmas.

In 1958, a new pad was evolved of a large format, with great clarity and space for notes.

The range of available Byatt originals came to an end in 1953. From that time the subjects have varied from H. M. Queen Elizabeth II, Winston Churchill, portraits of ladies, the Germans Surrender at Lüneburg Heath, country scenes, animals, air and military subjects, trains and a self-portrait of Terence Cuneo as the Deputy Marshal of Tombstone, Arizona.

These calendar subjects were always chosen from work by contemporary artists of the greatest repute. As a result, many of the subjects were framed later for home.

Framed early subjects now appear, by their rarity, at auctions. The rarity being caused in that the company never issued more than 800 calendars in any one year.

JAMES HAWORTH AND BROTHER LIMITED
DESIGNERS · LITHOGRAPHERS AND FINE ART COLOUR PRINTERS · LONDON AND LEICESTER

JAMES HAWORTH AND BROTHER LIMITED
Calendar
MARCH 1955 - FEBRUARY 1956

JAMES HAWORTH AND BROTHER LIMITED
CALENDAR

JAMES HAWORTH AND BROTHER LIMITED
DESIGNERS · LITHOGRAPHERS & FINE ART COLOUR PRINTERS · LONDON & LEICESTER
MARCH 1953

APRIL 1954

JAMES HAWORTH AND BROTHER LIMITED
CREATIVE PRINTERS TO ADVERTISERS
Calendar

APRIL 1961

JAMES HAWORTH AND BROTHER LIMITED LONDON
CREATIVE PRINTERS TO ADVERTISERS
MARCH 1966

FEBRUARY 1961

JAMES HAWORTH LIMITED
DESIGNERS · PHOTOGRAPHERS & COLOUR PRINTERS
CREATIVE PRINTERS TO ADVERTISERS
MARCH 1972
APRIL 1972
MAY 1972

James Haworth
CREATIVE PRINTERS TO ADVERTISERS
MARCH 1988
APRIL 1988

Returning to the more mundane items of the company image.

The eagle emblem for our labels, seemed dated by the end of the 1940s. To record our origins with the North of England, the Tudor Rose emblem was selected. Without revision, the design was to last 35 years, which must be a record for a company label.

Our own transport has always played an important part of our image. First, to make sure that the goods we manufacture, or parcel service, reach our customers safely in the minimum of time. Secondly, carrying the company's name on a well-built vehicle, combining by its lettering and colour a sincere indication of quality.

New vans after World War II were always Ford, painted black lower half and maroon top half, with gold lettering. This colour scheme stood the test of time for 35 years.

To competitively handle our increasing distribution service, more standard vehicles were required. These could be purchased finished in white. Consequently, the new label design was adapted for company recognition on our not inconsiderably sized transport fleet.

Many of the vehicles cover the entire British Isles to a fixed monthly itinerary, delivering marketing merchandise to depots and salesmen.

The company's image and wish was always to buy British vehicles and machinery. The shrinking commercial world and Britain's membership of the European Economic Community, enforced on us a fundamental change.

The lack, in recent times, of a British-made product, especially printing machines of all types, has forced us to buy overseas. Likewise in obtaining reliable goods vehicles and cars.

The 1980s has seen very much a change in Britain's prowess and world standing. It is to be hoped that it will only be a short time before British manufacture will once again be available and be the best that money can buy.

Above: 1980's transport.

Below: 1936 - 1982. A small selection from the range of company cars.

. . . giving consistent service today and . . .

Extract from our 1988 company brochure.

Design

Our purpose-built Studio is staffed by an imaginative team, experienced in providing the necessary design expertise and understanding required by advertisers at the point of purchase. The team is capable of handling any project comprising promotional advertising, marketing literature and all forms of point of sale material.

Photography

Facilities comprise two large custom-built Studios with ample private parking for visitors cars and commercial vehicles. The Studios are staffed by photographers and technicians whose abilities are matched by the very best in modern equipment. They can handle any subject in any format (35mm to 10″ x 8″) – roomsets, cars, models, still-life, or pack shots – within the Studios or on location, as creatively or as objectively as the occasion demands. The department's capability also extends into the area of audio-visuals, where it is equipped to undertake total direction and production.

Processing

To fully achieve and realise the ability of the photographer at his camera, the Studios are backed by in-house laboratories to provide E6 colour transparency processing. Alongside this service is also a computerised laboratory providing machine prints up to 20″ x 16″, hand prints up to 40″ x 30″ in quantities of from one print to 5,000. This service is carefully monitored by our technicians to ensure the optimum quality and fast processing, including where practical, same day service if required. This service is offered not only to James Haworth's own clients but is available to outside photographers.
An additional black and white laboratory produces high quality prints, copy negs, film positives and PMTs on a fast turnaround basis.

Lithographic reproduction

The Reproduction department at Leicester is equipped with its own Laser Scanner enabling individual treatment to be given to transparencies and flat copy artwork. Input size is 500mm x 710mm and has an output size of 636mm x 700mm. This is backed up by modern camera facilities up to 610mm x 762mm output to enable oil paintings and other artwork to be colour separated. Platemaking and proofing (both Cromalin and Press) complete the facilities. This combination of services under one roof and working closely with the printing department enable us to give a unique service, aimed at providing a fast and efficient turnaround to our customers, whilst retaining the high standards which we have built up over the years.

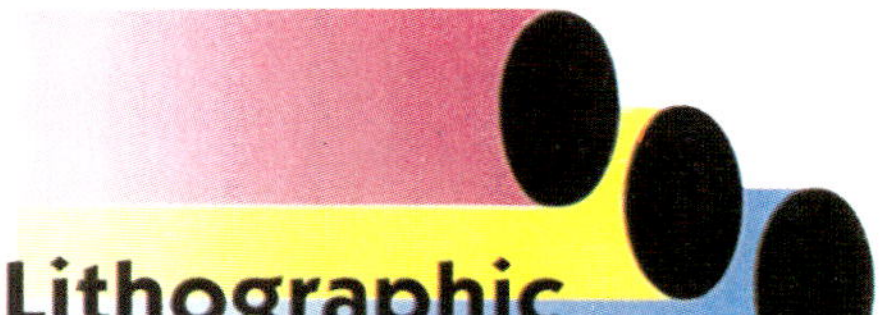

Lithographic printing

The Leicester division undertakes lithographic printing of the highest quality on single – two – and four – colour machines, handling any sheet size up to 800mm x 1120mm and stock up to 750 microns. Close co-operation with the reproduction department enables work to be turned around very quickly to meet the increasingly tight deadlines required by modern marketing, whilst this close liaison enables us to maintain the quality of the final product. A varied range of materials is also used at Leicester, from plastics to paper and board which enables us to give a better and more varied service to our customers.

Finishing

All sheet print finishing is carried out in the Leicester division with a similar service being offered to the trade – folding, stitching and three-knife trimming of brochure work, Wire-o binding and metal rimming of calendars and literature, rotary creasing and perforating of folders and programmatic cutting of labels and posters etc.

Fine art prints and publishing

The utterly uncompromising approach of the Leicester division to the quality and image reproduction equips it well for the reproduction of works of art, a specialist craft which it has performed for publishers and painters of repute since the company's foundation. James Haworth itself publishes a limited but varied range of fine art prints, for which a separate brochure is available on request.

Screen Printing

The Screen Production Unit, which is situated at Southgate, has earned itself an excellent reputation for quality and reliability for delivery, both for line-work and Screen Process printing. It has the ability to carry out its own reproduction and provides for the printing of single to four-colour printing up to 60″ x 40″ in any quantity on to paper, board, PVC, PVA or any other practical specialised material.

Display Manufacture

Strategically sited close to the M25 at Southgate, North London, this department provides comprehensive finishing facilities for specialised point-of-sale display material including mounting, platen cutting up to 1524mm x 1016mm sheet size, gluing, stitching, hand assembly, packing and despatch to specification.
Production encompasses a wide range of work with particular expertise in prepacks, dump bins, turn-over-edge show-cards, lightweight showcards, mobiles, dispenser units for both product and leaflets, life-size figures, large format window displays, profile-cut window decal, profile-cut self-adhesive stickers and clingfilm stickers, free-standing and counter display units.

. . .ever increasing service for the future.

Packing and distribution

Over the last 15 years the company has been able to offer a most successful proven contract service for the storage and repacking of clients' Point of Sale and Marketing material, including product samples, which is combined with a continuous or periodic distribution service by our own vehicles to addresses throughout the United Kingdom. We are able to undertake such deliveries to precise timings and dates as the client requires, as well as being able to undertake all the necessary distribution, stock control and record-keeping.

Trade work at Southgate

We are able to offer the following finishing services to printing and display industries – mounting, platen die cutting, wire stitching, drilling, remus bending and hand bench assembly.

Exhibitions

This self-contained section within our factory complex at Southgate has achieved a consistent and excellent reputation over the last 20 years in the designing, construction and erecting on site Exhibition stands ranging from a small display in an hotel, to a major complex at national Exhibition sites for leading exhibitors.
The small team comprising this department has been in receipt of many awards given by Exhibition organisers for design excellence.
Delivery to site and stand assembly is always carried out by our own transport and staff throughout the United Kingdom and E.E.C. countries.
By way of economy, we offer storage facilities to our customers for the subsequent reuse of their stands during a continued campaign.

For 75 years we have enjoyed a family firm image. Four generations have been in the "firing line", so to speak. From James Haworth's decision to "go it alone", the family members have had to justify their positions of command by proven ability and achievement, - the fourth generation being no exception to this expectation.

The "family" has a wider concept. Members of staff, in a few months of joining, identify to be within a family group. This has always enabled any grievances and problems to be discussed from a view of fairness. As a consequence, the Company has never lost a day's production, in any department, by way of an internal dispute. A record of which we are very proud.

In return for this harmony, the senior management have striven to ensure that all members of the Company may expect continuous employment - not only for the next month, next year, but for the foreseeable future.

In consequence, many members of the large "family" of over one hundred have spent a great proportion of their working lives in giving service to the Company and its customers.

Orders are our life blood. To see they are handled profitably, both to the customer and ourselves has required their progress to be supervised always by senior staff.

Our medium size, combined with the autonomous direction of the London and Leicester Companies, enables every order and instruction to be received by those with authority to execute the required action. Almost unknowingly, this policy of keeping to a medium-sized group based on London and Leicester, has kept us in business.

Staff numbers have remained constant for the last 40 years. This fact may have restricted the Company in terms of turnover, but as a result we have remained an individual company, in the same basic line of business for 75 years, a feat which very few, if any, of our would-be competitors can claim to equal.

James Haworth

THE CUSTOMER

On reflection, "The Customer" should be the most important subject of this book.

Without him or her having the confidence to place business with James Haworth, we would not have existed.

I mention "him" or "her". In the final analysis it is always a person authorising and placing orders, as the customer, never a company, no matter how large or complete with sophisticated computers.

To my grandfather and father, the customer was supreme. Business, in their time was to be obtained solely by service, quality and price.

To achieve the service, holidays, other than perhaps a "special occasion" day would have the lowest priority in personal plans.

I recall as a young boy, it would always be late September or October for a break. A week, or if time allowed, two weeks at St. Mawes, Cornwall.

This lateness was forced on the family by the fact that Ever Ready "selling fortnight" display material had to be delivered complete by the end of the 3rd week in September.

Prior to this, would be a hectic time. Arrangements had to be made for the despatch, by ship, of the many thousands of Exide and Huntley & Palmers calendars.

Orders for the Exide Battery Company could total 100,000 12-leaf calendars, going to a thousand addresses throughout the world.

With 1989 office machinery this would be relatively easy. In 1938 it was an enormous task, demanding constant supervision.

James Haworth during May, June and July would be a hive of industry involving directors, travellers and studio artists.

This lovely summer period (we always seemed to enjoy long hot summers prior to 1939) was the prime time for submitting ideas and designs for autumn and Christmas campaigns.

A time of long and intense preparation. The constant interest by the representative would be required to ensure order-winning designs.

All representatives, including my father, depended on commission from orders for a living. Summer holidays, as a consequence, would never be taken for fear of missing the opportunity of more and new business.

Pre-1939, a representative offering a good product or service, would almost without exception, be seen by a member of the buying department, even without an appointment.

Above: A customer's "Head Office". A building typical of the 1930's in which the buying department was located.

Bottom right: A typical, but late produced Exide calendar.

December 1965

OXO EXTRACT

Number 10

DURING THE LAST FEW MONTHS, *you have all received a copy of the Company's Golden Jubilee book, " . . . About Oxo." This was sent, not only to retired and present members of the Staff, but to those outside the Company who have close contacts with it.*

Among the many firms with whom we have long associations is James Haworth & Bro. Ltd. and when Mr. John Haworth, the present principal (RIGHT), received his copy it set him reminiscing on the early days of Oxo. At that time, as now, his firm supplied us with printed advertising material, such as showcards and booklets, and he was good enough to commit to paper some of his

MEMORIES OF OXO

YOUR BOOK ". . . ABOUT OXO" revived many memories. In 1908 my father had already spent a year in London and had made contact with the Liebig's Extract of Meat Co. and the Managing Director, Mr. John Maltwood. They were two of a kind—not in appearance, for Mr. Maltwood was tall and my father was just 5 feet, but both had an abundance of energy and drive.

This was just before the Oxo Company was formed and Mr. Maltwood encouraged my father to start his own business, which he did in January 1914. The group of commercial artists and designers which he had gathered round him joined the firm of James Haworth & Bro.

I should mention here that Mr. Maltwood—who I understand is still alive*—was a tall, aristocratic figure, always in a silk hat and morning coat, and my father, rather short, but also with a silk hat and morning coat. The secretary of the new Oxo Company was Mr. Hay. He was dressed immaculately in morning coat with tails and a high collar and cravat. There was an air of good old-fashioned dignity about the place. The offices were on the fifth floor and on the right a line of desks near the windows with various people working there. The first one was occupied by Mr. Barnes who was responsible for all label work

"Two of a kind . . ."

Mr. John Maltwood and Mr. James Haworth

* Mr. Maltwood was sent a copy of the book and wrote in October last to acknowledge it and to say he is in his 100th year.

3

Above: Wartime 1916 Oxo Cube Recipe Book designed and produced by James Haworth & Brother.

Left: Copy from the Oxo company's house magazine 1965.

This ease of entry to show or explain your company's product or service, could be achieved by the following ritual:-

Walk into the entrance of your chosen firm. Entrance halls of famous companies had the appearance and size of old railway station terminals. There would be a greeting by a sergeant from the Corps of Commissionaires or a uniformed doorman.

On learning your reason for entering such august portals, an outstretched arm would point to the entrance of a rather large sparse room across the marbled hall. In this room one would see an ageing notice, stating that company travellers were seen without an appointment from 10.30a.m. to 12.15p.m. and 3p.m. to 4.15p.m.

Two walls would be lined with a row of hard chairs. A third of the chairs would be occupied by impeccably dressed salesmen. Soberly suited, standard white shirt, quiet tie and shining shoes. Without exception, a hat on the lap; black bowler or homburg for city and big town calls, trilby for outer London and country calls.

Beside him on the spare seat, a briefcase, sample bag or for display printers a very large, thin, carefully wrapped parcel or samples. This last item would indicate great and rare status, - a company car! or at least a taxi from the station.

Eyes of sitting salesmen would look up as you walked towards an opaque glass panel in the bare wall. Upon pressing the bell, the panel of glass would slide with a rasping sound on its ballbearings and end with a wood-to-wood bang at the end of its run.

Thus exposed would be one to three telephonists, headphones and telephone mouthpiece hanging by a strap on her bosom. Facing her would be the standard GPO switchboard, with its maze of connecting cables and plugs.

Scrutinising your business card, the telephonist would, with deft movement, put a plug into one of up to 300 holes, flick a switch and announce your company and name. Then, turning her head to you, give the name of the buyer you would be seeing.

Taking a seat, it is now your turn to watch salesmen disappear to explain their wares to patient buyers.

Your turn comes, taking the gated lift or stairs to the appropriate floor you find the buyer's office, knock and enter. A hand beckons from one of the three or more desks crowded into the office. Each desk is piled high with paperwork and plain white card dummies. If the dummies are cartons, you, as a display manufacturer are in front of the wrong person.

LIST OF SALES LEDGER ACCOUNTS - JUNE 19TH 1959.

Aspro-Nicholas Ltd. Trading Estate, Slough, Bucks.
Ados Ltd., 84/8, Upper Richmond Road, S.W.15.
Aplin & Barrett Ltd., Newton Road, Yeovil, Somerse
J. & E. Atkinson Ltd., 24, Old Bond Street, W.
G. Bassett & Co. Ltd., Owlerton, Sheffield.
J. Blundell Ltd., 157a, King Street, Hammersmith,
Burndept Ltd. West Street, Erith.
Barlow & Jones Ltd., 86, Princess Street, Mancheste
Bovril Ltd., 148, Old Street, E.C.
British Vinegars Ltd., 87, South Lambeth Road, S.W.8.
H. Bronnely & Co. Ltd., Warple Way, Acton, W.
Brown & Polson (Ireland) Ltd., Terenure, Dublin, Ei
Barker & Dobson Ltd., Whitfield Road, Everton, Liverp
Beech's Chocolates Ltd. Preston, Lancs.
Beechams Pharmaceuticals Ltd., St. Helens, Lancs.
Batchelors Foods Ltd., Wadsley Bridge, Sheffield, 6.
British Thomson Houston Ltd., RUGBY.
F. Bryan Ltd., Bromyard Road, Worcester.
Alfred Bird & Sons Ltd., Devonshire Works, De
Beechams Foods Ltd., Beecham House, Gt.
Birds Eye Foods, Hesketh House, Po
Cadbury Fry Ltd., Bournville
Cunard Steamship Co. Ltd
H. & A. Churchman Ltd.
H. Comoy Ltd., 72, R
Connelly Bros Ltd. Char
Chiltonian Ltd. Manor La
Craigmillar & British Cre
Crosfields Ltd., St. Brid
J. & J. Colman Ltd., Carro
Chivers & Sons Ltd., Histo
Cussons Son & Co. Ltd., Ken
Colgate Palmolive Co. Ltd.
Coty Ltd. 3, Stratford Place,
J. & P. Coates Ltd., 155, St.
Dubarry Perfumery Co. Ltd. Gol
Dailley & Co. Ltd., 2-16, Gorma
G. A. Dunn & Co. Ltd., 335-343
Domestos Ltd., Newcastle on Tyne
Dunlop Rubber Co. Ltd., Fort Du
H. Denny & Sons Ltd., 102, Dean S
The Ever Ready Co. (Gt. Britain) L
The Eldorado Ice Cream Co. Ltd., 13
Evans Medical Supplies Ltd., Speke,
Exchange Publicity Services Ltd., Wh
Entwistle & Kenyon Ltd.,Acc
Foster Clark Ltd. Maidston
Fisons Ltd., Harvest Hou
Goodlass Wall & Co. Ltd
A. Guinness Son & Co.
H.J. Green & Co. Ltd.,
C. & J. Hampton Ltd.,
H.P. Sauce Ltd., Asto
Huntley & Palmers Ltd
W.P. Hartley Ltd., Gr
E. Griffiths Hughes L
T. Hedley & Co. Ltd.,
H.J. Heinz & Co. Ltd.
Hovis Ltd., 154, Gros
International Harvest
Imperial Chemical In
W. & R. Jacob Ltd., A
The Kellogg Co. of G
Kimberley Clark Ltd.
Lodge Plugs Ltd., Rugby.
Leyland Motors Ltd., Leyland, Lancs.
Laporte Chemicals Ltd., Luton, Beds.
Lambert & Butler Ltd., 141, Drury Lane, W.C.2.

Above: John J. Haworth (left) with the Head Buyer, Denis Hicks of Huntley & Palmers Biscuits Ltd., Reading. Year 1955.

Inset: Mr Michael Barber, who succeeded Mr Hicks to become principal buyer with Associated Biscuits.

Left: A 1959 'roll call' of active customers in supplying design, print and cardboard display. Sadly, many of the names have disappeared under modern trading conditions. Fortunately, however, the lost names have been replaced in number by many new businesses which we are fortunate to serve as suppliers of design, photography, print, point-of-sale manufacture, merchandising distributors and exhibition contractors.

-2-

J. Miller Food Products Ltd., Carnarvan St
Meltis Ltd., Miller Road, Bedford.
Mentmore Manufacturing Co. Ltd., Tudor Gr
Metropolitan Vickers Electrical Co. Ltd.
Morny Ltd., 22,WAdsworth Road, Perivale,
McDougalls Ltd., Wheatsheaf Mills, Mill
J.N. Nicholls & Co. Ltd., Britannic Wo
Northam Warren Ltd., 209, Blackfriars
Norfolk Canneries Ltd., North Walsham
J. Neill & Co. Ltd., Napier Street,
Needlers Ltd., Bournemouth Street,
Oxo Ltd., Thames House, E.C.4.
Optrex Ltd., Wadsworth Road, Periv
Parkinsons Biscuits Ltd., Phoenix
Peek Frean & Co. Ltd. Keetons Ro
A.F. Pears Ltd., The Soap Works, Is
John Player & Sons Ltd., Castle Tobacco
Godfrey Phillips Ltd., 112, Commercial Street,
Ch. Phillips Chemical Co. Ltd. 179, Acton Vale, W.3.
S. Parkinson & Sons Ltd., Royal Butterscotch Works, Doncas
Rowntree & Co. Ltd. York.
Robertson & Sons Ltd., 138, Bromley Road, S.E.
obertson & Son Ltd., Brislington, Bristol.
omes Sims & Jeffries Ltd., Orwell Works, Ipswich.
kitt & Colman Ltd., Carrow Works, Norwich.
kitt & Colman Ltd., Kingston Works, Hull.
Rose & Co. Ltd., Grosvenor Road, St. Albans, Herts.
Robertson (P.M.) Ltd., Golden Shred Works, Droylesden, Man
ger Evans & Co. Ltd., 14, Deptford Bridge Road, S.E.
uthon Laboratories Ltd., 84/8, Upper Richmond Road, S.W.
cott & Turner Ltd., Newcastle on Tyne.
pillers Ltd., 15, St. Helens Place, E.C.
Smith & Nephew Ltd., Park Mill, Hollinwood, Lancs.
Tanqueray Gordon & Co. Ltd., 260, Goswell Road, E.C.1.
Teleflex Products Ltd., Basildon, Essex.
Unilever Ltd., St. Bridgets House, E.C.4.
Van den Berghs Ltd., Kildare House, Dorset Rise, E.C.4.
Victor Products Ltd., Wallsend on Tyne.
J. Warburton Ltd., Sykeside Mills, Haslingdon, Lancs.
Walpamur Ltd. Darwen, Lancs.
J. Watson & Sons Ltd., Whitehall Soap Works, Whiteha
Welch & Sons Ltd., Norham Road, West Chirton, Tynem
T. Wall & Son Ltd., The Friary, Acton.
J. Williamson & Sons Ltd., Lune Mills, Lancaster.
A. Wander Ltd., 42, Upper Grosvenor Street, W.

On showing your display samples, this carton buyer would flick a hand towards one of the other equally crowded desks. A head would appear and look at your showcards and displays, now standing in colourful array on any spare floor space. Seeing that your company possesses the necessary competence in print and display, this second buyer would crisply reel off his requirements.

Pad in hand, make notes of his requirements. Collecting samples back into now not such a neat parcel, you remember just in time to ask the second man's name.

Down to the marble hall again. Your head is buzzing with the enquiry. 5,000 30″ x 40″ centerpieces: 10,000 showcards 20″ x 30″: 20,000 size 15″ x 20″ and 50,000 to size 8″ x 12″.

Their design is left to you and your studio.

Hopefully, in this short interview, you have gleaned the type and style of designs they have recently bought.

Back to James Haworth's art studio. Write the brief to convey to the best available artist what you think will be a winning idea and design.

Two weeks pass. 'Phoning, before calling on this occasion, you appear with your centerpiece display and one showcard.

In our case, we hope the standard set by our designs will produce a winner.

On exposing our designs, you look for a comment of approval, which might indicate we may have a chance.

Leaving behind your high hopes, you eagerly await the following Monday, when those making the decision will have selected their choice from the many competing entries.

Monday comes. A 'phone call to your company - success! If you have to 'phone it's most likely "thumbs down".

A large order is obtained. Delivery in five to six months. Nowadays in 1988 it would be five to six weeks, or even five to six days!

Commission received in nine months' time on this order will buy new curtains for the sitting room.

By the late 1950s, this method of placing display and print business was to undergo a swift and fundamental change. The science of marketing arrived, with commercial television and the self-service outlets.

'Original ideas from the Studio, and show the customer something he could buy', still held good to a certain extent in the 1960's.

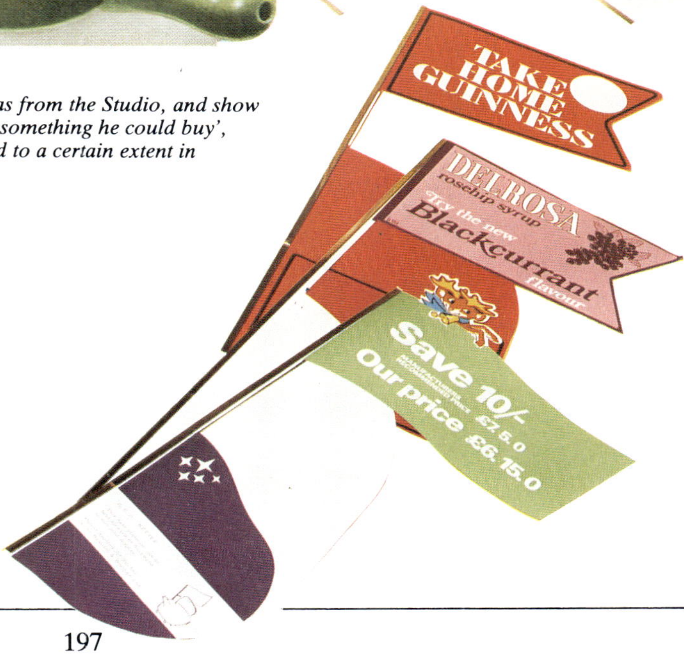

Selling print to new customers has become very much a public relations exercise. Considerable expense and time has to be spent to reach those placing work. Perhaps most frustrating of all, the knowledge that as many as four people will be involved in the placing of print work.

Each has to be made aware of your company's services.

Today, some national advertisers may be missing good suppliers in making it very difficult for a new alternative supplier to obtain an interview.

By not seeing at least once an untried supplier, who may have a genuinely new or better product, may, in some instances, be to the detriment of the advertising buyer's best interest.

Many national companies in the past and perhaps even in 1988, have not recognised the worth of their buyers.

The required skill to find suitable suppliers, ability to organise, integrity and, above all, financial responsibility, is not necessarily always recognised by their status within a company.

Past buyers have had to carry a very heavy responsibility on behalf of their companies. Many have saved their companies great sums of money by their dedication.

Compared to 1913, our customers, in 1988, range through many different fields of commerce, as a result of diversification over the years. Orders may range from a few pounds sterling worth, to many thousands, each requiring careful attention.

It would be invidious to mention by name any of our present-day customers. By way of historical interest, we record a list of our 1959 customers. Sadly, a good number have ceased to trade. Of those left, many are still our customers.

Successful companies, founded since 1959, have been introduced as new customers, making up for the loss of the almost forgotten household names of the first half of this century.

James Haworth & Company

The following illustrations portray a montage of a cross section of staff who have served over the last seventy five years at Chancery Lane, Soho Square, Southgate and Leicester.

Unfortunately, the majority of photographs are after 1945. Pre 1939 cameras were a luxury, and therefore staff were seldom photographed. Many members of the "Company" are as a result missing from the record both here, in these montages, and in the previous chapters.

Our story must be dedicated to James Haworth who had sufficient conviction in his ability to 'go it alone' and founded the firm of James Haworth Ltd. The dedication must be shared equally with the hundreds of staff, who over the past seventy five years, have given their best with their efforts to ensure we remain in business, often in trying circumstances and bad economic climates. Some gave their services for only a short period, but by far the greatest number have stayed, so that being with James Haworth has become the greatest span of their working life. Quite a few, as we have read, for over forty years.

A great number of our members were 'characters' in the very best sense. Sadly a great number are no longer alive to see us in 1989.

By portraying many of them here it is to be hoped that this family and company story will serve as a permanent memorial to their memory.

Ransomes

INDEX

Photographs and illustrations denoted in italics.

RYVITA
CRISPBREAD
How Splendid!
RYVITA
is now
BRITISH MADE
MAKES YOU FIT AND KEEPS YOU SLIM
Your Better Daily Bread

ACKNOWLEDGEMENTS

EDITORIAL PREPARATION

Janet Haworth for translating the author's writing into a typed manuscript and for much editorial assistance.

Gillian Meth for transferring the manuscript onto a word processor and assistance with the index.

HISTORICAL INFORMATION

Geoffrey Haworth for providing details of the family in their early days in Lancashire and for preserving many of the letters written by James Haworth to his father, Thomas.

Eric Latham for his description of his life and employment at Rossendale Works.

Vera Brown for the details of her grandfather, Richard Haworth.

Lancashire County Council and Mr K. F. Bowden, A.L.A., Bacup Library for the story of Chapels in Bacup before 1890 and for his time and interest in putting the author in contact with other avenues of historical research.

Mr Arnold Hargreaves, Secretary to the Bacup Natural History Society for the extracts from the Bacup and Rossendale News and the Bacup Times. Allowing the reproduction of the many photographs of Victorian Bacup from the Society's extensive collection.

Mr David Wigglesworth, Bemrose Corporation plc, who took the trouble to point the author in the right direction to obtain the historical information concerning Alf Cooke Ltd.

Mr Derek Box, Bonar Law Cartons Ltd., Manchester for kindly making the arrangements for the author to visit their factory at Hunslet Road, Leeds, formerly Alf Cooke Ltd.

Mr John Atkinson, Bonar Cooke Cartons and archivist for their company in Leeds. Acknowledging with gratitude the great trouble he took to ensure we had as much information and material it was possible to locate with regard to Alf Cooke Ltd., before 1914. For arranging the loaning of early examples of Alf Cooke's printing that appear on pages 18 to 22.

Enfield Public Libraries and their historical librarian, Mr Graham Dalling, for his interest in making available information in regard to Southgate's early days and to view the extensive collection of old photographs portraying the Borough in times past.

Mr Alan Dumayne for reading through the manuscript as it concerns Southgate, making historical corrections as required.
Alan Dumayne's books – Southgate - A Glimpse Into The Past, and Once Upon A Time in Palmers Green, are recommended reading for a comprehensive history of the Southgate area.

Kathleen Wheaton for historical details concerning her husband Geoffrey.

Ministry of Defence, R.A.F. Personnel Management Centre, Innsworth, for W.O. Geoffrey Wheaton's service record.

Royal Air Force Museum Hendon for 38 Squadron's World War II service record.

Cousins Audrey Straw and Pamela Boon for family information.

Brigadier G. M. Landy, O.B.E. for assistance concerning page 176.

Elizabeth Farrow of DODO for supplying original print material illustrated pages 10 and 11.

James Sharp for the apprentice indenture.

Pictorial Charts Educational Trust for the poster featuring the social background to the 1920's.

Palmers Green and Southgate Gazette pages 52, 153-154

PHOTOGRAPHIC ACKNOWLEDGEMENTS

Bacup Historical Society: Street scenes pages 3 and 4
Cotton mills, church and chapel page 5
Flood and old Post Office page 8. Burnley Road page 10
Bankside page 11. George and Dragon page 13
Todmorden Road page 17
Rear of book cover.

City of Manchester Central Library: Market Street page 15
Cannon Street page 16

Mr Christopher Makepeace B.A. Piccadilly page 16

Enfield Historical Library:
Southgate en fete, Palmers Green station
main line, New Southgate page 26
Chase Side page 29. The Cherry Tree, The Bourne page 30
Chase Side, Lee's Stores page 51. Roadworks page 54
Suburban train page 57. Enfield Road page 66
General bus, Railway, Enfield Road page 67
Lee's Stores interior, exterior page 76. War damage page 80
Chase Side page 148. Chase Side page 149. High Street page 149
War parade page 158

B.B.C. Hulton Picture Library: King's Cross page 56

Alan Dumayne: Enfield Police Station page 59
Geoffrey Haworth: Family pages 32, 86, 87 and 88
Vera Brown: Family page 96
Kathleen Wheaton: Geoffrey page 83. Wellington crew page 84
P.O.W. records page 85

Royal Air Force Museum: 38 Squadron page 84
Pandrol Ltd.: Terence Cuneo page 177
Mr Paul Marshall: Armstrong Siddeley page 152
Frank Wootton: Portrait page 178
Derek Johnson, Photoflair: Aerial Photographs pages 148 and 171
E.B. "Dick" Mann, Fleet Street Factory:
pages 139, 142, 143 and 144
H.R.H. The Princess Royal: page 176 (with permission)
Eric Latham page 147

DESIGN ARTWORK AND LAYOUT

Anton Scheck Ashley Riggall Lorraine Thornton

PHOTOGRAPHY OF PRINT MATERIAL

Diana Smith Arthur Barham

PHOTOGRAPHY OF EXTERIORS

Miles Winter Brian Mackett

COLOUR AND BLACK AND WHITE PHOTOGRAPHIC PRINTS

Andrew Johnston Brian Mackett

TYPESETTING

Chris and Jenny Easom, Easi-Set Ltd., Leicester.

BOOK PRINT PRODUCTION – LEICESTER

Michael Ludlow Derek Hardy Harold Williams

All staff at James Haworth – London and Leicester – whose work in preparation and production has resulted in this publication.

MAYPOLE
SOAP.
FOR
HOME DYEING
PRICE 4d. Per TABLET
DYES ANY COLOR.
DOES NOT SOIL THE HANDS.

- HAMER *married* BETTY TRICKETT *born: Mon 20th October 1794* *(Aunt to Sir Henry Trickett)* *2 children – JOHN-born: 3rd January 1816 at 3am* *MARY-born: 23rd May 1819 at 1am*
- GEORGE HAWORTH *born: Fri 25th March 1802 at 12noon* *died: 26th August 1868 in 67th year*
  - BETTY HAMER *St. Nicholas's Church* *Newchurch 12th August 1822*
    - MARGARET *born: Thur 1st May 1823 at 4am*
    - ELIZABETH *born: 13th May ? Year (died same year)*
    - SARAH *born: 20th May 1826 at 10am*
    - JAMES *born: Fri 26th Dec 1828 at 11am* *died: 11th January 1880* *married: 27th November 1862* ELLEN WALKER *born: April 1834*
      - ELIZABETH ELLEN *married* J.D. SMITH
        - IRENE *married* JOE SPENCER
          - GRAHAM *married* CHRISTINE HODGSON
        - LESLIE *married* DORIS
          - AUDREY *married* ROBERT HALLON
      - SARAH ANNE (SALLY) *married* JOHN HOLT
        - STANLEY *married* HARRIET
        - JENNY *married* FRANK RAWSON
          - MARGARET *married* PETER HOLLAND
        - TOM *married* EUNIS
        - JACK *married* DORIS INGHAM
      - ALICE MARY (POLLY) *married* HAROLD WITHAM
        - ALAN *married* ETHEL THOMPSON
          - NORAH
          - MARY
        - DENNIS *killed in 1914/18 War*
      - JAMES *married* ANNE UNWIN
        - LUCY *married* ALAN LORD
          - GARY *married* VALERIE
          - CHRISTOPHER *married* JOAN METCALFE
        - JOHN JAMES *married* FLORENCE WATTS
          - JOHN STEWART *married*
            - PAT
              - PAUL
              - ANNE
            - JANET
              - SIMON
        - HARRY *killed in motorbike accident 1921*
      - MARGARET *married* ERNEST HAYWORTH
        - EDITH *married* PERCY RAWSON
          - HELEN
        - PHYLLIS *married* GEORGE
          - GRAHAM
    - GEORGE *born: Wed 17th March 1831 at 8am*

A FAMILY IN PRINT